Isthmian Crossings

Isthmian Crossings

**FROM THE COLLECTIONS
OF RUTH C. STUHL AND
GEORGE M. CHEVALIER**

Enjoy your crossing
GMChevalier

Copyright © 2001 by Ruth C. Stuhl and George M. Chevalier.

Library of Congress Number: 2001117085
ISBN #:   Softcover   1-4010-0457-1

All rights reserved. No part of this book may be reproduced or transmitted in any form or by any means, electronic or mechanical, including photocopying, recording, or by any information storage and retrieval system, without permission in writing from the copyright owner.

This book was printed in the United States of America.

To order additional copies of this book, contact:
Xlibris Corporation
1-888-795-4274
www.Xlibris.com
Orders@Xlibris.com

Contents

PROLOGUE	7
PREFACE	11
ISTHMIAN SPANISH TRAILS	13
Oviedo-1521	16
Francisco Carletti—1594	19
Nicolas de Cardona—1619	34
Henry Morgan-1671	42
Philo White—1842	46
John H. Kemble 1848-1869	55
Elisha O. Crosby-1849	77
1849-Daniel Knower	85
Henry E. Davenport—1849	97
Theodore T. Johnson—1849	114
1850-Daniel Horn	192
Carl Meyers-1850	220
Bayard Taylor—1850	252
Mrs.D.B.Bates—1851	276
J.Bruff July 1851	304
Heinrich Schlieman—1851	331
Personal Memories of Capt.U.S.Grant: 1852	347
Crossing The Isthmus In 1852	352
L.M. Schaeffer—1852	367
Louis M. Gottschalk April 12, 1865	376
SS Ancon Transit—1939, 25th Anniversary	386

PROLOGUE

FIRST EUROPEAN CROSSING

OF THE ISTHMUS

The first city established by the Spaniards on the mainland of the Americas was Santa Maria de la Antigua de Darien in 1510. Founded by the lawyer Enciso who was accompanied by Vasco Nuñez de Balboa and from the beginning these two did not get along. Balboa was a natural leader and in the political maneuvers he took over as Governor and had Enciso sent to Spain.

Balboa was able to conquer a great part of the Darien by matching tribe against tribe and from these Indians he learned of a land to the south where its people sailed on large vessels on a very large sea. It was claimed that they ate and drank from vessels of gold and, of course, this was all the Spanish needed to hear.

Balboa learned of an Indian trail beginning on the Caribbean side and going southward over the mountains that was located only twenty leagues west of Antigua. From this starting point on September 6, 1513 Balboa set forth with a force of 190 armed men and guided by friendly Indians

The first two days were over rough and mountainous country with time lost pacifying local tribes with the journey continuing on September 20 taking four days to travel ten leagues over the worst trail encountered on their march. Many rivers could not be waded and had to be forded on rafts as they paused to fight hostile tribes and then pacify them to prevent further violence.

On September 25 Balboa reached a hill and climbing up a tall tree saw the Pacific Ocean for the first time. From here he sent out patrols to find the best route to the shore and water. A patrol reached the coast in two days and Balboa, after encountering more hostile Indians, reached the ocean shore on September 29 where he waded out to his knees and took possession for the King of Spain.

Balboa found native canoes and they proceeded to explore the coast line and islands until November 3, 1513 when they began the return transit over a different route. They contended with rough mountains, swamps and morasses while at other places suffered from lack of water. There was a scarcity of food in this region of their return because of a desert climate and no Indian villages to raid for supplies. Although the Spanish had been warned of these conditions they were not carrying the amount of provisions they should have carried. All their loot of gold and pearls could not purchase a single mouthful of food.

Finally on December 5, 1513 Indian villages were found and plundered for food and Balboa arrived back at the Caribbean starting point on January 17, 1514 and reached Antigua on January 19, 1514. They had been gone nearly four months and Balboa had been replaced by a new Governor known infamously as Pedrarias. Balboa was allowed to return to the Pacific shores and to continue exploring until the jealous Pedrarias recalled him in 1517 and had him beheaded. From these explorations the site for building Old Panama was determined which led to the construction of the permanent Camino Real connecting the two sides of the Isthmus.

PREFACE

These narratives tell of the adventures, trials and tribulations of early travelers crossing the Isthmus of Panama. Starting points went from Nombre De Dios to Porto Bello, to Chagres and finally Aspinwal which in time became Colon.

These stories were written by the participants in basically the same time frame in which they were experienced and they have recorded their impressions of what they saw and felt. For many these travels were of major importance in their lives as they ventured forth into an unfamiliar world.

Their thoughts and opinions reflect attitudes and language that were common place at that time among US Citizens travelling both in and out of their country. And of course cultural differences led to various forms of confrontation.

The discovery of gold in California and the resulting rush of humanity to seek their fortunes caught the Isthmus of Panama logistically unprepared to handle such an input which added to the many aggravations of Isthmian crossings.

It may come as a surprise to most readers to see how large and involved was the North American presence on the Isthmus during this period of US Western Expansion.

In modern times it has been possible to tramp over those old trails and find the campsites and debris as left by the "49ers" which greatly encouraged the hobby of collecting antique bottles.

In presenting these stories there has been no attempt to alter them to conform with todays trend of political correctness. What you see is what they said and felt.

G.M.Chevalier

ISTHMIAN SPANISH TRAILS

Until the completion of the Panama Railroad in 1855 travelers crossing the Isthmus of Panama used the roads that had been built by Spain soon after Old Panama and Nombre De Dios were founded in 1519.

The "Camino Real" from Panama to Nombre De Dios ran north to the Chagres River and on to the junction of the Pequeni and Boqueron Rivers. From there it followed the Boqueron and crossed the mountains into Nombre De Dios on the Caribbean Coast.

Today sections of this road are easily discernable while other parts have been obliterated. By the end of the dry season, when the level of Madden Lake has dropped, parts of the "Camino Real" stand out starkly against the bare earth as years of water actions have removed the layers of soil and humus.

Above Madden Lake, as the road begins to climb,

sections of it can be seen running through cuts thirty feet deep. This part of the road from the junction of the Pequeni and the Boqueron to Nombre De Dios was never considered satisfactory and there was much loss and damage to merchandise along this section of the route.

In the 1590's a branch road was built to connect Porto Bello to this road and although vast wealth was carried over the "Camino Real" to Porto Bello the road continued to merit the curses of those traveling it.

Because of these difficulties surveys were made for a new route and in 1533 the Licentiate Espinosa recommended to the King a route using the Chagres River to the site known as Cruces and then overland from there to Panama. In time this Chagres route became more important and the overland portion was paved and was known as the Cruces Trail and traces can still be seen today.

Because of a series of rapids below Cruces, and with low water levels in the Chagres, cargo would be unloaded at Gorgona which brought the establishment of the Gorgona overland trail. Coming from a more westerly direction than the Cruces Trail the Gorgona Trail eventually joined the Cruces Trail in what is the back area of Cardenas today. In 1735 engineer Nicolas Rodrigues recommended improving the Gorgona Trail and neglecting the Cruces Trail. Apparently his advice was not taken and very little of the old Gorgona Trail is to be seen today.

The Gold Rush brought the Gorgona and Cruces Trails to the attention of the press in the United States for travelers were sending home accounts of their harrowing experiences. The Panama Railroad and two steamship companies paid for road repairs which were finished in 1853. When the railroad was completed in 1855 the old Spanish Trails were no longer needed.

There was another trail built in colonial days, that was partially used by the "49ers", and this was the road from Panama to Chorrera. Travelers took the Rio Grande Ferry, which probubly was located near the site of the late Thatcher Ferry, across the mouth of the Rio Grande River. Then the road passed the old mouth of the Far Fan River, crossed the low area between Palo Seco and Fort Kobbe, and followed the coast to the Caimito River. The "49ers" only went as far as the hills above Palo Seco where they would camp in the woods while awaiting the ships for passage to California and remains of those campsites can still be found today.

MAPS AND ILLUSTRATIONS

1. Cover: Coat of Arms of the Old City of Panama.
2. Map of Porto Bello.
3. Map of Chagres, Yankee Chagres was on the west side of the harbor and river.
4. Map of Old Panama about 1671.
5. Plan of the New city of Panama.
6. Map of the Isthmus of Panama showing the main Spanish Trails and the new Panama Railroad.
7. Map of the Isthmus of Panama showing the Gorgona and Cruces Trails and the Panama Railroad.
8. Map of the first Panama Railroad line.
9. Section of the original Camino Real as it exists today.
10. Photograph of the SS Ancon in Gatun Locks on it's 25th Anniversary Crossing, 1914-1939.

Oviedo=1521

CONCERNING THE STRAIT AND PASSAGE FROM THE NORTH SEA TO THE SOUTH SEA

It is the opinion of modern cosmographers, pilots, and other experts on the sea that there is a water passage from the South Sea to the North Sea in Tierra Firme. But up to now it has not been discovered. Those of us who know that territory believe the narrows is land, and not a water passage. In certain places the land is so narrow that the Indians say that from the mountains of the province of Esquegna and of Urraca, which lie directly between the two seas, that a man standing on the mountain top there, looking to the north can see the North Sea, at the province of Veragua, and looking to the south can see the South Sea and southern coast of the province of Urraca and Esquegna. If what the Indians say is so, this must certainly be the narrowest part of the land, but since it is said to be so rough, mountainous, and rugged, I do not consider it the best passage or as short as the one from the port Nombre de Dios, on the North Sea, to the new city of Panama, on the South Sea.

The route is difficult to traverse because it is very rough and mountainous and cut by many valleys and rivers. There are also many thick forests. Some say that the distance from sea to sea is eighteen leagues, but I think it is fully twenty and I walked over this route twice in 1521. It is seven or possibly eight leagues from Nombre de Dios to the land of Cacique Juanaga (also called Capira); from there it is a like distance, or further, the Chagre river, the second day's journey. So to that point I reckon it to be sixteen leagues. That marks the end of the bad road. From there to Puente Admirable it is two leagues and from that bridge it is two more leagues to the Port of Panama. So according to my estimate, the total distance is twenty leagues. Since I have wandered about the world so much and have seen so much of it, it is very easy for me to estimate such a short distance as that between the North Sea and the South Sea.

If there is discovered, as we pray there will be, a water route to the Spice Islands, then the products of those islands can be brought to the Port of Panama and carried over land to the North Sea, in spite of the difficulties I have mentioned above. But there is a very easy way to go to the Spice Islands which I shall describe. From Panama to the Chagre River it is four leagues, covered by a very good road which loaded carts can traverse very easily. Although there are some grades, they are gentle, and for the most of the four leagues the road runs over treeless plains. At the Chagre River the spices could be placed in boats. This river flows into the North Sea five or six leagues below the port of Nombre de Dios. Where it enters the sea there is a small island called Bastimentos, and there it forms a very good port. Just imagine, your Majesty, what a marvelous thing it is for the Chagre River to rise two leagues from the South Sea and then flow to the North Sea. This river has a strong current and is quite wide and deep, all this being well suited to our desires. One could not wish a better arrangement for the purpose I have described.

The following is a description of Admirable or Natural Bridge, which is located two leagues from the above-mentioned river and two leagues from the port of Panama. Going towards Panama, one does not realize the bridge is there until one suddenly comes upon it. From one end of the bridge, looking to the right, a river can be seen below. Form where one stands to the water it is about two lance lengths or more in depth. The stream is shallow, about knee-deep, and thirty or forty paces wide. This river flows into the Chagre River, described above. Standing on the bridge and looking to the left there are many trees and the water is not visible. The bridge is about fifteen paces wide and seventy or eighty paces long. By looking underneath where the water flows, it can be seen that it is an arch of living rock, a sight at which any man would marvel, a thing built by the Creator of the universe.

Francisco Carletti
—1594

In yesterday's chronicle I left untold to Your Serene Highness the method of our debarking in Cartagena and of what occurred there. In that place, having cast anchor in the harbor, we debarked at once, my father secretly, and I, as the person named as agent of the business, there awaited the inspectors of arriving ships, as is the custom of that region. They, after having made the examination and having learned that we came from Cape Verde with Moorish slaves, ordered that I be taken from the ship, led ashore, and placed in prison. In the Spaniards' way of creating difficulties—at which, so as to extract money, they are good inventors—they accused me of having carried many slaves without His Majesty's license. I remained in that prison no longer than three days because of letters that we got there which the ships in a fleet arriving from Spain had brought.

These letters had been written by the Most Excellent Don Pietro Medici to the governor of the city, who at that time was Don Pedro Bravo de Acuña, a knight of the Cloak of Saint John of Malta.

Once those letters had been presented to His Excellency, he at once ordered that I leave the prison, in which I had been held though blameless, as I had twelve more licenses than were necessary for the Moors—that is, five left over from the eighty that had been bought, seeing that at Cape Verde we had not loaded or removed from the island more than seventy-five slaves, and the other seven licenses representing Moors who had died on the way. And we debarked with only sixty-eight who had remained alive. But many of them arrived badly treated, sick, and half dead. We tried to restore them, not so much out of charity, it must be said, as not to lose their value and price, and even though the supplies for maintaining them were in very short supply there, where we found at the time nothing but a little *cazzabe*, a food as poor as it is displeasing to the taste, being among the worst of all the things eaten throughout those Indies.

This *cazzabe* is brought thither from the Spanish island called Santo Domingo, and is made from certain roots of which the juice is said to be poisonous. But they are prepared by being cooked, and then they become health-giving. And those same roots being ground like sugar can, the mass of pulp is boiled and made into cakes or buns as large as desired, but only one finger thick. And they try to dry them out very well with fire, and then they eat them instead of bread. But one must be warned to have something pleasant and ready to drink near by, as this substance is so dry and gritty that it always seems to cling to the throat as if to choke one. But our slaves were given their portions softened in veal broth, in which it broke apart like a farina or polenta, and that way it was good.

We restored and maintained those slaves, but the weather and the season were not very favorable. In that climate it then was the rainy season, the rains being very unhealthful, though delightful for the tempering effect that they have on the air's excessive heat, which is hottest at that time because the sun is closer and strikes its rays down in a perpendicular line, so that at noon one has not a particle of shadow, all of which disappears under the feet.

Divine Providence and the reasonable order of Nature, as otherwise it would be impossible to live in those countries. And if things were not thus, that would bear out those ancient philosophers who said that the Torrid Zone is burned by excessive heat and lacks every good, and therefore is uninhabitable. On the contrary, it is very highly populated and overflowing with every and whatever thing is essential to living. And it abounds in waters from rain and snow and in huge rivers and in fresh pastures that are green the year round, and in forests, with trees of innumerable kinds and incredible, unthought-of size which differ from ours in every way, always being in green leaf the whole year through. Nor are fruit-bearing trees lacking to produce constantly either flowers or fruits at all seasons. For either summer or spring reigns there always, never winter or any other cruel season.

From those trees—that is, the largest ones—they make boats all of one piece, which the Indians call *canoee*, each of which carries twelve or fifteen casks of wine.

Returning to talk about the region, that was the first time that I, finding myself midway between the equinoctial line and the sun, came—when it was in the Tropic of Cancer—to make a shadow toward that part which we call noon, unlike those who live outside that Tropic, in our hemisphere, who always cast shadows toward the *tramontana*.

Further, the Indians of that region are very few, it happening that the land is not well inhabited, the larger part of it being deserted because of the great forests and the fevers that are there. Nor is it inhabited more numerously by Castilian Spaniards, the city being small and not yet walled, though in my time they were contriving to erect the walls. And it serves only as a port of call for the ships of the fleet which come from Spain on the way to Nombre de Dios, which therefore is called "The Port," whither they go to unload the merchandise, to be sent on to the province of Peru. Of that merchandise, a part is unloaded there in Cartagena—wines in particular, which then are transported to nearby places. They are sent, that is, to the mines of Saragossa, whence, by the toil of the Moorish slaves, they extract a great quantity of gold and, similarly, of emeralds. These are borne by sea to Margarita and to Santa Marta and to Riohacha, sites of the famous fisheries of Occidental pearls—and also to many islands and harbors all along the Cartagena coast. That coast is under the rule of the Crown of Castile, being among the first places conquered by their king in that New World discovered by Christopher Columbus, a Genoese, on October 11, 1492. Every three years, a governor is sent out from Spain with the title of captain general of this city of Cartagena and the galleons, which are to guard against corsairs. And in those galleons they say that the slaves to not generate lice because of the excessive heat and continuous sweating.

We received many courtesies from the governor out of respect for the abovementioned letters of protections, and with him we arranged to be able to stay, travel, and negotiate in all those West Indies just as though we had been native Spaniards of the kingdoms of Castile and had come there with a license from His Majesty. At that time, such licenses generally could be obtained for all those countries mentioned in the Indies, including all the foreigners to be found there, the ones who were classified as foreigners being all who were not native to the kingdoms of Castile, Aragon, Valencia, and Catalonia, that being the order that the King of Spain had given to all his viceroys and governors. It had been considered that by such a thing the said King was in a position to extract a good treasure, as took place, and with good justice, as from all who came to those areas from Spain without the license, His Majesty was able to take all their goods by confiscation according to the prohibitions made and published concerning those voyages and navigations.

But the King desired to perform an act of mercy toward his vassals and toward the foreigners. So he contented himself with having the tenth part of the riches that each acquired in those lands, and thus, he ordered and commanded his ministers, who were ruling for him. But if we had had to give the tenth part of what we had earned, we should not have paid anything, as rather than gaining, we lost on the slaves more than forty per cent of our capital. Instead of selling them, as was usual, at two hundred or three hundred scudos each, we sold them for less than one hundred and eighty scudos each, not to mention those, who died after being landed. But so that each time we moved from one place to another we would not have to contend with other ministers of the King who were deputed to make such arrangements, my father made one for only five hundred *reales*, which may be worth forty-five scudos. And in that the governor of Cartegena acted in a friendly manner. No additional arrangement had to be made in my favor, as I passed as a Spaniard in everything.

We stayed in the city of Cartagena until August 12 of the abovementioned year of 1594, almost constantly ill of a most malignant fever, and it was not a small grace on the part of God that we were not buried there, seeing that so many of the others died, particularly among those who had come with us and in the ships of the fleet. Of these latter it is a certain thing that more than half die each year as soon as they reach that land or that of Nombre de Dios, a place much more damaging to health and having a pestiferous air.

But the treatment and manner of medication is so strange that perhaps, because of its difference from the European usage, I shall not be believed while recounting it, and yet it is the exact truth. And, presuming that my chronicles need not be of anything but those things which I have seen and done, believe me, then, that this thing is entirely true. In the place of pullets and hens, which we are accustomed to eat when unwell, the doctor allowed and ordered that we should eat fresh pork, which in that land, not to tell a lie, truly is as excellent to the taste as can be imagined. And thus they hold it to be excellent for the health because it is formed in the dampest and hottest region and, furthermore, fed on the good things and fodder of that land. Convalescing invalids also are permitted by them to eat fish, which is very good to the taste and perhaps the best there is throughout all of the West Indies, especially the spiderfish and those which they call *musciarre*, which resemble the *dorado*, but are longer and have, when cooked, very white and agreeable flesh of the most delicate flavor. For the rest, the medications for those fevers are to let much blood and very often to give purgatives and emetics, for which last, during the decline of the fever, the patient is given as much fresh water to drink as he wishes. And thus, besides producing vomiting, they get them to sweat. And with such remedies and manner of treatment we finally escaped it.

Putting together the little that remained to us of return from the slaves sold, we invested it in merchandise that had arrived there from Spain in the fleet, which had come in during the month of February of that year. With that, we embarked, having the idea of transporting it to the city of Nombre de Dios, located toward the west on that same coast, at ten degrees, 230 miles distant from Cartagena. It was at that time the port to which the ships of the fleet from Spain usually went to unload their merchandise, which then, having been transported overland to Panama, the port of the other shore of the sea of noon, called the Sea of the South, was shipped in other vessels to the province of Peru, as we wished to do with ours.

Today the fleets go farther down, still on the same mainland coast, to a place that they call Porto Bello, located at nine and three quarters degrees, distant about twenty-five miles from Nombre de Dios. That port, at the moment when I passed it, was beginning to give instructions for settling and building its city, and thus starting to demolish that of Nombre de Dios, which consisted entirely of wooden houses situated in a place as unhealthful and conducive to sickness as can be imagined. It was uncomfortable and lacked all commodity for living, all necessities having to come from outside and by sea because its surroundings consisted of nothing but the densest forest and unhappy, uninhabitable deserts. In that city of Nombre de Dios we stayed perhaps fifteen days, most inconveniently and in extreme want of everything necessary for living—especially bread, which no one could find, so that instead of it we ate that which the Indians make of maize, which we call Turkish grain.

But what was worse was that at night we could not defend ourselves from the mosquitoes, which molested us terribly, those of that place not lonely occurring in great quantity, but also being much more troublesome than our mosquitoes and producing much more poisonous punctures. And this is true throughout the Indies to such an extent that in many places the people abandon those regions for a time and in other districts anoint the whole body with certain juices from bitter herbs in order to defend themselves from those tiny animals. Also in that city of Nombre de Dios there is an uncounted quantity of frogs and toads frightening because of their size. They are met with at every step through all of the streets and they get under people's feet, it being the opinion that they rain down from the sky, or rather, that they are born when the water falls and touches that arid land, which might better be called burned. Also, there are many bats of a very strange nature even though they are formed like ours. At night, the houses being made entirely of wood, they easily enter the rooms and bedrooms, windows and doors always being kept open because of the great heat.

And while the people sleep, these bats come in to find them and, flitting around the beds, make a soft breeze. Without one's feeling it, they bite one at the extreme ends of the fingers and toes or on the forehead or the ears. And then they feed on that tiny piece of flesh which they bear away and on the blood sucked out with it. And there is no way to protect oneself from them, for because of the great heat no one lies covered or enclosed within his bed, so that many people, wanting to hear them and so frighten them off when they come, hang many strings of leaves up around the bed, in the space between one post and another. and when the bats fly into these, they make a noise and are frightened off, so that either one hears them or they go away and do not molest those who are asleep.

Then we embarked again with our merchandise in certain small boats propelled by oars. These are steered and commanded by Moorish—that is, black—slaves, who, twenty-five of them to each boat, navigate along that coast, staying close to shore for sixty miles, and then enter a body of fresh water called the Rio de Chagres, the mouth of which lies at ten degrees toward the *tramontana*. With those small boats, one goes up that river against the current, with unspeakable fatigue and in incredible danger because in many places it is very shallow. And if the weather is dry, one nevertheless must expect rain, which at that season infallibly follows from noon onward each day, with incredible noise and the terror of lightning and thunder and heavenly rumbling, in such a manner that I may say that one feels all that more terrifying there perhaps than in any other part of the world. Or, at least, it is more fearsome than any I ever have heard anywhere else I have seen.

What is more, many stones fall, those which we call thunderbolts, mixed with fire and water, descending in sudden downpours so great that they very swiftly bring on floods, against which it is necessary to struggle with the poles if one is to advance and win one's way until that torrent shall have passed. And if, out of bad fortune, the small boat should be stove in or one should be placed in peril in some other manner, it would be impossible to save the people. No place to land appears long the river, the banks of which, from time to time, are closed in and barred by forests so thick and formed of such huge trees that one can neither land there nor find a foothold on shore. All to the contrary, the growth of those same branches forms a bank so impenetrable that it is impossible in anyway whatever to reach shore, where the sun's rays cannot penetrate, not to speak of men. It is believed—in fact, it is held completely certain—that those same trees never have been cut down or penetrated by anyone. It is not known whether there are paths or roads to follow, and it is believed that time alone is renewing the trees, as happens with other things in this corruptible universe.

These forests include a large proportion of areas that remain fresh and green throughout the year and, it is said, are full of various animals—in particular, wild swine and mandril cats or, as they are called, apes. These, throughout the night, make themselves heard in a strange, big noise that seems, in that solitude and forest thickness, to be a roar issuing from the Inferno. They say that those apes, in order to pass from one side of the river to the other, link themselves together by their tails, taking hold of one another. then, emerging on the tops of the trees, they cling to the branches, which, as has been said, project. Then, they having let themselves dangle from the branches, the one lowest down launches himself by means of their all swaying together and tries to gain a foothold on the opposite bank of the river, or to catch hold of the other branches and pull all the others over behind him. And they do this when fleeing or overcoming the current of the river, which is very great.

Finally we navigated that river for nineteen days. Living was very difficult because of lack of bread, instead of which I had to eat some of the bananas mentioned above, which are roasted while green and cooked under embers after being peeled.

Then we reached a place called the House of Crosses, where Hi Majesty has certain magazines for the reception of merchandise, which is transported thence little by little on mule-back to the city of Panama, distant from that Casa de Cruces or magazine by fifteen miles, and from the aforementioned Nombre de Dios sixty miles, traveling across the land that prevents the tramontane sea and the Sea of the South from joining. And because in that season it does nothing but rain, as happens all over the Torrid Zone, and especially in its northern part, in the already mentioned four months of May, June, July, and August, and because the route is so bad that nothing worse ever can be imagined, they put all of the aforesaid merchandise into certain bundles or small parcels. These are put together so that each weighs no more than one hundred pounds, so that each of the beasts can carry two of them despite the terrible route, which they can cover, with great difficulty, in fourteen or fifteen hours. During that time, the beasts move along constantly sunk in mud up to their bellies. It is so narrow that if two of them meet, it is possible only with great difficulty for them to step to one side and pass. Both sides of the path are wild, shut-in, solid forest containing no path other than this one, which was made by hand to permit passage.

The drivers who lead the mules all are Moorish slaves, naked and going along behind, constantly sunk in the mud up to mid-thigh, beating the beasts. And this labor is performed only by them, being a fatigue and torment that never could be borne by white men or done by others the way they do it, on foot. But not even they last long in it, but soon die, miserably paralyzed and covered with sores, which in that climate become incurable with a little scratching because of the heat and the excess of humidity of the region. And the beasts too very often are left behind, skinned along the way, there where their loads likewise remain even, as often happens, if they are of silver or of gold. But these are in no danger of being stolen, there being no place to bear them off to. So they must perforce be returned to Panama, whence they come, or taken to Nombre de Dios, to which that same path leads.

The rest, as has been said, is all a thicket of impenetrable forests. Besides which, throughout all the West Indies one finds this happiness, that there one encounters neither assassins nor people who commit robbery on the way or even in the houses. And one can go from one place to another with silver and with gold, as they say, in hand without carrying arms of any sort for defending oneself. For the

Indians do not carry them either, not being given to it, and sword and other instruments of war as used among us are new things to them, as before the Spaniards reached those regions there were no metal arms of any sort, and they used as knives certain sorts of stones, which cut like razors. And the Spaniards do not give themselves over to the infamy of robbing, not even those who have been known as disreputable men in Spain, but who, it is observed, having reached the Indies, are completely changed in character, becoming virtuous and trying to live civilly. So it often happens that he who changes skies changes, besides his fortunes, the nature of his character also, being driven to it, I believe, by the stars.

But to return to the subject of the bundles. I say that in order to protect them from the rain, which is certain, they wrap the bundles up in certain leaves that they call *biao*, which Nature has provided and caused to grow there very large and therefore suitable or such a need and a result. And with one *giulio* of them, each bundle is protected from the water. And for three scudos, two of these bundles, forming a load, are transported from the abovementioned fifteen miles with such weariness and misery that we thought never to reach the desired city of Panama. Yet on the very evening of the day on which we set out from the aforesaid Casa de Cruces, we arrived, soaked and melancholy. And that was in the month of September of the said year of 1594.

The city of Panama is situated on the other side of that strip of land which divides the western ocean from the ocean called Pacific. And it is distant from the equatorial line by nine and one half degrees toward the tramontana. It is the noblest port of call for everything that goes to and comes from the regions of Peru. All the silver and gold brought back from those regions is unloaded there, and this usually amounts each year to three or four million gold scudos. And thence it is taken to Porto Bello, on the shore of the other sea, whence, loaded onto the King's galleons, it is borne to Havana, a port and fortress situation on the island of Cuba, opposite the mainland of Florida, at twenty-two and one half degrees of the northern part and distant 850 miles, more or less, from the said port of Porto Bello. Thence, thereafter, together with other treasures arriving from the provinces of New Spain and other parts of the said Indies, these things finally are transported to Seville, in Spain.

The houses of this city of Panama are made of wood, and the men who live in them all are Spanish merchants who are very rich, especially in cattle. And some of the men there cannot count their cattle, which are too great in number. The city, which is governed by a number of judges who make up a tribunal that they call the Audiencia Real, is without other outsiders or any other sort of men except the slaves who serve the Spaniards. Of those slaves, all of whom are Moors, many have fled, having retired to a strong location in the midst of those forests, where, so as not to be oppressed, they have founded and constructed a settlement. And the Spaniards are content to let them live in their manner, in that liberty which they have taken, under the condition that they remain peaceful and do no harm and do not receive new fugitives into their settlement.

This port of Panama is marvelous for the enormous flood and ebb of that sea, which, when retiring, leaves bare three or four miles of that coast. And then the new water returns with such fury every twelve hours—taking six hours to wane and six to wax—that a man on a running horse could escape only with great difficulty from the waves at the beginning of that flood. For that reason, large ships cannot remain in that port, but stop at the islands that they call Las Perlas, so named because of the fishing that they do in that sea, about forty-five miles distant from Panama. Then, wanting to take on cargo for Peru, they approach another island, which they call Pericos, named so because of certain small parrots that are born there in abundance. That island is much closer and handier to the city of Panama.

There we stayed until the month of November of the aforesaid year, enjoying the veal that, in abundance and at very low prices, they also eat on the Sabbath Day and three days each week during lent—that is, Sunday, Tuesday, and Thursday—by permission of the Church. This is permitted because of the lack in that place of fish and of every other sort of Lenten food. No sorts of vegetables grow there. Everything is brought in from outside, even the wheaten flour for making bread, which comes from Peru and is cheaper when it reaches there than that which is brought from Spain. This is a result of the great expense there is in transporting it by land from Porto Bello to Panama. And from that place, if thus Your Serene Highness will be served, tomorrow I shall narrate our departure and the navigation that we made over that Pacific Ocean of the South, toward Peru, until we reached the city of Lima, the chief one of that very large and very rich kingdom of infinite provinces.

Nicolas de Cardona
—1619

In the month of July of the year 1619 I arrived at Portobello, having sailed from Cartagena with a frigate carrying supplies to cross Panama and begin construction of ships to again carry out the exploration of California. With the jurisdiction of Veragua I encountered two ships and a boat manned by the enemy. They were rather distant and thus we were able to enter this port where the silver galleons and convoy were preparing to sail for Cartagena. After the fleet sailed there were no ships or boats of importance left in the port. The enemy was in control. Of the seas of the region, showing his strength by sailing through the area and capturing some frigates. He was established himself in the mouth of the Rio Chagres and there was no way that a ship could pass nor maintain communications, thus causing great harm to commerce. Trade vessels were halted because they could not enter the river and goods could not go overland due to the great difficulties that will be explained below. When the enemy withdrew from the Rio Chagres the water level was so low that ships could not reach the Casa de Cruces, the mercantile custom house. Since it is necessary, I shall present a special document relative to means for the remedy of this problem which is of no minor importance to good communications.

Between Portobello and Panama there are sixteen leagues of very poor road which passes through ravines where the water reaches the chests of the pack horses. It is a difficult and laborious journey due to the lack of comforts and shortages of supplies available to the leaders of the pack trains. During the rainy season there are flash floods in the rivers which drown the mule trains along with their drivers and destroy merchandise, making it no longer usable. This happened in 1619 when I was in Panama, and over one hundred thousand ducats worth of property was lost. Finally, Panama is a small city built on the shore of the South Sea, and its only function is to receive the ships from Peru and dispatch those of Castile. The climate is the worst and its jurisdiction is limited. The costs of sustaining a fortress and law court are high, and only a black beach where boats and frigates drop anchor. Ships remain off the Islas de Perico, and to transfer cargo to and from the city it must be high tide so that boats may enter and leave. Occasionally the boats are swamped and the men are drowned for the sea bottom is rough (an insufferable labor). The Islas de Perico have no fortification and there the ships tie up to the best of their ability. There are enemies also, and the ships escape as they are able but if they cannot, they are captured. I could present a special document giving methods to improve this port from the standpoint of both the North and South Seas. This would be a safe port with a healthful climate, an abundance of inexpensive supplies, lumber for shipbuilding, rigging, tar, carpenters, and many other qualities which will be evident if I am ordered to present this document. I saw this area as one of the reasons for my lack of success on my voyage of exploration in 1620 because the enemy prevented the passage of my supplies from Portobello via the Rio Chagres as has been stated. Because of this, I was forced to buy ships already built in order to leave Panama in fair weather, having been advised accordingly. Then reports from Peru from the Principe de Esquilache arrived stating that twelve enemy ships had appeared at the port of Cañete en route to Panama, and that caution should be taken in guarding the city. At that time I had two ships and a boat with over one hundred sailors and soldiers, and President Don Diego Fernández de Velasco ordered me to postpone my sailing and aid His Majesty. This I did, remaining over two months at my expense, and later when I left on my expedition I met fog and north winds which caused me to lose my ships as will be seen below.

The coast of the jurisdiction of Veragua runs almost northwest-southeast. The sea is rough and there are some ports and a new settlement next to an island named Coiba which is some forty leagues from Panama. This is where the pearl fishing brigantines go to search for pearls, and there are harbors, fresh water, and wood available. From this island mangrove wood is taken for shipbuilding. The island is eight leagues in circumference.

This is the coast Called Chiriqui or Santiago de Alange. It is in the South Sea in eight and one-half degrees north latitude. The lagoon has two entries, one to windward and the other to leeward, the latter being safer than the former due to the sand bar located there, for it is a difficult passage and if high tide is not present there is a great danger to ships. The port is two leagues from the city called Santiago de Alange, which has a bare six houses with the principal church. It is within the jurisdiction of Costa Rica and the Audiencia of Panama. There are many cattle raised there, and they are slaughtered only for their tallow, which is shipped to Sonsonate and other places. Six leagues inland the Indians are warlike although at times they come in peace to barter, bringing cacao and taking knives and hemp. At this place I ran before a heavy storm and my captain's frigate foundered, forcing me out to sea. I miraculously escaped, but the boat was sunk and the admiral's ship was burned in port when a sailor left a handful of foul tobacco burning on top of some cotton sails in the hold and there was no way to stop the fire. There is a shipyard there for there is abundant cedar and a good supply of oak.

AN ANONYMOUS ACCOUNT

BY A PORTUGUESE TRADER IN 1620

The Negroes which the inhabitants of Panama had for slaves served them and they used them as mule drivers who go from here to Portobelo with mule trains, and others who go in the Chagres River with boats, and others load the merchandise which goes from one place to another and the merchandise costs more going from Portobelo to Spain than from Sevilla to Lima. In this road they treat you very badly if you do not take great care with them because the heat and humidity does a lot of damage (to the merchandise) and if water touches them they rot unless they don't wash them off, and as a protection against water they grow in this land some leaves called *bigau*, very large and stiff, and these leaves they wrap up the bamboo with a kind of string and then cover it with a kind of clay and even though it rains a lot they do not get wet.

From Panama to Portobelo are 18 leagues and the mule trains cover the distance in four days, and even they can do it in two days. The first day's journey is 6 leagues to the River Chagres and they ford over the river and from there you go to the Inn of Carasco and you cross the River Pequeni which comes down from the mountains of Capira, and here in this day's journey is the Fort of San Pablo which with 80 men and four pieces of artillery were able to stop Francis Drake and he could go no further and re returned to Nombre de Dios where he died.

Another day's journey brings you to the Inn of Caño. In this journey the biggest part of the trail goes in the river going upstream and you reach the inn and then you go up a mountain of small bluffs and you go down hill and you enter a stream of the other river and you go down stream to Portobelo and going in those two rivers you go more than 7 leagues and it is the worst road there is in all the 18 hills and many rivers, and they increase with great suddenness and catch the mule trains in the middle of the water.

The mule trains have their places where they can go inside and wait until the rivers go down because with the suddenness that they increase they also go down again because the water comes from very near and it happens that some times mules and men are drowned. The whole road is full of high and thick woods, cedars and oaks, which always have green leaves and the moisture is such within these forests that you cannot penetrate them, and the sun almost does not reach the earth because they are very thick. There are in this road many savannas which are meadows where there are many cows feeding. In these places there are very few Indians. The people who go over this road wear a shirt and undershirt and drawers and long stockings and alpargats and they wear other pieces of clothing as I have seen because they always arrive at the inns wet and they take off all their clothes and put dry clothes they bring. Between the sea and this road in one part there is a place called *Lugar Nuevo* where a lot of Negroes live who ran away in past time and the Spaniards could not dominate them and the King pardoned them and made them all free and gave them this part where they made their town and live, and this is 4 leagues from Portobelo.

Another road leaves Panama for Portobelo and you take the left hand near the Hospital of the Spaniards and the Monastery of the Franciscans and you go to the House of Cruces and the trip is 6 leagues of 9 hours and you go through a deep path through which is a small river, and you go down this river two leagues and it happens that the river increases rapidly and drowns a few mules. Although it is a rough road it is not half as rough as the other one mentioned. The Casa de Cruces is on the edge of the River Chagres and is made of wood with many warehouses where they store the merchandise which comes from Portobelo by the River Chagres coming up stream. These boats are very big and leave Portobelo and go along the coast of the sea until they reach the mouth of the River Chagres and then they come up stream navigating in the river up to *La Gatun* which is in between the two leagues of Chagres and Pequeni and between the Chagres which is the river on the right hand side you go to Cruces. Each one of these boats has at least twelve strong Negroes who with poles and by rowing take the boat upstream and the least they take is 9 days because the river has many rapids where the current is swift and many flash floods and a number of trees which the river brings down or which are in the deep part and cannot be seen, and thus a few ships are lost. Near the river they raise an harvest a great deal of sarsaparilla and very excellent, and that is why they say that the water of this river of Chagres is very fine and healthy to drink.

All the river is surrounded by forests very high, green and close together. Up above are many kinds of monkeys . . . When they wish to cross from one part of the river to another they look for trees that are nearest together and they take hold of their tails one after another and they hang from the trees and they give a push and the one that is in front catches on to the other tree and so they all pass over the river, all who wish without wetting, until they are safe; and they make fun and screech at the people who are navigating nearby and they throw sticks at them, . . .

. . . this road from Panama to Portobelo. They work hard at paving it and all the merchandise pays ½ per cent for the repair of the road and also the bars of silver and gold which pass over here pay the same.

Portobelo is a city of 400 Spanish inhabitants and some Negroes . . . . This land used to be full of sickness. Many people died here of those who came from Spain. For the last 20 years this part is very healthy and very few people die because they have cut down forests and with time everything changes . . .

. . . All the support and the wines come here and to Panama from Spain, and the King does not consent to allowing wines from Peru to enter so as not to lose the trade with Spain.

They grow in this land much chocolate and the whole land is full of oranges and lemons and cidras.

Also a few frigates come here from Lake Maracaibo carrying flour and others bring anise and cochenilla.

Henry Morgan = 1671

Emboldened by his earlier capture of Porto Bello Morgan decided to cross the Isthmus and attack Panama. After recruiting pirates from throughout the Spanish Main he mounted an expedition of 37 ships and some 2000 men.

After leaving Jamaica they stopped to capture and plunder Santa Catalina where he frees, from the island dungeon, three Spanish felons from Panama. These men agreed to act as guides for crossing the Isthmus.

It was dry season, so the way to Panama overland from Porto Bello on the Camino Real was at its best, and the river route via Chagres at its worst. Morgan was so advised of this by the guides but suspecting treachery he chose to go by river and the Cruces Trail.

This route required the taking first of Fort San Lorenzo at the mouth of the Chagres River. Trying not to alarm the Spanish to his true purpose Morgan only sent in a small force to subdue the fortress. After the capture the main body arrived with a storm hitting them as they entered the harbor which caused four of their largest vessels to hit Sentinel Rock and sink.

Knowing that Panama had now been warned the pirates set out up river with around 1200 men, five large boats and a number of canoes. At each village they found no sign of life and by the second day they realized the Spanish strategy was to leave nothing for the pirates to eat or use. Grain fields burned and orchards picked clean of fruit and so the foraging parties returned empty handed. They had expected to live off of the country and had not packed any food items. They were laden with only their armaments for war.

At the village of Cruz de Juan Gallego, which they reached late on the second day, they had to abandon the large boats for the river was now too shallow and only the canoes could continue on the river. Over 1000 men were forced to take to the trails with empty bellies and heavy back loads.

The third day came and went and still no food was to be found. By the fourth day they began to eat their leather pouches. On the fifth day as they stuggled through a narrow defile they were showered with boulders and arrows that resulted in several casualties.

On the sixth day a cave beside the trail was found to contain two jars of wine, several baskets of plantains and two sacks of meal. This was distributed as far as it would go mainly among the ill. At one point the men talked of eating their own dead but Morgan forbade this practice.

The next day they reached Las Cruces and found a binful of maize and a cellar of wine that had been overlooked by the Spanish. Each sick man got two ears and the others got a half ear with the wine being distributed in the same ratio. Some of the men found several old dogs and cats which they tore apart and ate raw and it made them violently ill.

The marchers now struggled up and over the divide and came upon a rancho where a herd of cattle was grazing. They fell upon the animals hacking them to pieces and eating the meat raw. After wards they built fires and roasted the meat for their second course.

The next day with the city of Panama and its cathedral tower in sight the battle began with the pirates outnumbered 4 to 1 not counting a herd of 2000 wild bulls the Spanish planned to turn lose on the pirates. When the tide of battle turned to favor the pirates the raging bulls were turned lose but Morgans blaring trumpets turned the bulls around and they stampeded into the fleeing Spanish.

When a lull ensued over the bridge came a group of priests who walked out onto the field and were administering last rites to the dying. Morgan had the priests brought before him and then being a devout Protestant, Morgan shot them one by one.

After occupying the city fire broke out and for a week pirates and Spaniards fought the common enemy. Having spent four weeks on the town Morgan decided it had been bled white and it was time for them to leave. On 24 Feb. 1671 a train of 175 mules and some 600 prisoners left the murdered city and filed out across the sabanas into the jungle on the trail back to Fort San Lorenzo.

After the pirate garrison of the fortress had taken its turn with the female captives Morgan shipped them to Porto Bello under a flag of truce and demanded a ransom of 100,000 pieces of eight. The Governor of Porto Bello conveyed his compliments to Morgan and told him to go to hell for not a real would he pay. Expecting this might happen Morgan had given instructions to turn over the captives ransome free.

Back at San Lorenzo Morgan put the French pirates to work mining the fortress walls and setting charges. The English he assigned to loading all the loot and provisions into their ships. Suddenly, when ready, Morgan sailed out of Chagres and made straight for Jamaica leaving the Frenchmen marooned in hostile territory with out their share of the loot or provisions.

Morgan was arrested on arrival in Jamaica and sent back to England in chains but he shared his wealth with King Charles 11 and came back with knighthood as the Lt.Governor of Jamaica.

Philo White—1842

ON THE US SLOOP OF WAR *DALE*

[PANAMA]

Saturday, Sept. 24: After having been for several days much baffled by light and adverse winds, we have finally succeeded in getting fairly into Panama Bay; and, at 9 o'clock to-night, we came to anchor near the Island of Tabóga, some 9 or 10 miles from the City of Panama.

Sunday, Sept. 25: The wind being favorable this morning, our ship was got under way, and run up within 2 ½ or 3 miles of the City, and anchored close in with a small Island: This is as near as vessels of any considerable size can approach to the Town, as extensive reefs of rocks run out to a considerable distance in front of the landing. A Boat was lowered, and several of us went ashore. Aside from the long distance we had to row, the landing was extremely inconvenient, by means of the ledge of rocks above mentioned. The usual landing place, is at a flight of stone steps, leading up into a kind of Portal, of the front buildings, and where the *markets* are held: But owing to the shallowness of the water in the inner cove, and the lowness of the tide at the time, we could not approach within 300 yards of the steps, and were obliged to land on a ledge of rocks, and walk some distance to reach the City. We were met by the Capt. of the Port, and some other Officers, who escorted us to the Governor's Chambers; where, in the absence of the Governor himself, we were introduced to Genl. *Mosquéra*, commanding Genl. of this Military Department. He is a tall, dignified man, about 55 years of age, speaks French (but not English) and appears quite accomplished in his education and manners. Dr. *Mosquéra*, late President of this Republic, (New Grenáda) is his brother: and the Genl., besides being commander in chief of this Military Department, holds at this time the commission of Minister Plenipotentiary to a "Congress of Nations" which as contemplated shall soon assemble in the City of Lima. The objects for which this Congress is to assemble, appear to be laudable and benevolent: The Spanish American States are nearly or quite *all* victims of anarchy or civil war; a deplorable spirit of dissention, national and domestic, is really devouring them: The *good* and really patriotic statesmen of the respective States anxious to arrest the downward tendency of political events, and to stay, if possible, the destructive elements that must, if unchecked in the course, soon sweep these young Republics out of existence; and reduce their hapless people to the extremes of want and misery,—have concurred in the expediency of convening this Congress, at which all the Spanish American Republics are to be represented, with the hope of being able to devise some system of international *government*, or municipal *law*, which shall secure peace to the several States, and the blessings of liberty and good government to the people. God grant that they may accomplish so truly benevolent a purpose,—and heaven forbid that *this* may eventuate in so miserable an abortion as did a former project of the kind,—the famed "Congress of Panama," into which our Government was wheedled to depute a Plenipotentiary, (Mr. Sergeant) who, some way remarked, was obliged to make the Sheriff's return on his commission,—*nonest inventus.*

From this interview at the Governor's house, we repaired to Mr. Nelson's, U. S. Consul for Panama. We did not find him at home, but the old woman in charge of the Key, (living opposite) admitted us, where we made ourselves easy, until Mr. Nelson was sent for at a quinta about two miles out of Town, where he boarded and lodged with a friend, altho' he kept a house and store in the City. Mr. *William Nelson*, the Consul, is a young man, (English born, I believe) and keeps a small store for a living: He is sedate in his disposition, and unpretending in his manners, yet is friendly and polite in his attention to us. As our Consuls receive no compensation aside from fees of office, and there being little or no American Commerce or other business for the official action of a Consul, the office is an empty honor here, and of course no man of much consideration will accept it.

Sickliness: Of the 2 ½ years Mr. Nelson has been here, he has been afflicted with intermittent fevers, and argues, about 20 months! and is yet suffering from the remains of lingering fevers. It is said, however, that a three years residence will so acclimate a resident, that he will seldom suffer from these pests, which may be said to prevail, to a greater or less degree, the year round in this place, or its neighborhood; so that Mr. Nelson takes comfort to himself, that his probation is nearly at its termination. And yet the Panamanians will not acknowledge that theirs is an unhealthy city! They attribute the origin of all (or nearly all) their sickness to Chagres, just over on the other side of the Isthmus, or to Buena Ventura, to the south of this on the Pacific coast. But the faces of most of the population bear a sickly hue, and the emaciated forms of a larger portion of them betray the absence of robust health. Yet there are some rotund figures among the men, and pretty faces and graceful bodies among the women; the most charming of the latter, however, have "delicate" complexions. Both men and women, however, of the native Panamanians, are of pleasing manners,— hospitable, and attentive to strangers.

The Weather is hot and rainy at this time, and continues thus about 6 or 7 months out of the year: Of course, it cannot be healthy with such a temperature. The rains are very frequent and copious during this season: Altho' the sun may shine with all its brilliancy and power, at one moment, it is seldom safe go out without an Umbrella, for fear of being caught in a shower before you return: Indeed, so far as comfort and health are concerned, protection against the rays of the *sun* are as requisite, as shelter against the peltings of the storm.

Mr. Nelson had neither eating nor sleeping conveniences about his house, as he himself performed those requisites out of Town,—as I have before stated; yet he managed to have dinner, supper, and breakfast prepared for us, and lodged Capt. Dornin and myself very comfortably over night, the others of our party having returned on board the ship. Mr. Nelson visited the ship, and received a Consul's salute.

Monday, Sept. 26: A boat having come ashore early this morning, I procured, *in the rain*, a supply of fresh beef and vegetables, and sent them aboard for the crew. After promenading over the city two or three hours, and making some purchases for my Department, I by invitation, took breakfast with the family a Mr. *Lewis*, an Englishman born, but who has been long resident of Panama, and married into the family of *Herreras*, a family of high consideration in this country,—and one of whom, brother-in-law to Mr. Lewis, was recently Governor of the State of Panama. I found Mrs. Lewis very lady-like, and agreeable. Lieut. Green makes this family his home while he remains in Panama, as he did some five years since, on his return home by this route. On the evening previous, Capt. Dornin and myself were invited to the house of Mr. *Perry*, English Consul for Panama, and sort of the celebrated periodical writer, and late Editor of the *London Morning Chronicle*. His salary, (of some 2000 or 3000 dolls. a year) enables him to live in quite a comfortable style: He is a widower, and has with him two or three small children, and a quite lady-like Governess, of say 25, to teach their young "ideas how to shoot." Mr. Perry furnished us some late English Newspapers.

During the forenoon, a good portion of our Officers came ashore, to see the City, etc. Lieuts. *Shepard & Griffith,* (who go home as invalids) came ashore with their baggage; and quarters were provided for them in the house of Mr. Nelson, until a passage can be procured for them at Chagres for the U. States: Lieut. Green will of course accompany them, and minister to their wants, etc. By the way, a vessel is expected at Chagres from New York, within 10 to 12 days, in which they expect to take passage; but should they be disappointed in this, they will doubtless find passage to Jamaica within that time; so that it is not probable they will be detained here more than two weeks.—In the afternoon, (Monday, 26th) we all repaired on board; and Tuesday morning the ship was got under way, and ran down to the Island of Tabóga, 9 or 10 miles, where there is excellent anchorage close in shore, and where there is abundance of water, and easily to be got on board.

City, and Commerce, of Panama: In the last century, a good portion of the Spanish trade to the Pacific, was carried on across the Isthmus, and thro' this City; and Panama, being thus made the general Entrepot of the Commerce from both seas, it thrived, and became a Town of much commercial importance, evidences of which still remain, in the crumbling relics of extensive warehouses and bodégas, large public and private edifices, et. Etc: But the City *now* affords one of these pictures of *dilapidation* so frequently met with in these Spanish American countries. The commerce of the Pacific has entirely passed into the channel by way of Cape Horn; and Panama, thus left without commerce, or much business of any kind, was obliged to go down,—and down it's going.

Pearl Fishery: The principal branch of the little commerce yet carried on here, is the *Pearl Fishery* of this Bay. There is an English ship here now in that trade: She lies at "La Isla de las Perlas," where the most successful part of the Pearl-catching is carried on: This Island is about 15 miles down the Bay, where divers are constantly employed: These *Divers* are native Indians, and are practised to the business from their youth; of course they become very expert, and will dive to the depth of 25 to 30 feet, and bring up their hands full of the Pearl Oysters. I bought a dozen oyster, for two reales by way of experiment, and had what was called pretty good luck,—five *small pearls* having been found in the dozen oysters: Some other officers had several dozen opened, without finding scarcely a single pearl: Sometimes, however, a single shell will contain pearls to the value of $100: So that the business is very much of a lottery.

The "*Panama Chains*," of such peculiar and delicate workmanship, as well of gold as of silver are manufactured here, (and I believe exclusively here to a considerable extent: Large quantities of the *Panama* (grass) *Hats*," and *Grass Hammocks*, are also the fabrick of this place. These, with a product of the pearl fisheries, constitute the principal articles of export from Panama.

The *City of Panama* could formerly boast of a population of some twenty thousand inhabitants; but I doubt if there be, at this time, an aggregate of more than six or seven thousand souls, all told; and the insalubrity of the climate is uncongenial to the propogation of the human animal. There are still, however, some wealthy families remaining, whose dwellings are large, well built, and tastefully furnished: Indeed, it was a very substantially build City in the day of its prosperity, will well-paved streets, etc. But it is doomed to dilapidation.

Taboga is a pretty large Island, and very fertile,—everything that is put into the ground growing luxuriantly, and requiring very little labor to produce most abundantly. Yams, plantains, yugas, bannanas, etc. are among the vegetables produced here in great abundance; ad pine-applies, oranges, cocoa-nuts, nisperas, lemons, mame's, etc. are some of the fruits with which the Island abounds. The population of the Island is 400 or 500, about 300 of whom reside in the village near the usual anchorage of vessels, which resort here to procure fruits and vegetables, and fill up with fresh and pure water, which runs out of the hills and tumbles over the rocks in numerous crystal streams,—affording, in addition to a great many other conveniences in this hot climate, delightful *bathing* in the numerous deep holes in hits rocky bed: A large portion of the population are either Indians, or have a greater or less admixture of Indian blood in them; there are some descendants of Spanish families unmixed, however. The whole population, as they associate but little with the rest of the world, seem to be in a primitive state of innocence and happiness, and treat strangers with a kind of inquisitive attentiveness. Their food, consisting largely of vegetables and fruits, is simple, but wholesome and abundant: Maize, rice, and bread-fruit, constitute their bread-stuffs: Possessing no mills, they soak the maize, take the hull off, and then mash (or crush) it between smooth stones,—a slight admixture of milk and salt, prepares it for baking, enveloped with palm-leaves. A more delicate kind of bread, however, is prepared from green corn and green cocoa-nut: The corn is cut from the cob, rubbed thro' a split-work kind of sifter, and, mixed with finely-scraped new cocoa-nut, is reduced to a suitable consistence by fresh milk, and seasoned with agreeable aromatics; this "batter" is then enveloped, in suitable quantities for small cakes, and thus baked: It is very pleasant eating,—equal, perhaps, to the best of our *corn-pone*.

I bought two cows, and had them slaughtered, which, with an abundance of vegetables, supplied our crew with fresh "*grub*" during our stay here. We laid in a large supply of pine-applies, oranges, lemons, yams, etc. for the voyage: the yams keep a long time at sea; some of ours remained good till our arrival at San Francisco, about 80 days.

We got up a "party" on board the *Dale*, and invited every body in Tabóga to it. These rural "Beauties" were decked out in their best "bibs and tuckers," and appeared to be delighted with their visit. We entertained them with a little dancing and waltzing,—some drinking of wine, and eating of cake, and a good deal of chit-chat and "gibberish." The principal man of the village, a Sor Sebáyos who is "Alcalde" of the place, came to the party in his *shirt sleeves*, as the weather is melting hot! He was accompanied by the *Cura* of the Parish, a jolly young man of 25 to 28; who joined in the festivities of the party with much *gusto*.

One among the most emphatic evidences of the ruined condition of the *City of Panama*, its commerce and business, and of the absence of public spirit and enterprize among its citizens, is the fact, that there is no *Newspaper* published in the place! There is not a Town in the United States of an equal population (6000 to 7000) but what supports two, three, or four Newspapers. It is the curse of bad Government, (among other causes) that renders these people so unambitious, so listless, and careless of keeping pace with the improvements of the age.

John H. Kemble
1848=1869

Transportation across the Isthmus of Panama was a major problem for the traveler by that route. From the mouth of the Chagres River on the Caribbean, where steamers anchored in the early years, to the city of Panama on the Pacific was a journey of about sixty miles. Approximately two-thirds of it could be made in boats on the river; the remaining part had to be negotiated on foot or muleback over wretched trails. In the first years of the route's importance, it was a journey full of hardship and discomfort, not unattended by danger. Health conditions were bad on the Isthmus in the absence of much knowledge of tropical hygiene, and though the terrors of the journey have certainly been exaggerated, they were nonetheless real. At Panama, it was sometimes necessary to wait months for a ship to California. Most travelers were bored there, some fell ill or ran out of funds, and a few got into serious trouble with the inhabitants. The opening of the new port of Aspinwall on the Caribbean, and the completion of the Panama Railroad in 1855 removed most of the difficulties of the crossing, and the transit from ocean to ocean became a matter of only a few hours' train ride.

The maintenance of an open highway across the Isthmus was, of course, essential to the operation of the route as a whole. No matter how well the steamers on either side carried out their part of the service, they would mean nothing if the land transit between the oceans were closed. It was at this point that the traveler on a route essentially internal—since it served chiefly to connect parts of the United States—crossed foreign soil and came under at least the nominal jurisdiction of the Republic of New Granada or Colombia. The disastrous effects of internal warfare on the development and maintenance of the Nicaragua route have been noted, and the success of that by way of Panama was to a great degree due to the comparative peace which was maintained on the Isthmus and to the fact that internal dissension and local feeling were never allowed to close the transit.

By the treaty of 1846, right of way across the Isthmus had been guaranteed to the United States, and in the same year British interests pioneered a commercial route from ocean to ocean. When, however, the first Americans came to cross in December, 1848, they found little in the way of organization for the journey. What arrangements the British had made were not available to the travelers from the United States and they found it necessary to fend for themselves.

Until 1852 all the steamers and sailing vessels coming to the Atlantic side of the Isthmus landed their passengers and cargoes at Chagres, a village composed of unprepossessing huts located on the left bank at the mouth of the river of the same name. With the growth of the traffic, an American town of Chagres grew up across the river, consisting mainly of hotels and saloons, catering to the wants of travelers during their enforced stay between the time of landing from the steamer and starting up the river on the journey across the Isthmus. The mouth of the Chagres was somewhat sheltered by a headland, on which is situated Fort San Lorenzo, but the depth of the water there was not great enough for ocean steamers, which were forced to lie in the open roadstead, disembarking their passengers either in their own boats or in native craft coming out from the shore. In 1851 the cost per person for the landing from the steamer at Chagres was $2. When the seas were heavy, it was impossible to land, and at times steamers lay pitching and rolling off the mouth of the Chagres for days before the passengers could be put ashore.

The climate at Chagres was reputed to be the most uncomfortable and unhealthful on the Isthmus, and since accommodations for travelers were poor and the food available proverbially bad, they tried to avoid spending a night there, by arranging transportation up the river as soon as possible. For the journey on the river, native canoes or "bungos," hollowed out of a single log, some twenty-five feet in length and two and a half to three feet in width, were the chief means of conveyance. These boats were poled up the river by three or four natives, carried two to four passengers, and were equipped with canopies for the protection of the travelers and their baggage. It was common for passengers on the steamers to make arrangements among themselves before landing, organizing into parties for the journey to Panama and choosing one of their number to make the bargain with the boatmen. Arrangements were at first made with the men of a particular boat, but by 1852 most of the boats on the river were owned by a few men, and it was with these that the agreement had to be made. The first travelers found an unsophisticated lot of boatmen, whose usual rate from Chagres to the head of navigation of the river was $10 per passenger. They were very quick, however, in learning what was the demand for their services, and within a few weeks the price had risen to $40 and $50. In 1851 persons were advised to pay not more than $50 for the hire of a boat, which meant that the cost per person was still about $10, and by 1852 the fare up the river was $4 to $5, indicating an increase of facilities and a decrease of travel. The natives early learned that many Americans were not above cheating them when the occasion offered, and they retaliated in kind. Persons making the journey in 1851, were advised to pay only half the agreed price of the river trip at Chagres, holding the remainder as security for the performance of the journey and paying it only on arrival. Otherwise, boatmen often refused to continue above a certain point on the river without additional payment, and the travelers were helpless to do aught but accede to their demands.

During the dry season, from December until April, the head of navigation of the Chagres was at Gorgona, a village situated thirty-nine and a half miles up the river from its mouth and some twenty miles from Panama. The rains of the remainder of the year made it possible for boats to continue to Cruces, four and a half miles above Gorgona and eighteen miles from Panama. The boat trip up the river to Gorgona required three to three and a half days, depending somewhat on the skill of the boatmen in avoiding eddies and swift currents and in keeping the boat close to the bank where their poles would be effective. Layovers were made at night at villages along the riverbanks, where the travelers, if they arrived early, could often find a cot or hammock in which to sleep, and where meals, of a varying quality, were served. One traveler, George Schenck, who crossed the Isthmus in the fall of 1849, wrote vividly of a meal taken along the Chagres.

The next morning we started on our journey, and about seven o'clock we stopped at a little hut at Gatun to get coffee and something to eat, three of us, Mr. Swain, Dr. Dow and myself. I noticed that we used up all the sugar that they had in the cabin. Some other passengers came along after us, and I thought I would watch and see how they managed about their sweetening, and see if they got any. I presently saw one of the natives, a girl of about sixteen or seventeen years of age go out and get a piece of sugar-cane, and commence chewing it, and occasionally she would eject the juice from her mouth into the coffee while it was being prepared outside the hut. Swain asked me if I was going to have some coffee. I declined to take any under the circumstances.

People were advised not to depend entirely upon the provisions which might be purchased along the river but to carry with them a small stock of such eatables as dried beef, oiled ham, sea biscuits, sardines, and a dozen or so bottles of claret. According to some accounts, many Americans took more than claret, and the journey up the river frequently assumed rather hilarious character. the wide, tropical river, hemmed in by the vivid green jungle in which strange birds and animals were constantly to be seen, formed a sharp contrast with the previous experience of most of the travelers. Many of them carried firearms, and these received plenty of use in shooting at alligators and monkeys, which frequently presented themselves as unwitting targets.

Almost as soon as the route to California via Panama was opened, the improvement of the isthmian transit was undertaken. The second steamer to sail from New York for Chagres was the *Orus*, a wooden side-wheeler of 247 tons and a length of 158 feet, 7 inches, which had been in service in sheltered waters around New York since 1842. She had been purchased by Howland and Aspinwall, and was sent to the isthmus to carry passengers up the Chagres. She reached her destination on January 14, 1849, and immediately entered service. It was apparent, however, that the *Orus* was not entirely satisfactory for the river journey. Her draft was too great to allow her to go more than eighteen or twenty miles up the river, where her passengers were transferred to native boats of the remainder of the journey. The captain of the *Orus* was expected to guarantee passage from Chagres to Gorgona for $10, including transit in the canoes above the point at which the steamboat turned back, but he failed to do this, and passengers made their own arrangements for the last part of the trip. The *Orus* could carry only about 150 passengers at a time, and all available room aboard was used for them, the baggage being piled into bungos at Chagres and towed behind her as far as she went up the river. Since the *Orus* was never able to make the whole river voyage to Gorgona and in dry season was useful only as a towboat at the mouth of the Chagres, it was clear that, if the river were to be navigated by steamboats, it would be necessary to have some more adapted to existing conditions. In the summer of 1849 the stern-wheeler *General Herran* was built at Chagres. Entering service in September, she was able to make the run to Gorgona, but this was a performance not always successfully accomplished by even this smaller boat. The additional competition did serve to bring down canoe rates to $4 to $6 per person, and travelers praised the efforts aboard the steamboats to make them comfortable. In June, 1850, the steamer *Raphael Rivas*, built for George Law and the Panama Railroad, appeared on the river. She had an iron hull 110 feet long and 23 feet in beam, and it was expected that she would not draw more than a foot of water. It was found that the *Raphael Rivas* or the *Ralph Rivas*, as she was called by un-Hispanicised Americans, drew between twenty and thirty inches of water and could ascend the river above Palenquilla, eleven and a half miles below Gorgona. She made a speed of about three miles an hour against the current, however, and her passengers were often able to reach Gorgona in one day from Chagres. In the summer of 1850, also, Adamson and Company of New Orleans bought a little forty-six-foot, twelve-horsepower steamboat, named her the *Harry Gleason*, and placed her on the Chagres. Later in the year the Panama Railroad built another iron steamboat, the Gorgona, sending her to Chagres to tow barges of materials up the river to be used in the construction of the railroad. Before the close of 1850 still another small steamer, the

Swan, appeared on the river. The steamer *William H. Aspinwall*, seemingly built on the Isthmus at Navy Bay, made her first trip up the river on February 6, 1851 going every other day from Chagres to Gorgona. It was said that the trip in her was very pleasant. There was room to walk about and her rain-tight covering and sides might be opened or closed at will. Although in the rainy season the *William H. Aspinwall* passengers had to go from Gorgona to Cruces in canoes, the trip from Chagres to Gorgona was made in seven and a half hours.

American enterprise was not devoted entirely to steamers. Captain Abraham Bancker, onetime shipping-news collector for the *New York Herald*, organized a line, under the name of the Isthmus Transportation Company, of some forty new ship's boats said to be well covered and well manned, and in time carried on a successful freight and passenger service up the river.

From the head of navigation at Gorgona or Cruces, depending on the season, travelers went overland to Panama. The roads of either route were not wider than trails, and only persons afoot and mules passed over them. Although the Gorgona road was longer than that by Cruces, it was generally considered the easier and pleasanter of the two. However, since it had no paving, it became an impassable morass in rainy season, and travelers were then obliged to go by the way of Cruces. This trail was a part of the paved road between Panama and Porto Bello which had been built in the colonial period. Though it had not been well maintained and in parts was in shocking condition, the rains did not put it completely out of use. Gorgona and Cruces were supplied with hotels and saloons, generally operated by Americans, which catered to the wants of travelers on the their overnight stays in transferring from river to road. The accommodations were reported to be fairly good and the climate at this higher altitude was often quite pleasant. When the city of Panama was known to be crowded with Americans and no prospect of a ship for California was in view for some time, travelers sometimes remained at Gorgona, camping on the shore of the river or staying in a hotel, until the arrival of news that transportation to San Francisco was available.

Persons were advised not to attempt to complete the journey on foot after leaving the boats, although some did so. Most travelers hired mules to carry themselves an their baggage and proceeded from Gorgona to Cruces early in the morning, since thus the journey could be made in one day. A great deal of baggage was so carried on the backs of natives. Even persons were transported thus, riding in chairs strapped to the heads of the surprisingly strong Negroes and Indians. For women the journey presented problems, which some met by wearing trousers and riding astride the mules, whereas others clung tenaciously to the long skirts, "preferring to die rather than to outrage modesty, shame their sex, and exhibit their large ankles even to the barbarians, among whom he who wore the least clothing was most in fashion.

At the beginning of 1849 the cost of a mule or horse for the day's ride from Cruces to Panama was $12 to $15; for the transportation of three packages of baggage, weighing in all about 180 pounds, one person paid $44, which by exchange became $56. At the same time travelers were being advised to bring with them only a single trunk and enough to make only one mule load, which was about 250 pounds. The cost of transportation overland fluctuated. In February, 1849, a man paid three natives $15 to carry his baggage from Gorgona to Panama; the next month it was said that a mule to carry two trunks from Gorgona to Panama should not cost more than $10. At that time there were some two hundred pack mules engaged in freighting goods across the Isthmus, the charges for their use varying with the demand. For one person with one trunk and one bag, the rate ranged between $15 and $30; for each additional 100 pounds $5 to $10 was charged. In 1851 the usual charge was $16 for the hire of a mule and $10 per 100 pounds for baggage. The rate for passenger mules in 1853 was $18, and the cost of transporting baggage had gone up t0 17 cents a pound. Travelers were strongly advised to be sure of the reliability of the person to whom they entrusted their baggage for the transit from the river to Panama. A recognized local express carrier like Zachrissen, Nelson and Company, Ran Runnels, Henriquez, or Perez was recommended. Even then a written contract was advised, with the stipulation that the baggage be delivered at Panama by a stated time, and persons were warned to pay no more than half the charges until the transit was completed. It was suggested that, if an individual carrier was engaged, he should be taken to the alcalde of Gorgona or Cruces and an assurance of his good character obtained before he was entrusted with baggage.

The transit of the Isthmus, which had been characterized by lack of any sort of uniform management during the pioneer years, began to assume regularity by 1853. In that year the Pacific

Mail concluded a contract with Hurtado y Hermanos, the largest mule owners on the Isthmus, to convey passengers and baggage through from one ocean to the other at a fixed rate. This made it possible for passengers to purchase tickets covering all expenses of the transit and to be freed from many of the cares formerly attendant on the journey. The contractors took charge of the baggage on board the steamers and delivered it aboard ship at the other side. At the same time, the independent mule-owners met at the Pacific Mail office in Panama to establish a fixed tariff for passengers and baggage across the Isthmus. It was stated at the beginning of 1854 that the transit was entirely in the hands of James S. Hermann and Company and Messrs. Hinkley and Company and that, in view of stiff competition between those firms, it was possible for passengers to purchase through tickets across the Isthmus—including a ticket to the end of the incomplete railroad plus river and mule transportation—for $25 to $30.

In traveling from the Pacific to the Atlantic, it was possible from the beginning to make a much quicker trip. Counting a day from Panama to Cruces or Gorgona, the boat trip down the river took only another day, making the entire transit about two days as compared to the four or five days usually consumed in going from Chagres to Panama. In 1854 it was reported in the *Panama Weekly Star* that the journey across the Isthmus had been made in the short time of seven hours.

An important part of the isthmian transit in the period before the completion of the Panama Railroad was the safe conduct of specie exported from California. It was generally sent through in charge of an express or steamship company, being packed on mules from Panama to the Chagres and then send down the river in boat. The primitive facilities for transportation, the poor roads, and the lack of adequate policing made the trip at times a dangerous one, and the attacks on the treasure trains and robbery of specie were not few. In August, 1850, the conductor of Howland and Aspinwall's specie train was robbed of $30,000, and on December 23 of the same Zachrissen, Nelson and Company's treasure train was attacked a few miles out of Panama, and $120,000 in gold dust seized. Parties were sent out immediately, however, and most of the gold was recovered.

In August, 1850, Henry Tracy, who acted as isthmian agent of the United States Mail Steamship Company and the Law Line, wrote to Marshall O. Roberts in New York, saying that in the future it would be necessary to have the treasure trains well guarded in order to get them safely across the Isthmus. To do this, he requested twelve Colt revolving rifles, twelve pairs of dragoon-size revolvers, twelve pairs of smaller revolvers, twenty-four Bowie knives, one case of powder and ball and two buckshot guns. A cargo of specie would require forty mules, and for each five mules, Tracy said, there should be a mounted rifleman, and each mule should be led by a *peone*. He went on to say:

> That robberies have but just commenced, and that there are from 50 to 100 as precious villains on the Isthmus as ever went unhung . . . That there will have to be bloodshed before matters become regulated. As I have no doubt, within six

months there will be an attempt to seize one of the large, but half-guarded trains.

In a letter written the next month, Tracy reverted to the subject of the treasure trains and their guarding:

> I am determined that there shall be none [treasure] stole [sic] from your trains except there be several funerals, and think you can rely upon good care being taken of it. But I do need the arms I wrote for, and hope they will come on by the "Georgia." I never wear pistols or knives, except I am conducting specie, or am expecting a fight; and therefore hope you will not think what I wrote about arms, the effect of fear so much as of caution. I risk my life, and wish, if it is to be sold, to have it go at a fair price; yet I have less fear of robberies than thefts; and as most thieves are cowards, like to have it distinctly understood that the train I conduct is ready for a fight, as I believe the rogues will always attack the poorest guarded train."

In September, 1851, there was great excitement in the city of Panama when news arrived that the Pacific Mail Steamship Company's treasure train, consisting of between seventy and eighty mules and carrying about $2,000,000 in specie and gold dust, had been robbed some seven miles from Panama. In the fight two men, probably native muleteers, had been killed, and seven mules returned to Panama without their packs. The sum supposed to have been taken amounted to $250,000. A large armed force of Americans, together with fifty or sixty of the National

Guard of New Granada, started in pursuit of the robbers, whose escape was held to be an impossibility. The Pacific Mail's treasure was transported across the Isthmus under contract by the house of Mosquera, Hurtada y Cia., and as the contract included insurance, there was no possibility of loss to the company or the shippers. Since the government seemed unable to control affairs on the Isthmus, an extralegal organization was set up under the leadership of Ran Runnels, an American merchant and shipper resident in Panama. An armed guard was organized, with the tacit consent of the governor, which had authority to punish all those guilty of crimes, even to the death penalty. Working with great effectiveness but little publicity, the Runnels Isthmus Guard, which was financed by the Panama Railroad, existed until March 1, 1855, when, with the railroad in operation and treasure carried by that means, the need for it decreased, and it was discontinued.

There were some attempts made before the completion of the railroad to improve the land transit of the Isthmus. In 1850 the Panama Railroad made plans for a plank road from Navy Bay to Panama, with the construction of the railroad itself postponed until later. But after some two miles had been graded, the project was abandoned, and the whole of the energy of the company was turned toward the building of the railroad. In the summer and fall of 1853 the United States Mail Steamship Company and the Pacific Mail Steamship Company, together with the Panama Railroad, agreed to assist, with repairs to the Cruces-Panama road, which was in particularly bad shape. The work was first carried on under Edward Allen, a contract being later awarded to Ran

Runnels to complete repairs. That had been hitherto bottomless mud holes were filled with stones, after the mud had been cleared away to a solid bottom; holes were macadamized, and sewers built along the side of the road to carry off the water. With the completion, on October 27, 1853, of work on this necessary link in the isthmian transit it was asserted that one of the forcible arguments of those competing with the Panama route had been answered.

Arriving at Panama, the traveler found himself in a city nearly two centuries old, with great stone buildings, paved streets, and an established society. During the years in which the Panama route flourished, the population of the city was between eight and ten thousand inhabitants, but it gave the impression of being larger. Of these, in 1868, about 2,000 were whites, including 300 resident foreigners, 100 of whom were from the United States, 100 French, and the remainder English, Italians, and Spaniards. A few of the Americans who remained at Panama for sojourns ranging from a day to three or four months waiting for a steamer to carry them to California interested themselves in the city and people, making excursions to the ruins of the old city of Panama and beginning the study of Spanish. By far the majority, however, were entirely intolerant of the civilization in which they found themselves; they made every effort to live as they did in the United States and became almost frantic with impatience if the ship which they expected was delayed. For much of the time down to 1852 there were enough emigrants in Panama to give them a feeling of independence and to make them bold in disregarding local custom and law when it interfered with their wishes or desires. As early as the spring of 1849 a traveler could write:

> Panama is thoroughly Americanized; has stores for the sale of meats, groceries, bread &c.; the auctioneer's voice may be heard at all hours of the day, in the disposal of assorted lots, placed in his hands by those who must raise funds to get to San Francisco. Brokers' officers are established for buying and selling passage tickets. One announcement I enclose literally:
>
> STEAMER and other TICKETS
> BOT and SOLD ON COMMISSION
> MONEY LOANED on Steamer Tickets
> Enquire Room No.-
> AMERICAN HOTEL

A good deal of drinking, gambling, and shooting went on among the Americans. But when the bishop died in the spring of 1850, the tolling of the church bells of the city annoyed them and caused much grumbling.

There were near-riots when drunken Americans entered the cathedral wearing their hats and showing the utmost disrespect for the character of the building and the feelings of the worshippers there. The reaction of many Americans to Panama was reflected in the following characterization of the city:

> Here I find myself again, for the third time, in this far famed city of New Granada—the same dirty, noisy, and unpleasant place to stay in. There is no comfort, no pleasure—nothing which in the last degree tends to make the time pass lightly, but everything is dull, heavy and monotonous. If it could

be Yankeeized, there might e some hopes of it; but as it is, it is deplorable.

While they waited in Panama, travelers either stayed in hotels or *pensions,* where board and room cost in the neighborhood of $8 per week, or camped outside the city walls. The number of Americans in the city fluctuated greatly, since a succession of ships might carry northward all who wished to go, whereas a series of delayed sailings would again crowd the town with emigrants. Thus in April, 1850, it was estimated that there were three thousand Americans in Panama, while in February of 1852 the number was said to be nearly four thousand. After 1852, however, there was seldom any large number of travelers waiting in the city, since with the improved coordination of the lies on the Atlantic and Pacific the facilities for travel on both oceans tended to become equal, and the number crossing the Isthmus could be cared for as they came.

THE PANAMA RAILROAD

The original stock issue had been for $1,000,000 of the $5,000,000 allowed by the charter of the company. In May, 1852, a second stock issue of $1,500,000 was placed on the market. Two issues of convertible bonds, in May, 1851, and January, 1854, brought the total capital to $5,000,000, and in 1855 the company requested an amendment to its charger, allowing the capital to be increased to $7,000,000. This amendment passed the New York legislature on April 12, 1855, and the additional stock and bonds were placed on the market. The first dividend of the Panama Railroad, amounting to 10 per cent, was declared on December 3, 1852, payable in stock on January 15, 1853. And additional 5-per cent dividend was voted in July, 1853, and 7 per cent was paid in 1854, with 3 ½ per cent in January, 1855. The dividends were 12 per cent annually from 1856 through 1860, and in 1868 they were 24 per cent, with an additional 20 per cent, making a total of 44 per cent. Stock of the company generally remained above par after April, 1852, with infrequent drops below par during and after construction days. Not until 1864 did it go above 200, but thereafter it rose rapidly, passing 300 in September, 1867, and reaching 348 in January, 1869. At the middle of June, 1869, it was the highest stock listed on the New York Exchange, standing at 295, the next highest being New York Central Railroad at 188 ¾. With the beginning of service in 1852 the Panama Railroad began to bring in money, the gross receipts for the six months ending December 31, 1852, being $250,161.81. Although the statement which has been made that the Panama Railroad paid for itself before completion is highly untrue—the gross receipts up to December 31, 1854, being but $1,037,556.92—this was rather a good record for a railway which was still under construction. Between 1856 and 1866 net receipts never fell below $656,517.60, whereas in five of the eleven years they were over $1,000,000, reaching their highest point in 1864 with $1,459,453. In this period, 396,032 passengers were transported over the railroad, $501,218,748 in gold, $147,377,113 in silver, $5,130,010 in jewelry, $19,062,567 in paper money, and 614,535 tons of mail, baggage, merchandise, and coal. The largest number of passengers to cross in these years was 46,976 in 1859; the smallest number was 20,420 in 1862. The rates charged and the profits which the company made for its stockholders were said by many to be unreasonably high. This may have been so, but the traveler across the Isthmus might well remember that, before the construction of the iron road from ocean to ocean, he had paid more for his transportation and had traveled with much less comfort and speed. Though the rewards of the railroad might be great, its service was great also.

When service by way of Panama was about to be opened in 1848, there was no provision for the transportation of the mails across the Isthmus. Although there were steamship lines on both oceans, and mail agents to accompany the letter bags, there was no one to carry them from Chagres to Panama. To remedy this, the Postmaster General, on October 25, 1848, ordered the extension of the Panama-Astoria mail route to include the isthmian transit, accepting an offer from the Pacific Mail Steamship Company to carry this out for $2,900 per year. In spite of this arrangement, the mail service across the Isthmus was very bad, particularly for the California-bound, since the contractors had no establishment at Chagres. In March, 1849, the mails from one trip of the Falcon took six days to cross to Panama, while those in the opposite direction reached their destination too late to catch the steamer. Later that spring, when there was no one at Chagres to receive the mails, Captain Tucker of the Orus gave them to a muleteer, telling him that when he reached Panama, he would be paid for his service. On arrival, the man could find no one to pay him and therefore offered the mails for sale to the highest bidder.

Late in 1849 the transportation of mail across the Isthmus was assumed by the government of New

Granada under the postal convention of March 6, 1844. By this, the payment for service was by weight, $30 for the first 100 pounds and $12 for each succeeding 100 pounds on a trip. Amos B. Corwine, United States consul at Panama, was appointed mail agent at $500 per year. This system proved to be little more satisfactory than the previous one. The government of New Granada farmed out the mail service to Panamanian business firms, with results which were not conducive to good service. Not only was poor service rendered but the arrangement also proved unprofitable to the government of New Granada, which was therefore willing to release the United States from its contract at the end of 1851. From March 13, 1850, until December 13, 1851, the United States had paid $70,585.31 for the transportation of the mail across the Isthmus.

To take the place of the New Granada service the Post Office contracted with the Panama Railroad to carry the mail from Aspinwall to Panama, this service beginning January 1, 1852. The rate paid was twenty-two cents a pound for first-class matter, with printed material considerably lower. As the railroad drew toward completion, the Postmaster General felt that the cost of transportation must be less, and therefore attempted to reduce compensation to eighteen cents a pound. The Panama Railroad objected violently to this, and the final outcome was a contract for service at the annual lump sum of $100,000 per year. This held until the expiration of the ocean mail contracts at the end of June, 1860, after which there was no regular contract. For the year ending June 30, 1861, the sum of $25,000 was paid for the isthmian transit of the mails, in 1866 it was $37,500 or $781.23 per mile, and in 1867 it remained the same. The mail service on the Isthmus underwent much the same experience as the ocean lines in the years between 1860 and 1869, being slighted in favor of the overland route and yet kept up because it was indispensable. With the completion of the overland railroad in 1869, mail between parts of the United Sates ceased to be send by way of Panama.

The attitude of American travelers on the Isthmus toward the residents and their civilization could hardly result otherwise than in friction. After 1850 there were frequent outbursts of violence between Americans and Panamanians at Chagres and Panama, for which the Americans were probably a good deal to blame. In May, 1850, a riot occurred in Panama in which two Americans and several natives were killed, the trouble arising from the accusation of a Panamanian boy of a theft of which others believed him to be innocent. The United States consuls at Chagres, Aspinwall, and Panama were unremitting in their application for men-of-war to be stationed at each side of the Isthmus for the protection of the lives of travelers, emphasizing the chronic bad feeling existent. In 1854, a Vigilance Committee of twenty-three members was organized at Aspinwall to protect the lives and property of Americans, and Panama was urged to follow suit.

Although it might have been expected that the completion of the railroad would relieve this tension by removing the travelers from contact with the natives, its effect was quite different. The Isthmus, which had enjoyed an income estimated at $125,000 to $150,000 a month spent by those who passed over the route and paid for the transportation of passengers, baggage, freight, and specie, now found most of this revenue cut off. Travelers no longer lingered at Panama waiting for a steamer but were transported across the Isthmus and from one ship to another within a day. A deep business depression settled over the region almost immediately after the opening of the railroad and caused bitter feelings among the natives toward the railroad and those who traveled over it. The bad feeling engendered resulted in a serious riot at the Panama terminus of the railroad on the evening of April 15, 1856. It was said to have started when a drunken American quarreled with a fruit vendor over a watermelon and drew a pistol, whereupon the native drew a knife and a fight resulted. There were some 1,950 Americans on the Isthmus at the time, travelers from both coasts, and those at the Panama station were attacked by a mob of the lower element from the city. The police were called out, but sided with the mob, and the affair ended with the killing of fourteen Americans and the injury of twenty-eight more, besides the looting of the station and baggage room and two hotels. About three natives were killed and twelve injured. There were no further serious disturbances after the "watermelon riot," and, as the Isthmus became accustomed to the changed condition resultant from the railroad, relations between natives and Americans tended to improve.

Thus, after half a dozen years of development and change, the transit of the Isthmus of Panama settled down after 1855,and 1856 to a seldom broken succession of short crossings of passengers and freight from ocean to ocean, a passage which formed a satisfactory and dependable link in the chain of communication between the coasts of the United States by way of Panama.

Elisha O. Crosby = 1849

When the news of the gold discovery in California was promulgated and it became known, as a reliable fact, every body seemed anxious if possible to make the transit of the Isthmus of Panama, to intercept the steamer when she should arrive there, if indeed she should be fortunate enough to get there safely. One or two vessels left New Orleans during the month of Dec. 1848 for Chagres; the steamer *Quaker City* left New York for Chagres about the 20th of Dec. 1848, being the first from New York. The second was the old steamer *Isthmus* which left on Christmas day 1848 for Chagres. I was a passenger on that steamer. I think the *Quaker City* carried about 200 persons, and we had something like 120 or 130. Some other vessels were fitting out for ports in Mexico and Central America about that time, when they proposed crossing the continent and taking the chances of getting passage on the Pacific side to California. These trips were wholly experimental. The *New York Herald* of that time sought information, and tried to discourage people from going by the way of Chagres, on account of its great unhealthiness, declaring that the adventurers would be destroyed as fast as they landed there.

They urged the people to be patient until some accurate information about the best route was obtained, and advised them to wait until it was known that the steamer had arrived at Panama. That was the prevailing tone of the New York papers at that time; but they might as well have attempted to stop a band of wild horses as to stay the emigration which had already commenced. The day the steamer *Isthmus* left New York, a cold half melting snow storm prevailed, and a more forlorn and half frozen crowd you never saw than filled the deck when she left her berth at the foot of Cortland St. on Christmas day 1848. On the morning of the 26th we passed Sandy Hook and to sea. This was my first experience of sea life, and the sea sickness that followed for some days brought many regrets for the quiet home I had just left and determined resolutions never to venture again at sea if I once gained a safe footing on land again. How well I kept my promises may be answered by the fact that I have since made eleven sea voyages.

The second day out we began to experience the softening influence of the gulf stream, and the third, fourth and fifth day brought us quite within a new and spring like climate. Our coats and heavy woollen[s] began to be laid aside, and the horror of a northern winter gave place to the delightful spring and summer clime. Our steamer was in command of Capt. Baker, familiarly known on this coast afterwards as "Lying Jim Baker, as he held a divided command with a Capt. Wood who professed to have been at the Port of Chagres, sometime in his early life as a sailor. Woods was then quite advanced in years. I never saw or heard of him after leaving the steamer. Both he and Baker were free drinkers, and much of the time pretty drunk We made the Bahama Banks in due time and as we had lost the usual ships channels we meandered the shoal and often dangerous channels among the coral reefs. I may mention an incident that occurred when we were well out to sea off Cape Hatteras. A severe gale had driven the ocean into high waves, and our old steamer was labouring heavily, when an alarm of fire was given and smoke began to issue from the hold of the vessel. Much confusion followed and after search was made for the location of the fire, it was found to be under that part of the hold where our trunks and baggage was stowed, and seemed almost beyond human reach. It was pretty well known that every passenger had stowed away his small arms and enough powder for a California campaign and any one of these trunks continued enough powder to blow the steamer to atoms. I remember setting on the taf rail with E. V. Joyce Esqu. a fellow passenger from New York, and contemplating the chances of our being very soon blown up. Fortunately however a gleam of hope came to us, in the proposition to scuttle the ship, and let it sink far enough to stop the fire, and this expedient was actually commenced, but one of the firemen (by the way a colored man) succeeded in opening a passage to the location of the fire, and we all took a hand in pumping water into the hold which soon extinguished its ravages. It was a pretty close shave, and for one I was thankful to be so fortunately out of it.

 We navigated pretty nearly around the island of Cuba, and finally stopped in Havana. The contrast of climate and scenery between New York in the middle of winter and the tropical beauty and foliage of the delightful island of Cuba, produces the most agreeable sensations. I advise you to try the experiment. We were not permitted to land although we stayed in port two days under the guns of the celebrated "Moro Castle."

The Isthmus then put to sea and made way for the Island of Jamaica, and for what reason I could never divine our Captain went entirely around the Island, and finally put into the Port of Kingston for a supply of coal, water and provisions. There we were permitted to go ashore and were received very kindly, and the "boys" had the free run of the town. The scenes and the occasion were as much enjoyed by the people as by the passengers, who were mostly young men full of life and hilarity. The contrast between the rigors of the northern climate we had so lately left, and the soft tropical atmosphere of Kingston seemed to inspire them with unusual animal spirits, and they had a "high time."

A good many took occasion to lay in a supply, not only of provisions, but of summer clothing, and as this trade proved so profitable to the merchants of Kingston, the authorities gave us the liberty of the city and country.

Santa Anna was then living near the city of Kingston and I went with a party to call upon him. He received us very kindly chatted familiarly; entertained us with refreshments, wish us a prosperous voyage and success in our new adventures, and said he esteemed it quite an honor that he had so brave an enemy to deal with during the Mexican War. He is a fine type of Mexican General and President, polite and courteous to all and well calculated to intrigue his way into power. We left him with our best wishes and highly delighted with our call.

The coaling of a steamer at Kingston presented a new feature of tropical life to most of us. The work was done at night, and the coal carried on board in buckets on the heads of the negroes. The blazing sun is too powerful for even negroes and they took the cooler time at night for this labour, by forming two lines, one going on board with tubs of coal on the head, depositing it in the bunkers and returning in another line, to the shore. The torches that lit up the scene and the chanting of their wild melody presented a weird picture not easily forgotten. Kinston life and coaling must have an end, and notice given to again go on board, and try again the delightful Sea life on the old *Isthmus*.

The passage of the Caribean Sea is generally disagreeable because of its shallow water and short chopping seas, and woe he who has the slightest tendency to sea sickness, that most vilanous of all sensations to head and stomach, and all to be laughed at, for nobody gets the least sympathy, for all his woes from his fellow passengers. By way of a remedy I advise "Champaign Cocktails." It is not bad to take and did me on many voyages much good. Try it.

We reached Chagres about the 20th of January 1849, the steamer running right into the harbor. The *Quaker City* was lying outside, when she discharged her passengers. The entrance is very narrow, with rocks on both sides, and it was dangerous passage. I have often thought that Providence protected that wonderful emigration that came by sea and land to the Pacific coast, during that eventful year of 1849, and was the cause of our safety, for both our captains were in a condition not to exercise much if any discretion. We went in however safely nearly touching and grazing the rocky points on either side.

The passengers of the *Quaker City* and those who came by the vessels from New Orleans had already disembarked and had disappeared on the *Isthmus*. I associated with ten or twelve of our passengers, and we hired a large bungo, for our bagagge, and a smaller one for ourselves from the natives, and the same day got our "traps" from the steamer, and stowed them as best we could, on these dugouts, and commenced our ascent of the Chagres River, the natives rowing or paddling, with an oar like a pointed long handle shovel, or poling by long poles resting on the bottom of the river, and occasionally getting into the water & dragging our boats along. We got up from Chagres five or six miles that evening and camped on the bank of the river. In about three days we reached the end of navigation on the river, at the settlement of Cruces. The natives at that time were very civil, inoffensive and obliging. We got supplies of Poultry eggs and vegetables, meat, rice, and such other articles as they had, and at very low prices, compared with the enormous prices afterwards paid by passengers who swarmed upon the Isthmus, a few months later.

With another companion, I hired a couple of mules for our trunks, and we were fortunate enough to secure another animal to ride alternately, "ride and tie," as it was called. In that way we made the trip across the Isthmus to Panama, some twelve or fifteen miles. We did not enter Panama immediately, but camped outside, as the cholera was said to be prevailing at the time, and several hundred emigrants there already. The second day after we arrived, news came of the sighting of the Steamer *California* of the Port of Panama. That was on the 25th of January I think. I went into town and presented my letters to the agents of Howland & Aspinwall, Zachrison & Nelson. These letters directed their agents at Panama to put me on board the first steamer than came round to Panama. Mr. Nelson very kindly and considerately took me in charge, and furnished me with a box of provisions, and a large Mexican Hammock for he said he could do very little else than put me on board; that there were only cabin accommodations for 25 persons, and they had already been taken up, and besides that, some 60 or 70 Chilenos had been taken on at Valparaiso; and how the passengers were to manage, was more than he could tell. But he said he would put me on board with that little box of provisions, and what I could not get from the general mess I must make out of my box. It was a very thoughtful thing in him, and I have often called to mind his kindness with much gratitude. He also advised me to take the Hammock, which I did, and had it hung in the rigging of the steamer, and slept there most of the way from Panama to San Francisco. The hold of the steamer was fitted up with temporary bunks, and as many passengers taken on as it was thought possible to accommodate, and carry with safety. We left at Panama about 300 who were anxious to go, but were refused, much to their regret and disgust. I think we had about 450 on board including the Chilenos and crew. Capt. Marshall was taken on board at Valparaiso to navigate the steamer, and Capt. Forbes who brought the steamer from New York around Cape Horn looking after the passengers &c. Alfred Robinson who came out as the agent of the Pacific

Steam Ship Co. was on board. He had previously lived in California.

We left Panama on the 1st of February 1849, and every one of the passengers were in good humour, as they all expected to become rich and happy; the scenes and incidents of that voyage were varied and comical in the extreme.

1849 = Daniel Knower

I sailed on the steamer which left New York at 5P.M., July 1,1849. friends were there to see me off, but there were no persons on the boat that I had ever seen before and I was wondering who would be my first acquaintance. Being very tired, I retired soon to my berth, and woke up the next morning on the broad ocean. Two days of sea sickness and I was all right again. There were about one thousand passengers from all parts of our country.. I tried to fathom the motives and standing of different ones. Col. B. from Kentucky,an aristocratic looking man, with his slave for a body servant, who could not have been bought for less than $1500 in Kentucky, where slavery existed at that time. Why a man in his circumstances should be going to California to seek gold I could not fathom. One day a party of us were seated around the table talking matters over and it was proposed that each should reveal what he expected to do and his motives for going. We each related our expectations and motives with Col. B.

stating "I am going to California to deal Faro, the great American gambling game , and I don't care who knows it".

The fourth day out being the fourth of July, was celebrated on the steamer in true American style. Our course was to the east of Cuba. We passed in sight of the green hills of San Domingo to our left, and in sight of Jamaica to our right. In crossing the Caribbean sea whose grand and glorious sunsets I shall never forget.

I could not buy a ticket in New York for the steamer from Panama to San Francisco, but was informed by the office in New York that sixty tickets were for sale in Panama by Zachrisson, Nelson & Co., the American Consul, who were agents for the steamer on the Pacific side. I naturally supposed that those who offered their money first for those tickets could buy them. The price was $300 for a first class cabin and $150 for the second class cabin from Panama to San Francisco but a fraction of the passengers did have tickets for the Pacific side.

The objective point was to get to Panama to secure a ticket so I made an arrangement with four others. Three were to take charge of the baggage of the five and proceed liesurely across. Lt. M. , of South Carolina, and myself were selected to run an express across the Isthmus and secure the tickets for the five of us. When we came to anchor in the bay at Chagres we two wanted to be the first to land. The captain announced that no passengers would be permitted to go ashore until the government officials had inspected the vessel. The officials arrived by boat from shore and after a short stay the officials went down the side of the steamer to their boat to return to shore. There was a guard on the boat to keep all but the proper persons from getting into the boat. With a small carpet bag in my hand I went over the side and slipped a $5 gold piece to the guard and took a seat passing as one of the officials which made me the first passenger ashore.

To secure a boat for passage up the river I was recommended to a Col. P. who was a colonel in the Granadian army and a full blooded African. I got his price for a boat and two of his best men and then offered double the price if they would row night and day for everything depended on securing those tickets on the Pacific side. With all arrangements made Lt. M. and I beheld our canoe or dugout with a little canopy over the center that you could crawl under to lay down with two natives clad only in loin cloths and communicating by signs since we did not know each others language.

At 4 P.M. starting for Gorgona, fifty-five miles up the river, where we were to land and take mules to Panama. We felt elated that we got so good a start over all the other passengers. The denseness of the vegetation first attracted our attention on the banks of the river. The trees, the vines, the shrubbery and the vines clinging to the trees, hanging in all fantastic shapes seemed to be impenetrable as an ocean of green unlike any thing we had ever seen before.

Early in the evening we arrived at the first stopping place, eight miles up the river, where we both made ourselves at home, excited at the strangeness of the scene, surrounded by the thatched huts of the natives who were having a dance on the square in the village. After we had been there an hour we thought our men had their rest and it was time to go on according to our contract of being rowed night and day.

In the meantime it seems the natives had taken some offense at Lt. M.'s familiarity and they appeared with the handles of long knives projecting back of their necks in a threatening manner. We likewise learned that this was the home of one of our men and that he proposed to stay there all night in violation of our contract. So we had a consultation to decide what to do and it was pitch dark as we laid our plan. Lt. M. beckoned one of the men away from the dance as if he wanted to give him something. He then drew his pistol on him and marched him down to the boat, while I with a pistol kept him there while he went for the other man.

After a while he came with him and we got them both in the boat and started. About this time a storm came up with rain, thunder and lightening, as only the elements can perform in the tropics. We were surrounded by impenetrable darkness in a river unknown to us with two naked savages we had only gotten into the boat by force and could not feel very friendly towards us. Expecting to be fired on from shore if they could see us in the darkness we took our departure from our first landing place on the Chagres river.

In a while the clouds broke away, the moon showed itself, and we made good progress that night. We had no trouble with our men after that for the colonel at Chagres had evidently given us his best men. They found we were masters of the situation and it was in their interest to submit. we treated them kindly after that and all went well as we passed every boat we came to. I shall never forget the look of despair of two Frenchmen as we went by them and they told us of how long they had been coming up the river and could do nothing with their men.

That afternoon we came in sight of a thatched hut on the banks and evidently a ranch. We thought it in our interest to rest and saw a man whom we took to be the proprietor, entirely naked, rubbing his back against a post. On landing and approaching him he excused himself for a short time, returning dressed and walking with the air of a lord of manor as his dress consisted of a course bagging shirt coming down to his knees.

We arrived the next day at 11 A.M. at Gorgona and took our dinner at the hotel kept by the Alcalde of the place and bargained with him for a guide and three mules to continue our journey to Panama. As soon as the guide and the mules were ready we departed around 1 P.M. for Panama. We soon got enough of our mules by being thrown a number of times over their heads. They did not understand our language for "get up "and "go along" was greek to them but when the guide said "mula vamous" they knew what it meant.

On reaching the place where we were to stay all night we got our rest and arose refreshed. We conclude to leave our mules and make the rest of the way afoot as we considered them a nuisance. We had no baggage but my little satchel in which I had bills of lading, the specifications of my carpenters schedule, my letters, a gold watch and a bottle of brandy. this bag I handed to the guide boy after taking out the brandy bottle for it was to be used for warding off fever during the crossing.

We were walking on at a free pace with our guide boy following behind and looking back after a while we could not see him. We stopped and waited for some time, but he did not come, so we thought to go on and he would follow. The result was we lost our way and craved for a sight of the Pacific ocean and after wandering all day, almost without hope, until four in the afternoon when we came to a stream of water where oppressed by heat and fatigue we threw ourselves in to get refreshed.

As we lay there we heard voices and in looking back who should we see but one of our countrymen and we felt saved. We, by chance had struck the Cruces road and were but ten miles from Panama. We joined our new friends and arrived in Panama that evening.

Lt. M. and myself were the first of the one thousand passengers on our steamer to enter the city but the office of the agents of the Pacific steamers was closed and so I went the first thing in the morning to purchase the five tickets for our party. Alas for human expectations! I was informed it would be several weeks before the steamer would sail for she had not yet returned from the first trip to San Francisco. They said there were but sixty tickets for sale and they would not be offered untill a few days before the departure of the steamer. Of course all we could do was to abide our chances of getting them.

The city was walled around and dyked like those of the Middle Ages. Toward the bay the wall was one hundred feet high and by twenty broad. The city had been on the decline for most a hundred years and we could see the ruins of what it once had been. At one time Spain had owned all South America, Mexico, California, Louisiana and Florida. Panama was the only port of entry on the Pacific coast and controlled its commerce. As you enter the gates of the walled city there is a chapel just inside where the lights are always burning on its altars. The first thing all good Catholics do on entering is kneel and make their devotions while seeking the protection of the patron saint of the city.

The head alcalde of the city was a Castilian Spaniard and the second alcalde was a negro as black as I have ever seen. In the city of Panama in its days of prosperity under Spain the higher classes must have lived in great luxuries with the negroes as slaves. The natives or peons were in a condition similar to slavery as they could not leave the land as long as they owed any thing. But the despotism of old Spain became so great that when they struck for freedom all classes united. They gave freedom to the negroes and peons and even the priests, who had been tyrannized by the mother church in Spain, joined the revolutionists and all classes are represented in the government.

Two brothers had furnished rooms like a parlor but I could not speak Spanish nor they English. I could speak a little French and I found they could speak it fluently. When I asked them where they had learned it they said at the Jesuit college at Granada. Then one of them, when he learned that I was from the United States, went to the piano and played Hail Colombia as a compliment to my country.

There are now great trees growing up in the ruins of what was once its great cathedral. The freebooter Morgan is said to have plundered one of its altars of a million of gold and silver. The new city of Panama is a healthy city to those acclimated and facing a beautiful bay and unlike Chagres which is the most unhealthy spot on this continent.

I stopped at the American Hotel for I was somewhat in a dilapidated condition from the experiences of my trip from Chagres. The waiter in my room at the hotel took the best care of me and I soon found he was no ordinary waiter. He had resigned a position in Washington of $2000 a year to go to the gold Eldorado. He had been taken down with the fever twice which had exhausted his funds and was working at the hotel for his board but never thought of turning back. He was quite enfeebled from the effects of the fever and he got hold of my sympathies and secured my friendship.

I had been here four or five days without seeing our guide who had my satchel containing my valuables. I was in a quandary and anxiety about it when one day as I was going to dinner I felt a tug from behind and there was our native boy with my satchel with contents there all safe. It was an instance of honesty that would do honor to any nation. I gave some honest Catholic priest credit for the boy had evidently been well instructed.

The great objective point now was how to get to San Francisco. There was no hope for a sailing vessel from this place, for we saw one return for water that had been out three weeks, scarcely out of sight of the city. There is very little chance for a sailing vessel until they get west several hundred miles and strike the trade winds. So the only hope seemed to be the steamer with its sixty tickets and with from one thousand to fifteen hundred passengers waiting to buy them.

I saw in the office of the steamer agent a young man whom I took a fancy to and sought his acquaintance. I found he was from Hudson, N.Y. and I from Albany and it ripened into a warm friendship. I explained my situation to him and my desire , if it was possible, to get off on the steamer but did not venture to ask his influence to try and get me a ticket.

At this time the cholera and Panama fever was

raging in full force and unacclimated Americans were dying in every direction. I was conversing at 8 A.M. with a healthy looking man, one of our passengers from New York, when at 5 P.M., the same day, I inquired of him and was told that he was dead and buried. He had been attacked with the cholera and it was the law of the city that they must be buried within one hour of death from a contagious disease. I was finally myself taken down with Panama fever, lay unconcious and unnoticed in my room at the hotel for a long time. I then came to and found myself burning with the raging fever, had a doctor sent for, and after a time recovered so I could venture out.

In the meantime the steamer Panama had arrived and its day of sailing for San Francisco announced. Zachrisson, Nelson & Co. had issued an order that the sixty tickets would be put up to a drawing with the winning numbers having the privilege of buying them. Probubly one thousand names and but sixty tickets and the chances small but the only hope. I was still very week from the effects of the fever when I went to register for the drawing. As I was about to put down my name I looked behind a desk and saw my friend who shook his head for me not to sign. I backed out knowing that meant something favorable and returned at once to my hotel room.

That evening about 8 o'clock my friend came to my room with a second class cabin ticket. I was overjoyed and asked him to tell me how he had been able to obtain it. He said he was about to resign his position and go on the same steamer to California. The night before the drawing he asked Mr. Nelson if his services had been satisfactory and when the reply was yes, they had been, he asked for a favor upon his leaving. When Mr. Nelson replied he would grant the favor he then asked for a ticket for a friend. Mr. Nelson said, "If I had known what you were going to ask for I could not have granted it; but since I have pledged my word I shall give you the ticket."

The next day passengers would be received on the steamer, which was anchored out in the bay, some distance from shore. It was announced that no sick persons could go on the steamer. As I was quite enfeebled from my sickness and at my best in the morning I wanted to make an early start so as to be sure and get aboard the vessel which was to sail early the next morning. As I was going along , some distance ahead of me, sitting at the doors of a doggery, with his head between his knees, the picture of despair, was my Washington friend. He who had waited on my room at the hotel when I first arrived and done me many favors. I said to my self, poor fellow, I can do nothing for you. I must not let him see me so I dodged and passed him. When I got some distance passed him my conscience smote me and I went back to speak to him.

I had advised him a few days previous to see some officer from the boat and offer to go as a waiter without pay. He said there was no hope for they told him they had been offered $300 for the privilege of going up as a waiter. I then told him I had a ticket and was going then for a boat to take me aboard. That his case was desparate and desparate cases require desparate remedies; that he had been down twice with the fever and the next time he would probubly die; that he had no friends or money; if he would do as I told him I would stand by him but he must have nerve. He said to me: " How can a man have nerve without a dollar in his pocket?". I asked him to hire a boat to get him out to the vessel and gave him the $2 it would cost and told him to get his baggage but he replied that he had none.

I told him to come out about 11 o'clock and go to work among the hands as if he was one of them for all were new hands and officers and would not know the difference. He said that the captain had said that if any person was caught on board without a ticket they would be put ashore at the first uninhabited island. I told him I would attend to that if it happened in his case. I went on board and got my berth and baggage all in and about 11 o'clock I saw my friend coming over the water making for the vessel. There was considerable confusion on board at the time with passengers constantly arriving, he was not noticed, and he went to work among the hands as if he had been regularly employed. In the evening he came and spoke to me and I said all right so far. But in the morning he told me they were going to examine every person and then they will put me ashore. I told him to keep a stiff upper lip and if you get into trouble come to me.

The next morning the gun was fired , the anchor raised, and we sailed down to Taboga where the health officers came out. Then my friend trembled and thought the day of judgment had come to him but the health officers were on board but a short time and no examinations took place. The signal gun was fired for departure and we passed with the bow of our vessel pointed north. I said to him that this vessel is bound for San Francisco and you are aboard and will get there as soon as I will.

A few days after that the mate was arranging the employment of the men and when he came to my friends turn he asked him as to who had employed him for he was not an able-bodied seaman. The mate could see he was a man of intelligence and his pale look showed he had been sick. It may have moved the sympathies of the officer who then said to him. This vessel is crowded with people and it won't do for us to be short of water so I will put the water in your charge. You must not let any passenger, or even the steward, have any except according to regulations and if you attend to that properly no other services will be required of you. Of the one thousand passengers desirous of getting on that steamer, and there was room but for sixty on the day of departure, his chance looked the most helpless being penniless. But he was one of the fortunate ones while those who had plenty of money were left in Panama. It illustrates the old maxim, "Where there is a will there is a way."

THE RETURN VOYAGE

Arriving safe in Panama we found they had commenced building the railroad over the Isthmus but as it was not finished we crossed to Cruces and then down the Chagres. I there took the steamer Georgia for New York. It was commanded by Captain Porter of the United States Navy who commanded your admiration with his skill of his management of the vessel.

There were on the vessel well-dressed pickpockets, who went from New York to the Isthmus and return by the steamers for the chances of robbing the returning Californians of their gold dust as most of them carried it on their persons. I had deposited mine with the ships purser for safety.

Henry E. Davenport
—1849

We left New York on the 17th of July; and on the 28th of the same month cast anchor before Charges, one of the eastern ports of the Isthmus of Panama. A leaden sky, a humid and oppressive atmosphere, and peals of thunder, that were echoed from the depths of the close woods, contributed not a little to give a melancholy aspect to a port whose reputation for unhealthiness has eclipsed even that of Senegal.

Though Chagres is so conveniently situated between the two oceans, and the two lines of steam navigation that connect the United States with California, it is but a miserable village, composed of a few Indian huts, which are constructed of wood and stubble, and stand on each side of the river. The streets are complete puddles during the rainy season, which occurs in winter. This season is most fatal to health, because of the humid heat that prevails, and the mysterious miasma which is disengaged for all parts of the soil. Serious maladies may be contracted within a few hours; and strangers are eager to leave this inhospitable place. The boatmen of the river Chagres, who were formerly hard put to earn a miserable subsistence, now gain very considerably by the American emigration to California, and the haste of travellers to leave this noxious coast and get up the river to Panama. In order to secure their own price from the poor strangers at their mercy, they take care only to exhibit a small number of boats while there are plenty more out of sight along the opposite bank of the river.

We left Chagres on the 30th July. The entrance of the river presented a most rich and beautiful aspect. Palms and cocoa-nut trees, and other gigantic productions of the climate, made two barriers on either side the stream of impenetrable verdure. Their long branches, gracefully inclining over the water, projected afar their splendid shadows, but which the voyager was only too happy to profit. The first impression produced by the sight of this luxuriance of nature is that of profound admiration; to which shortly succeeds a vague sinking of the spirits. This doubtless procceds from the enervating odors sent forth by tropical vegetation, and from the gases produced by the soil of the plants, whose absorption, emission, and flow of sap, acquire, in the heat and humidity to which they are constantly subjected, an extraordinary energy. Alternately peaceful as a lake, and impetuous as a cataract, this river seems to pride itself in its violent contrasts. Its habitual visitors were more surprised than frightened by our approach. Here the wild turkey-hen, with plumage of ebony, sailed round a palm tree, slowly beating the air with her heavy wings Further on were clouds of paroquets, gay with a thousand tints, and uttering their sharp, provoking cries. From time to time we could distinguish, in the middle of the thickets, the scaly and yellowish bodies of alligators, which are very common on the borders of the Chagres, where they wait entire hours for their prey, in a state of perfect immobility.

We were not long in arriving at a filthy hamlet, named Gatoung. There are few things so comical as a disembarkation in this country. The moment you place your foot upon the soil, which is nothing but mud, it sinks beneath your feet; and it is not without a great deal of trouble, and often at the sacrifice of your boots, which are left imbedded in the dirt, that you at length gain the top of the slope. We were ignorant, when we quitted New York, that the Isthmus of Panama was altogether without resources. We had not therefore been careful to lay in a store of victuals necessary for our journey; and a little sea biscuit and a few pots of preserves composed all our stock. Our halt at Gatoung gave us the opportunity of visiting several Indian huts, where we met with the most hospitable welcome, and we profited by this reception to try to procure some food. They at length directed us to a habitation where the inmates had a pot on the fire; the preparation of an *otta* of rice was quite an event in the district. A few crown-pieces obtained us a portion of this modest repast, and we succeeded besides in discovering in a neighboring hut a stray bottle of Xeres. Having forgotten to bring rain-water from Chagres, we found ourselves reduced to quench our thirst with the unhealthy water of the river, the crudity of which it was well to correct with a few drops of a spirit-wine liquor, even after it had been filtered. One of our number had fortunately brought with him a filter which enabled us to obtain a passable draught. Thirst is perhaps the most dangerous enemy one had to encounter on to the Isthmus of Panama. I have seen more than one American pay with his life for the fatal habit of listening to the temptations of this demon.

Continuing our route, night surprised us, and lent a new aspect to the surrounding scene. The majestic shadows of the huge trees upon the waters—the pale rays of the moon, that made the river like a sheet of silver—the silence around, uninterrupted save by the regular strokes of the oars, and the cries of the night birds, all contributed to the fascination of the hour. At length we arrived at a small creek, where our old pilot made us remain until sunrise.

Towards the evening of the second day, we arrived at the village of Pedro Blanco, where, after long and troublesome negotiations, we succeeded in obtaining a little rice for supper. Two of my travelling companions, who had been exploring the neighboring forest, brought in a couple of pretty paroquets, which were soon plucked, and added as a relish to our rice. But the flesh of this bird is far from equalling its plumage; and, notwithstanding the good-will of our sportsmen, they were compelled to pronounce their game horribly tough.

The next day the boatmen substituted the palanca for the oar. The *palanca* is a long pole, terminating in an iron point, which is pushed into the bed of the river, or into the roots or trunks of the trees, in such a manner as to shove the boat onwards, as much as possible avoiding the current. This mode of propulsion, more efficacious than the oar, has likewise the merit of being less fatiguing. But it exposes the passengers to certain danger, and this was to be our day of misfortunes. One of the boatmen, by some awkwardness, lost his *palanca*. The boat, which had been adroitly guided close along the bank of the stream, ceded to the impetuosity of the current, which was not to be mastered by an unequal number of *palancas*, and was driven against an enormous trunk of a submerged tree in the middle of the river. The frightful force of the shock staved in our front plank. The water began to pour in, and we saw ourselves on the point of capsizing, without the power of leaving the boat, shut in as we were by its roof of branches and our numerous packages. But we escaped this danger by a species of miracle, and the current, carrying us rapidly on, left the poor Indian, who had lost his *palanca*, suspended in the air to the bough of a tree, which he had seized with all his strength to avert the violence of the shock. Seeing us leaving him rapidly behind, he at length allowed himself to drop into the water, and swam ashore. The two men who now remained shoved the boat towards a creek, where we found a shelter for the night, and where the other Indian shortly afterwards rejoined us. Here we repaired the damage we had received.

This night, another boat, containing several Americans, was moored beside ours. The desperate condition of one of their number had compelled them to halt. The unhappy man had been suddenly attacked by cholera, after drinking a little milk and eating several oranges. I shall never forget the night that we passed beside the poor sufferer, who, far from his family and all remedies, was fast approaching his end, without even a bed to lie upon. His companions unceasingly administered eau-de-vie, which had no other effect but to accelerate the disease. The plaintive groans of the wretched man hindered us from shutting our eyes for a moment, were exposed in the frightful climate. The next morning he was no more; and his friends were obliged to get the assistance of their boatmen, and of some inhabitants of the neighboring hamlet, in rendering the last duties to his remains.

Having now repaired the breach in our plank, we would have continued our route, but one of the men, retained by the hope of participating in the benefits of the interment, opposed our departure. Hoping, doubtless, to moderate my eagerness to continue the journey, he said, pointing at the same time to the corpse of the American with a significant smile—"Este muerto y usted esta enfermo" (he is dead, and you are ill); an observation far from reassuring to a traveller laboring under a slight attack of fever in an unhealthy climate. The interment over, and the piastres pocked, our phlegmatic boatmen decided upon continuing the voyage. The banks of the river now began to lose their grand and picturesque aspect, which they had owed to the beauty and density of the woods with which they were clothed. We terminated happily a day so ill commenced, and arrived at night at the village of San Pablo.

The next morning, at a little distance from a small town named Gorgona, we perceived an American steamboat abandoned in the river. The numerous obstacles it had encountered had completely disabled it after only a few voyages. In order to secure a safe navigation for steamers of the very smallest dimensions, the Rio Chagres ought to be completely cleared. It is obstructed, throughout the whole extent of its course, by trunks of trees, often hidden by merely a few feet of water. While waiting for the great roads which the Americans intend to establish through the isthmus, it is urgent that the Rio Chagres should be rendered navigable. The emigrants and the country generally have the greatest interest in this measure.

The Chagres rises near Cruces, a small town situated about six leagues from Panama and two from Gorgona. Its course is nearly seventeen leagues. Travelers, en route for Panama, sail up it as far as Cruces, which, besides being two leagues nearer than Gorgona to Panama, possesses also an ancient royal Spanish road—a very bad one, it is true, but much better than that of which we shall have occasion to speak. Most of the Americans who landed at Chagres at the same time with our party went on the Cruces, which was likewise our first intention. But our boatmen and other assuring us that the means of transport were very rare, and cholera and fever rife, we determined to land at Gorgona—a resolution of which we afterwards had reason to repent. In this country a stranger cannot be too much on his guard against the misrepresentations of the boatmen, on the one hand, whose interest it is to shorten the voyage, and of the inhabitants, on the other, in order to secure to themselves the advantage of his sojourn in their locality. There is a regularly organized conspiracy against his purse.

Gorgona is, like Chagres, an irregular assemblage of from sixty to eighty huts, intersected by steep streets, where mud and water replace the pavement. These habitations are but one story high; they have neither flooring nor ceiling, and they are frequently flooded during the rainy season. The town has already its hotel, which possesses four beds, a few hammocks, no windows, but numerous holes in its thatched roof, which permit one to contemplate the firmament when the weather is fine and favor the inmates with gratuitous douches when it rains. The food corresponds with the lodging.

Contrary to what one usually remarks in unhealthy climates, the natives of New Granada appear equally exposed with strangers to the reigning maladies. There is scarcely a hut where one does not encounter some poor wretch trembling with the calentura or the fever. The cholera, likewise, in 1849, made terrible ravages. The physical characteristics of the population are easily enumerated. They possess finely-formed limbs, equally vigorous and supple, copper-colored skins, tolerably regular features, and black hair, but not crisp like that of the negroes. The men are generally clad in a species of shirt, which descends a little way down the leg. The women add to this a petticoat. Both sexes wear straw hats, with broad brims to shade them from the sun. The inhabitant of the Isthmus of Panama is kind and hospitable. In great matters he may be entirely trusted, but it is well to place tempting trifles out of sight. He wants energy and character; there is no very decided leaning to good or evil. An extreme filial tenderness, as among the Chinese, is the sole peculiarity that breaks in upon his habitual indifference; all his faculties seem to languish under the enervating effects of the climate. Nothing is more monotonous than rural life in these countries. With the exception of some rare excursions, the people pass their time in smoking, and sleeping in a wretched hut, scarcely sheltered from sun and rain by a roof of palm-leaves. Many huts are formed of nothing but four stakes supporting a species of loft, where the family pass the night extended upon mats, and to which they mount by the trunk of a tree notched at regular distances, so as to serve for a ladder. The domestic utensils consist of one or two kettles, and a few large jars, of a spherical form, which hold rice and rain-water. They light a fire on the ground, and cook in the open air. Men and women eat squatted upon their heels; and the use of tobacco is common to both sexes.

Gorgona possesses an alcade, to whom we were obliged to address ourselves for the fifteen or twenty mules which were needed to convey us and our luggage to Panama. The complaisant magistrate placed himself at our service, and promised us an unlimited number of these rare and indispensable quadrupeds. But time passed, and the mules did not appear. The travellers who had preceded us had engrossed them all. We were consequently obliged to separate for a time, much against our inclination, and to hire the mules as they returned by twos and threes to Gorgona. The hire of a mule varies from eight to sixteen piastres.

Our advance guard, composed of two mules, two Indians, and the youngest of my fellow-travellers, set out on the 5th of August. Impatient to arrive at Panama, I followed the next day, the landlord of the hotel having procured me a little mare, and a guide twelve years of age. Furnished with some sea-biscuit and chocolate, my fusil strapped to my shoulder, and hunting-knife at my side. I mounted my pitiful beast, after having disposed of a waterproof cloak of its croup, and placed under the saddle a blanket, which had been of the greatest service. In this fashion I left Gorgona, after having bidden adieu to my remaining comrades, who were to rejoin me at Panama as so as possible, bringing with them our luggage. From the beginning of my journey, we traversed most abominable roads. Steep and slippery declivities, rivulets, precipices, narrow passes, where the rocks approached each other so closely that the mare could not advance without the greatest trouble, and at a sore expense to my poor knees, which were every moment grazed against their sharp edges, all announced a tiresome journey. I could not avoid making comparisons between my guide and my horse. The east greatly exceeded the boy in topographical knowledge; and, with a modesty for which I gave him credit, the latter at length resigned himself to the leading of the former, walking in the rear, and only crying out, from time to time aqui (here), or acà (there). When the branches of the trees or their overgrown trunks barred further passage, my young native resumed the lead and speedily leveled the obstacles by the aid of a cleaver, without which an Indian never sets out on a journey. Sometimes the mare would stop and inflate her nostrils at the sight of a half-devoured mule, regretfully abandoned at the noise of approach by the vultures that disputed its remains. The poor beast was constantly knee-deep in mud; for what they call a road in this country is simply the bed of a river, more or less dry in fine weather, but filled again by the first heavy shower. Divers claps of thunder now announced the approach of one of those storms which take place every day during the winter, and in a few minutes inundate the country. Urged on by the pouring rain, we reached, just in time, a tolerably large river, which was now forded without difficulty, but would have been impassable an hour later. We were luckily enabled to take refuge in a shed, when

I dried my clothes, and determined to remain for the night.

The next morning, at an early hour, we continued our journey. In place of the good road I had been led to expect, I still encountered these muddy plains, and eternal hills bristling with rocks. At length we reached a house situated upon an elevation half-way between Gorgona and Panama. Here we obtained some coffee, without which I could scarcely have been able to endure the fatigues of the journey. At four, we arrived at the last dwelling before reaching Panama. For one instant I thought of passing the night here; but my guide hindered me from following this happy inspiration, solemnly assuring me that we should reach our destination the same evening. We therefore continued our way through a prairie where the road from Gorgona unites itself with that leading to Cruces, which, though horribly uneven, is at any rate tolerably free from mud. Here a new annoyance was reserved for me. My wretched mare, accustomed to the worst roads, refused to advance now that there was a little improvement. I was reduced, knocked up as I was, to dismount and lead her. By blows and cries we contrived to make her advance a little way; but our progress was so slow, that some workmen occupied in repairing the road laughingly prophesied that she would never arrive at Panama. This prediction, confirmed as it was by a feverish trembling of the animal, was far from being agreeable. While thus slowly progressing, night surprised us—a night of clouds and rain. The obscurity was such that we could not have told where we were, save for the ignis fatuus, the fire-flies, and the lightning. At length, unhoped-for happiness! We distinguished the barking of a dog, and soon afterwards a light. We had reached Panama. The reader may judge of my satisfaction on seeing the end of my eight days of painful journeying, accomplished under such disagreeable circumstances. I quickly made my way to the Hotel de France, where I found my young companion, who had set out the day before me; and there I speedily got rid of the fever that still hung about me.

Panama is a ruinous town, the population of which does not exceed 7000 souls. There is nothing remarkable about it but the immense number of churches, monuments of past grandeur, and now invaded by creeping-plants and turf. The bells of these venerable edifices are half rusty, and morning and evening ring the most lugubrious peals. There are, besides, some fortifications, and a dozen old guns, disposed along the rampart that faces the Pacific Ocean. This is a magnificent point of view, whence may be seen the church-steeples, the vessels in the roadstead, a quantity of plots, and, about two miles distant, towards the extremity of the peninsula upon which Panama is situated, the ruins of the former town, abandoned during the wars of the Hibustiers, in consequence of the reiterated attacks of a famous pirate.

Panama is traversed by two principal streets, containing a few tolerable ships, and a number of stalls, where they vend liquors. These last, kept by obliging *señoritas*, boast a sort of counter, and are separated by a screen from the bedchamber, where the indolent saleswomen swing in their hammocks the greatest part of the day, smoking their cigarettes, and waiting for customers. The houses are built of stone, and ornamented with wooden balconies. The walls present that beautiful whiteness which distinguishes Spanish masonry in hot countries. But there is nothing elegant about these buildings, and their interiors are deplorable. The rooms are almost destitute of furniture; curtains are unknown, even in the governor's palace; and it would be hard to find in the whole town a good bed or a safe lock. The pavements and footpaths respond to the houses.

The climate of this town is unhealthy, especially during the winter rains, which commence in May, and end in October or November. The complexions of the inhabitants evince the noxious influence of vitiated air. Fevers are very common among the natives as also mephitic colic, induced by the badness of the water, in drinking which one cannot be too cautious.

The population of Panama is composed of ancient Spanish families, natives, and half-breeds. The costume of both men and women is European, a little generated and simplified, to suit the climate. The women go with the head uncovered, and decorate their black tresses with flowers of penetrating odor. Without being beautiful, their features are agreeable enough, and they have a good deal of grace and coquetry about them. The habitual indifference of the inhabitants is strongly contrasted by the howlings and clamor that accompany their funeral ceremonies. These lamentations, however, appear to be hired. Their interments are managed after a singular fashion, as they employ a species of omnibus coffin, which they place the corpse, to carry it to the cemetery. Once arrived there, they take the body from the bier, and throw it at once into a fosse, returning with the empty coffin.

The natives patronize music, and other amusements, among which may be reckoned cock-fighting. But the sicknesses, which, in 1849, clothed nearly every family in mourning, have put an end to the fetes, and thrown over all a tinge of distress and fear.

The public works are executed by convicts, who are seen passing every instant under, military escort. These guardians appear very polite to their prisoners, for, if any of the latter are stopped in the streets by an acquaintance, the soldiers stop also, and wait very tranquilly until the convicts are pleased to continue their way.

Panama possesses three or four hotels, which, upon our arrival, we found crowded with travellers. Eight, ten, fifteen were sleeping in the same chamber, upon hard-rope beds, without mattresses. The charge of a week's board and lodging varied from $6.75 to $7.50 cents, without reckoning wine, which costs from 37 cents to 75 cents the bottle for ordinary Bordeaux. Meat and fruit abound, but vegetables are very rare. We had taken up our abode in the Hotel de France, situated in one of the healthiest quarters of the town; and here the companions whom we had left at Gorgona hastened to rejoin us.

The crowd of emigrants, though still very considerable, was infinitely less than it had been for some months previously, for thousands of Americans had been compelled to abandon the place, and return home, in default of financial resources, or means of transport to California. Never have I seen more deplorable figures than those of the poor Yankees, congregated in this little town, dragging themselves painfully along the streets, some under the influence of fever, others under the curse of idleness, disputing with oaths and imprecations upon the easiest and cheapest modes of reaching San Francisco, parading their bad-humor from stall to stall which they endeavor to dissipate by reiterated doses of brandy, and then hastening to throw away the little money they have left, in gaming-houses, the last hope of these poor idlers. Once ruined, the Yankee becomes himself again—that is to say, the most industrious and enterprising of men. He finds a thousand resources, he invents a hundred modes of making money. One will engage himself as a sailor, another as a cook, a third opens a shop at Panama, and, a few weeks afterwards, procures some lots of goods to be assigned to him. He then commences selling, at magnificent prices, assortments of American boots, harder than wood, and newly-invented coats, that would have mouldered away at San Francisco without attracting a single admirer. A number of articles, in fact, find a far readier sale at ports situated on the way to California, then in the country itself, which is inundated with products of all species.

In the mixture of the floating and the indigenous population of Panama there is a most striking contrast between an almost extinct civilization and a spirit of young and powerful enterprise, full of nerve and promise for the future. The hoary steeples, these deserted monuments, attest the former magnificence of the place, the wretched inhabitants of which are, without doubt, the descendants of the proud and brilliant chevaliers of other days. All is poetry and grandeur in the past; in the present, silence and decay. But mark those columns of smoke, those pantings proceeding from the huge lungs of the steam-monsters in the roadstead. Those large vessels are freighted with passengers furnished with every species of instrument. They go to acquire wealth, to organize a new state; how differently from the soldiers of Cortez and Pizarro! Happier than these, it is neither at the price of their own blood, nor that of the peaceable inhabitants of the gold country, they conduct their future operations. Thanks to them, Panama already beholds the commencement of a new prosperity. Whether the project of a railway through the Isthmus replace that of the Nicaraguan canal, or simply a good road for ordinary communication from Chagres to Panama, the future prosperity of this town is assured. A point of junction between the two Americas, a feeble barrier to the two oceans, it is one of the places marked out by the hand of Providence for the reunion of nations—a belt of land that will serve for the migrations of races, and bring the Untied States nearer to China by some thousands of miles.

The Isthmus of Panama, notwithstanding its extreme fertility, is but slightly cultivated; yet the rare agricultural experiments attempted by Europeans in these parts have been attended by magnificent results. With a little industry, some instruments of labor, and collected capitals, immense fortunes might be made. But there are no journals to record these facts, and no one dreams of settling there. The Californian torrent still rolls on, to endure privations and dangers in a country denuded of vegetation, the climate and salubrity of which even the Isthmus of Panama needs not to envy.

Sailing vessels frequently arrive at this port in search of passengers for California, and make a lucrative affair of it. Many travellers, disappointed in the regular means of transport, avail themselves with blind eagerness of any opportunities of quitting

Panama, without considering that sailing vessels are frequently, in these seas, exposed to dead calms, and are consequently incalculably delayed.

Theodore T. Johnson
—1849

"The latitude of Richmond and climate of Italy"—the gold of Ophir—the silver, red wood, and cedar of Solomon's temple—the lovely valley of the Sacramento—the vineyards of France, indigo of Hindostan, and what of America; and more magnificent still, the placers of golden rocks in the mountains, and rivers of gold in the valleys, who would not go to California? and echo answered, who? For not a ticket could be had in the Pacific steamers—not a Berks' washer, Colt's or Allen's revolver, spade, pick, shovel, tin-pan, or India-rubber outfit, but by contract, premium, or transfer.

Yes, the *yellow* fever was upon us; and in company with thousands of our go-ahead countrymen, we were off to the El Dorado of the Pacific, sure we were right, because we had a colonel's and governor's report in our pockets. Provided, through the influence of a kind friend, with a transferred ticket for the steamer on to the Pacific, I embarked, on the 5th of February, in the steam-ship *Crescent City*, Capt. Charles Stoddard, from New York, for Chagres. The thick-falling snow and sposhy wharf dampened not our ardor; but we only longed the more to be away from these inhospitable shores, where only common potatoes and similar products grew, and where gold could only had in the shape of alloyed coin; to the delightful region where the products of tropical and temperate zones outvied each other in the same genial soil, and where gold (except the two massive lumps) had to be removed from under the coulter of the industrious plough man.

Thus the fever raged; and there seemed to be no remedy but a change of air, climate, and diet. The scene of our departure presented a spectacle ludicrius, animated, and extraordinary. The decks of our steamer were crowded to suffocating with departing adventurers and their friends—our ribs were in danger of fracture from pressure of the crowd—our shins from contusion against the gold machines, forcing pumps, crowbars, shovels, axes, picks, pocket-pistols, and pickpockets, and our lungs of collapse from returning the excited cheers of the multitude. The wharves and shipping, in eluding three other ocean steamers, crowded with a dense throng to witness our departure—the firing of cannon from ship and shore, re-echoed by cheer after cheer—a vigorous snow-ball campaign among the b'hoys, mingled with the waved handkerchief of the gentler sex and the unuttered emotions of parting, fixed an abiding record in the volumes of our memories.

As we passed slowly out of the dock, the

excitement of the surrounding multitude was manifested by the most enthusiastic shouts, and many seemed ready to leap on board to accompany us to El Dorado. Imbued with a similar spirit and aroused by the glowing anticipations of the future, we commenced our long voyages and journeyings to the promised land, with upwards of three hundred passengers, composing no discreditable specimen of the energy and enterprise of the universal Yankee nation; and clad in all sorts of costumes from a Broadway top-coat and cloth cap, to a boatmen's pea jacket and norwester, and from a western hunting shirt and wild cat, to a *bona fide* Mexican blanket and sombrero. Pistols, bowie-knives, rifles and revolvers were slung over our shoulders or stuck in our belts; and the followers of the renowned Don Quixotte might well have claimed us as fellow adventurers, if variety and singularity of equipments as well as self confidence in expected achievements, entitled us to that distinction.

Steaming rapidly down the magnificent bay of New York, we met the long-expected steamer, *United States*, and welcomed the sea-beat home of the safe voyagers with enthusiastic shouts, which they returned with good will, no doubt congratulating themselves at bidding adieu to the world of waters on which we were soon to be tossed. The clouds which in the morning had filled the air with fast-driving snow, now betook themselves to the upper atmosphere, and soon we dismissed our pilot, charged with numerous farewell letters to our friends and families. Then, with giant arms, our gallant ship dashed on her course; and we turned our eyes for one more adieu to the eastern shores of our native land, conscious, as they disappeared from our strained vision, that the stormy Atlantic and wide Pacific, and our great western continent, with its towering peaks and rolling prairies must soon separate us from the loved thresholds from which we wandered. Few of our adventurers saw the glories of the declining sun on this our first day at sea; for the unrelenting misery of sea-sickness had seized upon most of them. Fortunately, exempt from this infliction, ample opportunity was afforded me for observing the scenes on board, and the magnificence of the surrounding ocean.

The horizon on every side shut in with dark wind clouds and the increased rolling and pitching of the ship, betokened a growing sea; and our anticipations of the sublimity of the ocean were thus realized on the following day; for on every side the white-capped waves were curling around our bark of safety in scornful defiance, while her ponderous wheels, with unceasing revolution, clove their steady course through the contending flood—on one side submerged in foam, on the other grasping with vain energy at the rushing waters.

It is not, however, my intention to inflict upon the reader a minute description of the voyage. On the following day we were in the Gulf Stream, and off the famous Cape Hatteras; the ship steaming and drifting with all sails set before a stiff norwest wind, which soon changed to the westward, causing a strong and heavy cross sea, and making it necessary for those on deck to hold on, keeping a bright look out to leeward; when a sudden arrival of some poor wight in the scuppers was announced by shouts of laughter from his more fortunate companions. In the cabin below the scene was ludicrous in the extreme; the chairs, settees, sofas, and carpet were strewed with pale, despairing castaways, to whom our polite and attentive stewardess, Mrs. Young, was a mother in gruel, not forgetting the continual gingle which she industriously maintained among tea-cups and spoons, and the fiz-whiz of Seidlitz powders, from which there was a perpetual outcry, or rather a dying moan, from floor and sofa. One poor fellow vowed he would be buried in the bottom of the Atlantic Ocean next day, and no where else, while several engaged their passage home from Chagres.

It was a subject of regret that there were no ladies on board to enliven us with their presence and conversation, and remind us of the home scenes we were so rapidly receding from. Nevertheless, among our large number of passengers, much order and harmony prevailed, and we could not but remark the general good conduct and character of all on board, representing as they did nearly every State in the Union, and most of the professions, trades, and pursuits of life.

Surely it is an extraordinary spectacle when men of industry, sobriety, talents, and good character at home, are willing to forego for a considerable period all the advantages which they there possess, and venture upon voyages and travels of danger and hardship, of more than six thousand miles, to the west coast of America, for the acquisition of gold as miners or traders only. Men of this class have gone out to California with the confident expectation of accumulating rapidly abundant means to liquidate honorably just claims upon some, and all with the hope of providing comfortable independence for themselves and families. And to them will be accorded all the commendation due to an enterprise unparalleled on so large a scale, in the history of the world.

In a few days we welcomed the balmy air of the South, and our invalid passengers, availing themselves of the smooth sea, thronged the deck,—some with books, some with amusements, all enjoying the scene according to their inclination.

We spent the lovely moonlight evenings with songs and chorus, or in listening to the flute and violin. When our national airs were played, enthusiastic cheers resounded through the ship; the Marseilles hymn elicited three cheers for the French republic; and when finally our gentlemanly and jolly captain performed a sailor hornpipe in the first rate style, nine cheers roared around the decks and up the shrouds, till the ship almost danced in chorus.

Though we were out of the regular track of coasting vessels we passed several sail, and spoke, second day out, a beautiful brig going right before the wind, with studdin' sails slow and aloft. She presented a most animated and beautiful appearance, rising gracefully to every wave like a swan, her snowy wings just opened to the breeze; we exchanged cheers with her passengers, and requested them to report us all well.

On the afternoon of February 10th, our fifth day out, we hove in sight of the Caycos Islands, a part of the Bahama group, covered with a range of low, undulating hills. The land was greeted by all as a pleasant sight, the first that met our view since the highlands of Navesink. This afternoon the awnings on deck shaded a merry and pleasant crowd; and all remarked the good feeling, order and sobriety, which universally prevailed on board. The call for gruel was over, and all betook themselves to knife and fork with a will, at which we few old salts congratulated them.

Again we beheld with admiration the gorgeous hues of the evening sky, and one by one the stars shone out, the heavenly host led on by Venus, now the evening star, whose effulgence in the tropics is so vastly superior to that in the North, as to cast its beams across the ocean in miniature rivalry with the bright queen of night.

Soon she rose and cast the light of her full orb upon the sea and ship, and this night she was indeed to us a messenger of mercy, for in half an hour after her rising, the engine was suddenly stopped, and the cry of breakers ahead passed with electric rapidity from stem to stern. Going forward, we beheld with awe the surf and white beach of a small island on both bows; the ship seeming to be in a little cove within a mile of the shore, and going stem on, ten knots an hour. The island proved to be Little Iñagua, uninhabited except by turtle, and our escape from wreck was most providential, as most of the Bahamas have coral reef extending far into the sea. The look out man in the fore top had gone to sleep, the first mate, who was officer of the deck, had failed to see the danger, and a sailor off duty first gave the alarm.

The following day we saw the granite-bound shores and cloud-capt hills of San Domingo, and soon after, on our starboard bow clearly traced the lesser heights of the east end of Cuba; thus having in sight at the time the two greatest and most perverted island paradises of the West Indies.

This day was our first Sunday upon the ocean, and nearly all attended divine service conducted by the Rev. Albert Williams, of the Presbyterian denomination, concluding with the beautiful tune of Old Hundred: "Praise God from whom all blessings flow," which from our united voices pealed out upon the sea, through companion, hatchway, and port-hole.

The east end of Cuba was now in plain sight, presenting a succession of rocky cliffs and barren mountains, intersected with deep, dark ravines running towards the coast. This end of the island is not susceptible of cultivation; but produces the well-known copper mines.

Being now well through the Windward Passage, we saw next morning the large and beautiful island of Jamaica; its villas and coffee plantations covering the hill sides in every direction. As we gazed upon the mountains capped with fleecy clouds, or diversified with sunlight and shadow, and beheld the beautiful valleys at their base, we felt that nature at least had done her part, in bestowing profusely her richest bounties and highest advantages.

Enervated by our sudden and rapid transition from the cold winter of the North to the uniform heat of the tropics, we now welcomed the refreshing trade winds; which, with the steady roll of the Caribbean Sea, its white-capped billows flashing in the bright sunlight, caused the most delicious exhilaration of spirits.

As we neared the termination of our voyage at Chagres, we were discussing all sorts of plans for crossing the Isthmus; and some of the great men among us, the militia colonels, doctors, and bearers of despatches, presided over our deliberations, or spouted in the most effective mass-meeting style. All this resulted in the appointment of mule, boat, and baggage committees, which ended only in delay, vexation and trouble, although they exerted themselves to the utmost.

At noon of February 14th, the cry of land O! announced the shores of South America, and we were quickly on deck gazing at the wished-for sight. We soon neared the coast and sailed some fifty miles in full view; the shores bold with high hills rising in broken aspect one above another, covered to the water's edge, and even the rocks in the sea, with the profuse and extraordinary verdure of the tropics; displaying every imaginable hue of tree, flower, and plant, giving to the whole coast a feathery appearance, for no other word will describe the exuberant growth. In the distance, we gazed upon the famous Andes, and at 4 P.M. came to anchor amidst a furious shower of rain; a sort of welcome from the Isthmus and specimen of the *dry season*.

We now occupied ourselves in closing letters to friends, and in preparing to disembark, after which we had leisure to view the entrance of the Chagres River, guarded by the picturesque old Spanish fort of San Lorenzo situated on a commanding eminence, and to watch the careening buzzards and clumsy pelicans for ever hovering over the town of Chagres, a few huts only of which could be seen from the ship, with the graceful palmetto and cocoanut trees in the distance.

A jabber of bad Spanish, intermingled with yells of *vamos* and *caramba* or another more common and vulgar oath, saluted us as we looked over the side next morning, at the strange scene below. Large dug outs, or canoes, made from the single trunk of the bay tree, or common mahogany, surrounded the ship, filled with Negroes, Indians, and Creoles, nearly or quite naked; rolling up the whites of their eyes at us, and vociferating for cargo in tones that were a caution of ourang-outangs. Their ludicrous gestures, mingled with the outlandish and eternal clatter of their tongues, afforded abundant amusement, which was further enhanced by their continual alarm at the frequent collision of their boats, and the raps which they received on the head or shoulders from descending trunks, bales, and boxes. The negroes appeared to be a mixture of the African and Moorish race, the thick lips and woolly hair being in many of them accompanied with straight or somewhat aquiline noses, while the nostril of the full-blooded Congo revealed an amplitude sufficient to indicate his unquestioned descent from the dusky children of Ham. The Indians were few in number, and diminutive in appearance, manifesting the common characteristic of their race—a dogged submission to the necessity of labor. Both negroes and Indians were evidently beneath the control of the Creoles, who were generally the patrones or captains, and owners of the boats—the least dash of the blood of the white man being sufficient to assert either the supremacy or tyranny of his race here, as in all other countries.

Having disposed of all our baggage in readiness for landing, and maintained possession of the lighter articles, we took our seats in one of the ship's boats, and were rowed ashore—a distance of some three miles, to the town of Chagres. As we bid adieu to the gallant steamer which had borne us with speed and safety over 2,200 miles of ocean, we realized more completely the nature and length of our journey. Now commenced the hardships and discomforts of our route: the comforts and luxuries of home were behind us, the dreaded Isthmus and comparatively unknown Pacific coast before. The only reflection, however, which we bestowed upon the matter was, that the way was before us, and we were going ahead.

As we approached the shore, we gazed with admiration upon the picturesque and romantic old Spanish Castle of San Lorenzo, whose dark and ruined battlements, crowning the bold buff at the entrance of the river, looked with proud desolation out upon the sea, which with the eternal war of breakers, was still bidding defiance to the hoary hand of Old Time, whose relentless grasp had thrown parapet and gun to the base of the cliff. The forsaken watch-tower of the sentry, covered with dank moss and crumbling decay, tenanted now only by the screaming wild fowl, afforded a melancholy lesson to us in the thought, that while the demon of war deserts his ancient abodes, it is only to gird his loins with new panoply; and aided by the science of modern times. We afterwards visited the interior of this fortress; and ascending the hill by the old paved road, entered at the principal gateway by a drawbridge extended over a wide and deep fosse encircling the entire work, but now quite dry and green with tropical verdure. Within the walls we found numerous old cannon, mostly dismounted and covered with rust; and on some of them could decipher the date 1745, with the Royal Arms of Spain. Beyond this outer fort was the main citadel, on the verge of the cliff, towards the ocean, and approached by still another drawbridge, isolated also by a separate fosse. Here were some brass cannon in better preservation, and the entrance to the magazine, containing some damp and useless old powder. The view from the battlements we found extensive and very beautiful. To the northward and eastward stretched away the blue Caribbean Sea, to the southward and westward rose the varied peaks of the Andes of the Isthmus, while at our feet lay the town of Chagres, with the mouth of the river almost concealed from view by the immense variety of tropical vegetation.

Such pleasing impressions, however, were soon forgotten on the occasion of our first landing in the far-famed Chagres. Here were, indeed, Pluto's dominions, and here was the veritable Styx. Amidst hundreds of canoes, our boat was forced up on the low sandy beach, and we jumped ashore to find ourselves surrounded by a host of Charons, whose dark visages and rude paddles belied not the comparison. As soon as we could escape from the yells of "*Canoa! canoa! a Cruces! a Gorgona!*" and the incessant demand for *riales* and *pesos*, we strolled into the town, which was found to consist of about two hundred and fifty bamboo huts, with high-peaked roofs of dried palmetto leaves, situated in a complete morass—the streets or lanes exhibiting the remains of a species of rough paving, and filed with a confused mixture of dogs, hogs, and naked children, negroes and creoles. All was excitement, wonder, and amazement at the tremendous irruption of Americanos. The women abandoned their corn-pounding, or relinquished hair combing in the doorways—the children, with a jerk, released their heads from the searching process, and gathered around us—the latter being *a la Cupid*, though not without dressing either, being enormously stuffed *a la Falstaff*, exciting our laughter continually. The women dressed suitably to the climate, with naught but petticoat and chemise, seemed transported with the novelty and excitement. The innumerable, lank, miserable dogs and pigs, left sole occupants of the huts, availed themselves with activity of the chance to play an extensive and voracious game of cribbage; and the disgusting but useful buzzards, gathered in solemn rows on the house-tops, to view the unwanted commotion in their favorite haunts.

Presently we saw approaching the tall and stately *padre* of the town, arrayed in his priestly robes of rich black silk and shovel sombrero. As he passed, every one bowed respectfully, and he returned all with courtesy. He was going to attend the funeral of a child said to have died from the bite of a centipede—a most unusual, and even in this instance, doubtful circumstance.

Not having the fear of the "Chagres fever" before our eyes, we wandered through the whole of this delectable village, and found scarcely a house but presented some new or ridiculous scene—some odd or disgusting exhibition. Very few of the huts contained more than one room. In the ground-floor in the centre were large rough stones; between these the fire was kindled for cooking purposes. An iron pot or pan placed upon the stones contained coffee, frijoles, or tortillas, while seated on the ground, the women attended to the cookery, and combed their hair at intervals. Pigs wandered in and out quite unmolested; and perros, or dogs, without number, thrust inquisitive noses into larder, pot, and pan, disturbed by rarely, and then only by a shout, as these people have a greater regard for their dogs than their children; which we could only account for by observing that the former being quite hairless, occasioned none of the trouble inseparable from the woolly crowns of the bipeds. Even this ingenious theory was subsequently demolished; for we saw some of the people living on pickings and stealings, in more senses than one. Laziness and listlessness seemed to prevail among all. Every house had the everlasting hammock, in which they sleep at night and lounge all day. The women were slip-shod or barefoot—the men ragged or hatless; and all were dirty and greasy. A flock of buzzards would present a favorable comparison.

Returning from our ramble we joined a crowd of our countrymen, congregated with indignant gesticulation around the large barn-like hut of an old creole trader and canoeman, whom we denominated by the soubriquet of Old Ram-Hos.

The committee sent ashore the previous day had made a contract in writing with them, engaging a sufficient number of canoes for a specified sum, to convey all of us with our baggage to Cruces or Gorgona. The terms were highly liberal on our part, being dictated solely by themselves. When the contract was signed, the committee proposed to have it certified by the Alcalde, or chief magistrate of the town, but to this very correct and usual procedure they strenuously and most indignantly objected: no indeed, they were gentlemen, men of honor; their word was as good as their bond. The committee finally yielded the point, chiefly relying upon the liberal sum agreed to be paid by us. Surprised at our facile compliance with their original demand, they determined at once to bolt from their contract, and had now don so, demanding the most exorbitant prices for canoes.

The remonstrances and threats of Captain Stoddard on our behalf were for a long time unavailing, when our patience becoming quite exhausted, revolvers were quickly put in efficient condition, and bowie knives made their persuasive appearance. Whip the rascal, fire his den, burn the settlement, annex the Isthmus, were heard on all sides. Fortunately for themselves the high contracting parties understood English, and their ears being sensitive at the moment, and their nerves more so, the dirty brown of their complexion speedily changed to a livid white, and they came down in their villanous demands, barely in time to save their shantee from a come down on their heads. Their rascality, however, was in the main accomplished, in the way in which they had cunningly foreseen and intended; for many of our impetuous young men, led by the example of a few selfish old travellers among us, and wearied with delay, had engaged canoes for themselves, making private bargains on the best terms they could; but even then they were frequently deprived of a canoe after the bargain was concluded, on the plea that others would pay more. As soon as this game was understood by us, we quietly selected and took possession of the canoes which we required, agreeing to pay them eight dollars each person for passenger canoes, and at the rate of about three dollars per hundred pounds for baggage to Cruces or Gorgona, half to be paid in advance.

Anxious now to be off, out party of four took possession of a light little canoe or dug-out, provided, as in all cases, with a bungo, or species of roof made of the branches and leaves of the palmetto, extending some six or eight feet in length, and just high enough to creep under upon our hands and knees; leaving space enough at the stern for the seat of the *patron*, or captain, who with a short broad paddle, both aided to propel and steer the canoe. The *patron* was a little nimble creole of Porto Bello, named Leon; his face strongly marked with small-pox, and seeming to be full of eyes, as the two small and piercing black orbs with which his countenance was garnished, were eternally dancing like fire-flies in every direction. Speaking a little English, of which accomplishment he was very vain, his tongue kept time with his eyes in an incessant fandango of bad Spanish and worse English. Stationed in the bows of the canoe was Pantaleon, a negro lad, silent, strong and industrious; and the poor fellow had need of all these qualities, for on him devolved the hard work of poling up stream against the rapid current. At length after two hours more delay in getting these worthies into the canoe, and providing bottles of water to last us above tide; in beating dogs, pigs, and poultry off from our provisions, and escaping from the crowd of *patrones* and canoemen, we commenced our voyage up the Rio Chagres, with our expert navigators surnamed Loon and Panteloon, both bereft of the latter article, but provided with a coarse short shirt, some sausages, and a bottle of Cogniac, which we observed was not long to last.

Rejoiced at our release from the vexatious annoyances and tedious delays of Chagres, we commenced our journey toward the Pacific with renewed spirit.

Entering the river immediately from the little cove at the mouth of which lies Chagres, our senses were entranced by the beauty of the scene that opened upon us. Every faculty was at once absorbed in admiration of the earthly paradise which surrounded us.

The river itself, a beautiful limpid stream about fifty yards wide, was dotted in every direction with the gondola-shaped canoes, some descending the middle of the current with great rapidity, others like our own, stemming the quiet water by the green shore; while from beneath the shady bungo we watched the flashing paddles, or gazed with unsated eyes upon the glorious scenery, listening amidst the thousand strange warblers of the groves for some familiar song, or startled by the wild cry of the canoemen as they shouted to each other from every turn in the perpetually winding stream.

Neither pencil or pen can do justice to the surpassing views ever present to the eye of the traveller on this river. Varying in width from fifty to one hundred yards, its crystal waters roll over a clear, pebbly or bright, sandy bottom pursuing a perfectly labyrinthine course, embracing here the entire base of some spur of the mountain, or there forming an island in the vale; thus traversing nearly fifty miles, when the direct course from the head of navigation to the coast is only about twenty miles.

The shores, at first low and marshy, soon become more elevated, and are crowned with the most exuberant and abundant vegetation. Nature seems to have bestowed here even more than tropical profusion; for, as in the forests of Brazil, there appears to be no space unoccupied by tree or plant, flower or vine. The banana and plantain, the palmetto, the graceful cocoanut and cabbage tree, the papa and mango, bearing their delicious fruit; the pine apple, orange and lime, were seen in all directions; while among the endless groves we could occasionally spy the tall sugar cane growing spontaneously and in the greatest luxuriance. The air was redolent with fragrance from innumerable varieties of flowers, and the wood resounded with the melody of feathered songsters of the most delicate or gorgeous plumage, or echoed with the noisy chatter and scream of monkeys and parrots.

Through such new and enchanting scenes we pursued our winding way, scarce conscious of the lapse of time, till the setting sun cast his crimson and mellow light upon hill-side, valley and stream, and the darkening shadows of wood and ravine recalled the wanderers of earth and air to rest and repose.

The transition from daylight to darkness is of course very sudden within the tropics; but although deprived of the delightful hour of our northern twilight, we were fully compensated by the dazzling beauty of the night. The moon and stars shone with wonderful brilliancy, and the air was filled with large fire flies, sparkling like gems of sapphire.

While enjoying the novelty of the scene, our canoemen struck up a wild nasal chant, a sort of Spanish improvisatore, which Leon informed us was about "de good canoe, de good casa, and de good muger," the latter lauding to house and wife.

Proceeding thus for three or four hours, we saw the lights of habitations on shore; and the barking dogs, crying of children and beating of drums, soon apprised us of our approach to the village of Gatun.

Forcing our canoe into a regular flotilla, we scrambled up the banks, and following the direction of the sights and sounds, were quickly in the midst of the villagers. Here we found others of our countrymen, and received, like them, a cordial welcome. A table was spread in front of one of the principal houses in the street, covered with clean cloth, and sundry odd-looking red earthern jugs, jacks, and jars. Acceding without ceremony to the polite invitation of a very pretty creole señorita,

"We each took a smack
Of the *blood-red* jack,"

And then fell to with eager appetites upon tortillas, fresh rolls, cakes, and, in fact, all eatables within reach, to the great dismay of the Gatunos. The cry for *café* meantime rose loud and long; but we found the only way to obtain it was to cease eating; for, like the Spanish, these people could not be made to comprehend that the Americanos drink their coffee with their food, instead of at the close of the meal, as is their custom. This afterwards occasioned many ludicrous scenes, and bothered both los Yankees and their entertainers more than a little.

Paying cheerfully the few riales demanded for our meal, we took our way further into the village, and found the principal street well swept, and crowded by the jabbering and merry natives. The beating of a small monotonous drum, betokened the incessant fandango; but the excitement about the Americanos and the pesos or dollars to be made out of them, seemed to absorb all else. We had determined, on first landing, to sleep here; but we had not yet become sufficiently accustomed to the miserable huts, dirty hammocks, and insects smaller but more dreaded by us than centipede or scorpion.

After some trouble e found Leon and Pantaleon, and to our orders to go-ahead, or *vamos*, they manifested much disappointment; but a cup of *café*, a fresh supply of cogniac, and a promise of a shirt for each, quite reconciled them to proceed all night. With the eternal cigar, which was as constantly in their mouths as the paddle in their hands, we were quickly in the stream; and now came the tug of war to poor Pantaleon; for the river being lower at this season, he was obliged to relinquish the easy paddle, an take to the laborious pole, forcing the canoe against a strong current by sheer muscular exertion. In this way we could only progress at the rate of one or two miles an hour, often being driven back—the strength of the current requiring the most unremitting effort.

Leon, the patron, now displayed his laziness and rascality, as he would do nothing but steer the canoe and urge us to land. We at once proposed to throw him overboard, duck him, flog him, tie him, and stop his grog; but the fear of "no cogniaca" restored him to duty. We, therefore, stowed ourselves away under our bungo, four in number, in a space eight feet long by two wide, the only way to manage being to "put our heads together," and lie "spoon fashion," and with heavy pilot coats on, the interstices were well filled. Once we were aroused by the clatter of branches of sunken trees against our canopy, and as often lulled to repose again by the rocking canoe and rippling stream. It being the dry season, the early part of night was free from dews and fog; but as morning approached the miasma from the shore was oppressive and offensive in the extreme. At this hour we were also aroused by the most extraordinary sounds, produced by monkeys, iguanas, and some of the larger varieties of the feathered tribes—the latter producing a noise resembling the violent collision of two stones under water, while the former seemed to have filled the forests with Chinese gongs innumerable, and thousands of steamboats, high and low pressure, blowing off steam in every direction. Beginning at a long distance, these sounds roared around us till echo herself was confounded.

We welcomed the morning light as it quickly dispelled the mist; and the rising sun displayed to our view the little village of Dos Hermanos, (or Two Brothers,) where we landed, and were speedily engaged in discussing our breakfast, consisting of thick black mud and water called *café*, which was not too hot to allow the dogs occasionally to stir it up with their noses. "Throw physic to the dogs" exclaimed one and all, as we turned our attention to claret and water for a time, and a coarse set of ragamuffin biscuits as a stay for our stomachs.

This day we got our fowling-pieces in order, and obtained some wild turkey—numerous here but quite small; a species also of wild peacock, some blue and white heron, besides having a shot now and then at long distance for monkeys, parrots, and other birds nameless and unknown.

Approaching near to shore at mid-day, we saw on the sedgy margin a strange and ugly-looking creature, exactly answering to our ideas of a regular Egyptian crocodile in miniature. Giving him the contents of one barrel, he made a desperate effort to escape into the bushes; but Leon, active for once, shouting, "*Iguana! Iguana!*" rushed after him and soon returned, holding him by the tail, with gloating eyes, exclaiming "*Bueno! bueno! hueros! hueros!*" It was of greenish bronze, and dirty yellow, with scaly skin, four short legs with claws, a tail like a serpent, and head of lizard or crocodile, and about three feet in length from tip to tip. After satisfying our curiousity, we handed it over to Leon, who valued it as a great prize: and as we discovered at dinner time, extracted more than thirty eggs from it of the size of a quail's, having a tough, white skin, but no shell. These he boiled and tied in a row like Weathersfield onions, for after entertainment, considering them a great luxury. We know not which string would be most wholesome, but think the Weathersfielders would "clare de kitchen" soonest. We mean no offence, however, to our Yankee friends, and hope they will not turn up their noses at the odorous comparison.

This afternoon, while two of our party were availing themselves of a sand-beach to walk and collect agates, we were aroused from our siesta under the shady bungo, by a low quick cry from Pantaleon, of "*Aligador! Aligador!*" and following the direction of his eager eye and boy finger, we saw what appeared at first to be the remains of a dead tree, gray from decay, lying near the edge of the water, about fifty yards distant, but which was really an alligator, and the first we had discovered. A ball was passed through his ugly head without further ceremony from Colt's large revolver, by one of the party who claimed to be a good shot, and proved himself such, at least on this occasion, for head and tail, mud blood, and water, flew up in the air, and the convulsed wretch floundered into the stream to meet a cordial reception from the jaws of his tribe. He was about five feet long, and the only specimen we saw, though some of our fellow-travellers saw them as long as nine feet, and quite in crowds.

Thus passed our second day on the Chagres; but the last incident caused us to defer our purpose of bathing in the clear, soft water of the river, which, at this season, is also sweet and delicious to drink. We now began to inquire of every passing canoe, "*Quantos leguas a Gorgona?*"—Spanish borrowed of lazy Leon for the occasion, and which answered for our inquiry of, "How many leagues to Gorgona?" But they seemed to have no idea of distance, some answering quite differently from others; and in fact, the number of leagues seemed to increase as we advanced. This was afterwards rendered more amusing by the explanation of an intelligent Spanish gentleman, that "down the river the distance was very short, but to Gorgona a great many leagues." Thus distance seemed to be measured, and pretty wisely too, by the difficulties of the way, and the time expended to overcome them. Full many a persevering or wearied traveller on the River of Life has found that, however laborious, tedious, or uncertain his ascent of that turbulent and winding stream during the active years of manhood, his descending bark, though guided, mayhap, by the steady hand of experience, floats noiselessly, yet swiftly, in the rapid mid-current, while years dwindle to months, and months to days, as he watches for his entrance upon the great Ocean of Eternity.

The rascally Leon had faithfully promised us to arrive at Gorgona that evening, is especial consideration of the two shirts begged the night previous; but the day declined into evening and evening into night, and yet the weary Pantaleon was straining to his bending pole, songless, silent, and now ominous extent, even cigarless. In vain we offered him one by way of encouragement, and his loved cogniaca lay neglected at his feet. Exhausted nature could accomplish no more, and we marvelled not, after twenty-eight hours incessant labor without sleep, and almost without rest; so we hauled the canoe up on a sandy beach in a bend of the stream and made our camp there, building a fire to keep off mosquitoes and reptiles. Here we were greatly incensed at the mean and lazy Leon, for leaving Pantaleon to aid in making the fire, he rolled himself up in his dirty blanket and quickly disturbed the alligators by his barbarous snoring. We seriously discussed the propriety of burying him alive as a warning to all lazy *patrones*, when the suggestion that he was already well covered with soil caused us precipitately to abandon our benevolent intention. Before morning another canoe joined us, and its people gladly gathered around our file. At two o'clock, the moon rising, we kicked lazy Leon into wakefulness and activity, ad resumed our slow and toilsome progress. The following day we reached Palenquilla, a picturesque little hamlet on an elevated and level part of the shore. Near it we saw a large and beautiful plantation filled with sugar cane while above and below, the margin of the river was gorgeous with every variety of tree, leaf, and plant, perfectly overgrown with wines bearing exquisite flowers; and one species of large tree was clothed completely with crimson passion flowers, in description similar to ours, but four times larger.

Just after our enjoyment of this scene, we were treated to another, highly ludicrous, and affording much fun and gratification. We had reached a short turn in the stream, where the current was very strong over a pebbly bottom; in fact, there were rapids on a small scale. Pantaleon, immediately depriving his ebony form of his fashionable short skirts, leaped overboard displaying above water only the outlines of a bust, capped by a pair of shoulders which, besides their dusky hue, were as rounded and shining too, as the back of the leader of a great school of rolling porpoises. Lazy Leon, obliged to follow his example, waded along for some time by the stern siding in the progress of the canoe, with vinegar countenance. Presently he relinquished his hold, intending to follow at his case in our wake, but the current was so strong that he could barely keep his feet, making no progress; then commenced a volley of vociferations, yells, oaths, prayers, and commands to Pantaleon to return for him, but all in vain, for fun we had, and mischief we were bent on. So we called out to him, no entender, (we don't understand,) speak English, Master Leon; come on board quick, quick, quantos leguas a Gorgona; all which increased his fury, till, livid with rage, and well ducked, by losing his footing and being carried down the rapids, we hauled him on board, with the aid of Pantaleon's pole, and he returned to duty an altered man, as his whitened skin plainly betokened.

We now approached bolder shores and observed trap rock on some of the banks, while directly in front of us uprose a mountain in the shape of an immense mass of conical verdure from whose bowels the river seemed to gush into sudden being; but we soon glided around its sweeping base and beheld on a high bluff beyond, Gorgona, "the place of rocks," and the welcome termination of our long pilgrimage of forty-one hours, for the accomplishment of as many miles in the tortuous and rapid Chagres.

We found at Gorgona, a collection of about one hundred houses; and natives in all respects similar to those of Chagres, except that among the former were few Creoles. The scene here partakes of a bolder and more varied character. From the high table-land on which the town is built, mountains rise in every direction, forming a complete amphitheatre perpetually reflected from the sparkling stream let in their midst.

Gratified, however, as we had been with the beauty of the river, we gladly escaped from our confined and cramped position in the canoe, and ascending the precipitous bank, preceded by a throng of natives carrying our traps, were ushered into an *adobe* house with tiled roof, denominated by the sounding title of Hotel Francaise. Here joining more of our famished travellers we made furious onslaught on mule steaks and other delicacies of the season, washed down by some very good coffee and tea or claret. Breakfast, dinner and tea were continually in progress from morning til night, and the "Francaise" was the crack Hotel of the place. As the sleeping apartments, *id est*: the hammocks and floors were all, however, "mortgaged" to previous comers, we were fain to take up our abode with the Alcalde, or chief magistrate, of the town; who, besides being the richest man, was notorious as the greatest rascal and cheat in Gorgona.

The fellow was a mixture of Spanish and negro, wore spectacles for dignity, and was deaf for convenience: all unmistakeable signs of a big bug. True, he did not drive his carriage, being unable to pony-up, for want of horse flesh, which was all made steaks of, for the only course furnished at his table.

He had, however, an extensive *turn-out* every day, as his lodgers testified that they were obliged to *flea* frequently, retreating from the boot avenue with *four-in-hand*.

We also discovered that he was a *large operator* in pork which had died a natural death, and, in fact it only remained for him to establish an extensive correspondence with the other side, and a well-sustained system of advances on "bills of lading," in order to rank as a very prominent man abroad as well as at home.

Of such a distinguished host had we now become the guest, sharing with many others, at a round sum, the hospitalities of his house, in common with sundry pigs, hogs, dogs, and naked children. The aforesaid house was built of adobe, or sun-dried bricks, or rather of mud-walls, which bamboo and palmetto thatched roof, extending over a space of about twenty feet in width, by sixty n length, divided at each end into two small rooms; while the grand apartment between, with doors and windows on both sides, served for eating and sleeping. The ground floor, swept only on saints' days or holy days, was garnished with a large, rough board table, benches of similar material, and a few chairs seated with mule or horse hide. From two rows of uprights that supported the roof, were suspended some eight or ten coarse and dirty grass hammocks, and in these such as were lucky enough to get possession, sought repose for the night. The first night of our arrival some fifty slept here, and besides two moored, stem and stern, in each hammock, the floor, tables, chairs, and benches, trunks and boxes, were occupied in a similar manner. The nights being cold in comparison with the day, we were obliged as well by other precautions to sleep in our clothes, retaining even overcoats, boots and hats. For though we saw neither centipede nor scorpions here, yet we considered some kind of covering for the head quite indispensable. The following day, becoming tired of eating mule steaks, dead pork, and iguana pie, we made a regular descent upon the villagers, in search of bread, eggs and oranges Of these we obtained some, though at exorbitant prices. Finding that we would be detained a few days, awaiting the arrival of our baggage, we now sought out an old hut in another part of the village, occupied by a live Yankee named John Smith, of course, and there we feasted, for the remainder of our abode, on eggs and slap-jacks. With his two big *b'hoys* to assist him, this enterprising restaurateur employed every moment in turning the pan-cakes, which were as rapidly turned down by his crowd of hungry expectants.

The old rascal of an Alcalde had yet the audacity to charge us one dollar per day for board at his barn or stable, begging his pardon for the appellation, yet doubting if any respectable American horse would enter there, provided he had any regard for his standing, and more especially his repose.

Wandering through the village we found a few little shops, embellished sometimes with fancy china ware, but chiefly supplied with *aguardiente*, wines and cordials; and the rows of empty and half empty bottles showed that the money earned from the Americans had not subserved the cause of temperance.

Situated on a rising ground, we also discovered the old church or cathedral; and a ricketty old building it is, a large part being entirely in ruins, and the remainder now in use, being enclosed on one side by a rude board partition, through the chinks of which we could perceive the altar and the images of various saints. The padre whom we met and conversed with was very polite, especially when he learned that we aboded with the Alcalde, with whom it was said he was a partner. He very kindly urged us not to go to Panama too soon, as the cholera and yellow fever would be there at this season. We thanked him, and played at the game of politeness so well, that one of our number obtained his horse for the journey; and a good one he proved to be, though at a good round price.

In this climate we were told it was unsafe for strangers to bathe much in cold water; but determined, at least, to try the experiment, we wended our way early one beautiful morning to a shady beach below the town, where the river makes a graceful curve, its rapid current subsiding quickly into tranquil repose. Here, in company with several others, we enjoyed a fine swimming bath in the soft and pure water, while farther down, the natives, men, women, and children, were indulging in a general paddle. The stream appeared to be filled with fish, some of which precisely resembled our specked mountain trout, and were so tame as to appraoch and rub themselves against our persons; but all our attempts at hooking them with the line were unavailing. Returning thence, we came upon a fine and quite extensive sugar plantation, where the cane, with as many as twelve and fifteen joints, was growing in the greatest luxuriance, and without apparent cultivation. We also saw Indian corn, the stalk several feet in height. This is a great article of food with the natives, who pound it between two large smooth stones, and after a further process make *tortillas,* and corn-cake, or bread

of it—both of which we found most agreeable to the taste. They also make a kind of cocoa cake of the coconut, pounded and gently boiled with the juice of the sugar-cane. Emerging from this plantation, we visited the rude sugar-mill employed to crush the cane. It is of the simplest and most ancient construction; and the juice being allowed to ferment in large wooden vessels, forms an intoxicating drink much liked by the natives.

Some of our party also ascended the high conical mountain seen as we came up the river, and were much gratified with the wonderful vegetation and fine view. A learned doctor who accompanied us, being also naturalist, botanist, and geologist, lingered long amidst these fascinating scenes; and it was only when our fears for his safety became intensely painful, that he returned to us laden with botanial and geological specimens, and his bowie-knife reeking with the blood of an enormous and dangerous repile which he had slain. Among his specimens was one of native lead of especial beauty and value, but which some of the Turks among us (for sceince has her opponents everywhere) basely insinuated was a stone rubbed by the kettle of an old camp-fire.

While here we witnessed an amusing and, to republicans, altogether a strange scene. The penal laws of New Granada are quite severe and summary; and to ensure their certain application, great power is confided to Alcaldes of villages and towns, who are amenable to the chief Alcaldes and governors. Hearing a scuffle and vociferous outcry, attended with the furious jabbering of the natives, we made a rush to the bar-room of the Alcalde, where both liquors and justice were dispensed at dear rates. There, surrounded by the oniferous and greasy crowd, stood a gigantic Othello of a fellow, charging *himself* before the Alcalde with shipping a diminutive little Creole at his side, who was livid with rage, and vehemently entering a similar complaint against his own prowess in thrashing Othello. The differeince of opinion as to who was vanquished was well-nigh coming to another fight, and the prospect for fun was believed by *the fancy* to be good. Meantime above the top of the adjoining partition, and over the heads of the crowd, appeared the heads of Madame Alcalde and her daughters—the former to see that her lord demanded enough pesos of the culprits, and the young *señoritas* to laugh and jeer at all whose attention they could secure for that object. The terrible Alcalde now put glasses across his nose and applying one containing *aguardiente* to his mouth, assumed pen, ink, and paper. Silence reigned throughout the court, disturbed only by the tittering of the women, scratching among the men, and loud yells of sundry naked little *criers*. The *Acalde* then writing down the names of the culprits, and nature of their offence, sentenced the big Othello to pay a fine of six dolars, and be placed in the stocks four hours. The little Creole, who was first to bring the case before him, he let off with a sentence *to treat the whole crowd*. This at once accounted for the tight squeeze in the courtroom; and if none were *tight*, it was only because the Alcalde filled their glasses himself.

But the most extraordinary part of this performance was to come; for Othello paid down his fine in hard dollars, gulped his *aguardiente*, (the Alcalde considerately allowing him to fill his own glass,) and walking deliberately to the prison, placed his feet in the stocks himself, where the fumes of the large draught of *aguardiente* which he took good care to imbibe, enabled him to snooze away his four hours very comfortably. Thus the cunning Alcalde secured frequent appeals to the bar of Justice, by favoring the first complainant, while his bar of Bacchus flourished, and his popularity increased, by the sentence of a general treat. O, Momus, hold thy side.

And yet we have seen similar leniency displayed to the complainant, before the magistrates of a certain city we know of in the Great Republic, were brotherly love most doth reign.

While tarrying here, we visited one day the camp of the engineers engaged in the great and important work of the survey of the Isthmus; and by the polite invitation of Captain Tilghman, who was then in command of the corps, we dined with them en famille. Their hospitality and kind attentions will ever be cherished by us with the liveliest satisfaction. The encampment was a very beautiful one, on a green plain, back of the town, near the skirt of the woods and a fine spring of pure water.

The last night we tarried at Gorgona, a grand *fandango* came off, and hearing the merry beating of the drums we joined the crowd. In front of one of the houses were seated two of the men, strumming a monotonous cadence on drums made of the cocoa-tree, half the size of a common pail, held between their knees, and another with the small Spanish guitar, which furnish the universal music on these occasions. The revellers form a ring, in the midst of which as many as choose enter into the dance. This consists generally of a lazy, slow shuffle, until by aguardiente, and emboldened as night progresses, the women dance furiously up to their favorites among the men, who are then obliged to follow suit, all joining in a kind of nasal squeal or chant. There is nothing graceful in their mode of dancing, but, on the contrary, their motions are often indecent and disgusting.

On our way through the village to this scene, we came upon a smaller affair of the same description of amusement, which was going on in front of one of the liquor shops, and with proportionate noise and confusion. Here a little Creole, who, from the restless flash of his coal-black eyes, might bear the cognomen of Diablo, was dancing with all his might and main. He was evidently a bully among the men, and cock of the walk; and seeing us in his audience, came up and began to dance close to us, with a sort of challenging, swaggering air. Watching him a moment, and seeing that he was half intoxicated, and would soon give out if put to the test, one of our party commenced a regular hoe-down, knocking his shins with heavy boots when opportunity offered, by way of *tattoo*, thus provoking him and keeping him to his own game, till, at last, he became quite exhausted, and fairly broke down. The yells of derision, the laughter and jeering of his companions, with his own chop-fallen aspect, were ludicrous in the extreme. "*Bueno! bueno! Señor Americano!*" shouted his rivals in great glee, in the midst of which we departed, having had our full share of the fun going on in that party. At a late hour we retired to our hammocks; and while listening to the distant drum and guitar, and watching the stars twinkling through the palmetto roof, fell asleep, to be aroused at daybreak by the same sounds, which the revellers had thus kept up all night long, literally amplifying the old song of "We won't go home till morning."

Next day, having contracted to have our baggage forwarded by an American within a specified time, and obtained one wretched little animal to ride, called a horse, we took our departure, two in company, for Panama the Pacific.

Once mounted on a miserable palfrey the size of a St. Bernard dog, and the delight of Sancho Panza, had he been there to see, and the other truding along with double-barrel on shoulder, we took a narrow pathway across the table-land, and speedily struck into the thick forest at the base of the hills. Glad to be again in progress, and to escape from the hot sun even at this early hour, we welcomed the refreshing shade, and listened with increased delight to the thousand songsters of the groves. Not a drop of rain had fallen since the afternoon of our arrival off Chagres; and we found the climate, at this the *dry season*, pleasant and salubrious. With perfectly clear skies, the heat of the mid-day sun was not so oppressive as we anticipated, as a pleasant breeze sprang up every day, and the nights were cool and bracing. The *dry season proper* is from the first of December to the first of June; but February, March, and April are the only months when the traveller may confidently rely upon little or no rain; and at this time only is the Gorgona road traversable with any degree of comfort.

This we found to consist of a mere bridle-path, worn in the mainly clay soil or soft calcarcous rocks by the feet of the horses and mules. The trees and underwood appear to have been originally cleared from a small space on both sides, through which the road winds among the mountains—enclosed by impervious banks ascending and descending perpetually, and sometimes very abruptly and precipitously. For many miles the path is worn into deep holes, the mules stepping continually from one to another, which, in process of time, have formed many narrow ravines, often feet in depth. When entering one of these, we frequently heard shouts of muleteers approaching the opposite way, and were obliged to wait till they passed—the way often being so narrow that we were forced to lay on the backs or necks of our horses.

Thus, amid solitude and shade, we pursued our onward way—now plunging into the deep and gloomy chasms of the mountains, and anon rising the opposite ascent, till the distant openings in the forest, gradually restoring the welcome sunlight, revealed also mountain and valley yet to be traversed.

Views, ever varying in beauty or magnificence, and partaking of all the forms of natural scenery, were presented on every side to our delighted gaze. Descending the step declivities with slow and cautious steps, the light of day imperceptibly faded away till twilight grew upon us; and the scream of the parrots, or twittering of birds, was exchanged for the low hum of insects or rustling of serpents, while the gurgling mountain rill fell like sweet music on the listening ear, or stole with silvery gleam and noiseless course, through the deep thickets, trellised with the wild flower and wine. Bathing awhile our weary limbs, and cooling our tired animals, we drank of the pure water, and again commenced our ascent to the realms of day, when, pausing upon the mountain side; we could see peak above peak rising to view, and the valleys between clothed with interminable forest, with here and there the brown palmetto thatch of a native's hut. Echoing, too, from every ravine or abrupt turn in our pathway, came the shrill cries of the *vaquero*, or hoarse shouts of the *cargadore*, mingled occasionally with our emphatic national *hurrah*. This the natives soon acquired, reiterating our shouts with *a hoo-rah*, which, though not quite the thing, seemed to afford them great glee.

Thus we met string after string of horses and mules, returning for fresh loads or *cargo*, tied each to the tail of the one in advance, the *vaquero* or muleteer riding behind with a long gad in his hand, his head covered with a broad-rimmed parti-colored, coarse straw *sombrero*, which, with a pair of dirty pantaloons, and form naked to the waist, often completed his costume. These fellows were generally merry and contented enough—when along, beguiling the way by some rude song; or when accompanied by others, jabbering, shouting, and gesticulating perpetually. But the poor *cargadores* seemed to share a sterner fate; for at each quiet nook or fallen tree, would we see some them resting with their weary burdens and panting for breath, with the perspiration streamed from every pore. During the dry season,, the natives who follow the business, are employed constantly in carrying baggage and freight on their backs. Lashing their burdens, which are commonly of about one hundred pounds weight, firmly to a kind of bamboo panier, with a band to the upper end to cross their forehead, and straps for their shoulders, they make the journey of twenty-four miles from Gorgona to Panama in two days, when not over-paid or over-worked; but since the great amount of travel across the Isthmus, they often consume several days.

After we had been sometime on the road, one of these muleteers overtook us, and with many exclamations seemed to wish to deprive us of the horse. Thinking him rather too familiar we gave him such unmistakeable demonstrations of our disapproval, that he quickly *vamosed*, somewhat weaker in the knees. We however recalled him, and gave him the receipt for the hire of the horse supposing he might perhaps be the owner, and this seemed to restore him to vitality, for he went off again at a round pace. Proceeding a few miles further the wretched brute deposited himself and rider—without ceremony—in the road, evidently resolved upon taking a *siesta*, but receiving a severe kicking instead, he finally concluded to continue his rambles.

But our adventures did not end here, for soon

four of the natives laid their hands simultaneously upon bridle and saddle, shouting and vociferating most furiously. Incensed at what we believed to be a new claim upon the miserable beast, for the hire of which we had already paid a most exorbitant sum, and supposing that they intended to get possession of him, the butt of a pistol was rapidly descending upon the pate of the nearest intruder, when he sprang aside like a monkey, much to our regret. Again, however, they all returned to the charge, when our *dander* being up high, the muzzle of the pistol was "in less than no time" in close range with his legs. Fortunately at this moment we were joined by another party of travellers, one of whom was well acquainted with the Spanish and at once explained. It appeared that the straw mat underneath the saddle had slipped from its position, and back of the poor beast was in consequency badly chafed, which had also caused him to lie down, and the excited natives were only anxious to correct the difficulty.

Upon comprehending this, our anger and vexation vanished into a general outburst of laughter, and our four hombres capered about in the greatest glee crying, *"ah mucha mala señor, mucha mala,"* to which we replied, *"muy bueno"* and *"mucha gracia."* Replacing the saddle and receiving some *medios* for reward, they bid adieu to us amidst general mirth at the funny termination of the adventure. The one who had been in close proximity to the pistol, however, was transmuted by his fright from a dark darkey into a milky Creole.

Soon after this occurrence we met upon the road two straggling horses without saddle, bridle, or *vaquero*, and knowing by the brand that they belonged to the same individual who had imposed upon us already, we selected the best one and placing a rope around his nose for bridle, and strapping an overcoat on his back for saddle, pressed him into the service for the remainder of our road, and he proved quite an acquisition.

The sun was high in the heavens and the heat beginning to be felt even in these shades, when we reached the summit of the mountain range. Here we found another encampment of engineers, and hard by a *rancho* of a native. Resting a short time at the camp and partaking of a lunch of pilot bread and water, we commenced the latter half of our journey, looking in vain ere we left the summit for any glimpse of either Atlantic or Pacific. On every side the view was shut in by the confused range of mountain above mountain, covered by the impervious woods. Thus we continued to jog on, riding and walking by turns, which we found a most excellent plan, occasionally making a detour into the woods on either hand. We saw great varieties of birds and insects, among the latter the large red and black ants with their hills several feet in height; and another of our party, who crossed a few days after, shot an armadillo, his coat of mail not being proof to powder and ball.

Late in the afternoon we began to reach wider valleys and less precipitous paths, until we finallly emerged upon a succession of savannahs or plains, dotted here and there with groves of mango, or crossed at intervals by belts of cotton-wood trees and underwood. Among these we noticed the black thorn tree, and many others unknown to us; gnarled and beautiful vines mingled with their branches, and the wild cactus grew all around, forming a complete chaparal. Through this we wound our way, appreciating more completely by observation, the nature of the difficulties so perseveringly surmounted by our armies in Mexico.

Leaving the Gorgona road, we now struck into the old paved road of the Spaniards, an odd wooden cross and pile of stone by the wayside indicatig either the grave of a robber, murderer, or suicide, or the junction of the two roads, as the imagination might determine.

We soon after crossed an old stone bridge over a beautiful little streamlet, and now began to distinguish among the distant groves the country houses of the citizens of Panama. Some of these were quite picturesque in the midst of large plantations, their foreground covered with herds of fine cattle. Day was now rapidly declining, and the crimson rays of the setting sun on tree-top, valley and plain, betokened the early approach of night ere we could reach our destination. From each new eminence attained, we eagerly strained our vision to catch the first glimpse of the great Pacific and our animals, more wearied than ourselves, permitted those of us on foot to keep the lead, now eagerly sought by all. At length we began to overtake the aguadores, or water-carriers, conveying to the town their last burdens for the day, and to see the twinkling lights of the suburbs, rendered necessary by the closing shoadows of night, which had settled over the town and country. These suburbs we found upon entering, to be quite extensive, the houses at first being of no better class than those on the other side of the Isthmus; but as we advanced nearer the walls of the town, we noticed houses of stone or frame, two or three stories in height.

Pausing at a little shop without the gates, we

refreshed ourselves with some very sweet oranges, biscuit and Madeira wine, after which, joining the current of stragglers, we reached the wide, paved street, with a low wall on each side, leading to the Gorgona gate, or Puerto de Tierra. The moon had not risen, but the stars brightly shining, revealed the high arched gateway, surmounted with tower and bell, and rude stone cross, with the massive old walls, and deep fosse extending on each side, encircling the whole town in their complete, but now useless embrace. Within them we could trace the confused mass of tiled roofs and crumbling ruins, with the towers of the great cathedral rising in the midst, while beyond all, and beheld for the first time, were the glittering waters of the Pacific, and Bay of Panama, with the bold islands rearing their verdant crests like mountains in the sea. Welcome, thrice welcome now, to us was the far-famed Panama, and right glad were we to find ourselves in comfortable lodgings with a bare cot on which to rest our weary limbs, after ten hours of journeying in the Andes of the Isthmus.

Travellers by this route will find it best to cross the Isthmus in parties of two, three, or four. Keeping aloof from all general arrangements, they will, on arrival at Chagres, engage a canoe alongside the ship large enough to land them with their baggage, which they will attend to in person. This plan will avoid the delay and confusion attending the general landing in boats and launches. Reaching what is called the American side of the river, opposite to Chagres, one or more can remain in charge of the baggage, while another of the party can select a canoe to ascend the river, in case there is no steamer. A canoe of the medium size, large enough to accommodate the party and their effects, will be chosen. Take care that it be clean and dry, and provided with a roof or bungo, impervious to sun or rain, with room for all to sit or sleep under. Make your bargain with the owner at the canoe, stipulating for three men, (a captain and *two* polesmen,) then take possession and *maintain it,* while one of the party goes before the alcalde and pays the *whole* amount agreed upon, taking a receipt in *Spanish*. Unless you pursue this course, the proprietor will not hesitate even to return your money and refuse the canoe, if he finds he can obtain a little more from others. Having completed arrangements as above, you will still be detained several hours, as neither solicitation or threats will avail to get the men to start, unless you promise them some *additional* reward to leave in half an hour. Two bottles of common Cogniac, and some common cigars, should be laid in at Chagres for the use of your canoemen under their severe labor in poling up the river, and you will facilitate your progress by treating them kindly. Whether you propose to land at Gorgona or not, contract to be taken to Cruces. Start as early as possible, but not later than 5 p.m.; about ten or twelve miles above Chagres you will reach Gatun; if you are early in the day, you can land there for lunch or dinner, but if towards night avoid it; otherwise you will have trouble to induce your boatmen to tear themselves away from the fandango and aguardiente.

Proceeding ten or twelve miles further, you arrive at Dos Hermanos, where you can obtain eggs, chocolate, and other refreshment. Piño Blanco is the next point where refereshment may also be obtained. Palenquillá comes next in order—two-thirds of the way to Gorgona, and rather more than half way to Cruces. Above this point on the stream, are some powerful currents; and a little below San Pablo there is a single rancho a short distance from the river, where supplies can also be had. After leaving there, do not land again till you reach Gorgona.

The Gorgona road is best in the *dry* season; and if there is not a great throng of passengers, it is well to depart thence to Panama. Otherwise it is better to continue up the river in your canoe to Cruces, which is about eight miles farther, and where, under *such circumstances*, mules will be obtained more readily, and at more reasonable prices, thus facilitating your progress. You will find two or three hotels or boarding-houses both at Gorgona and Cruces; and if in the *dry* season, you can rest with some satisfaction at either place for a day or two, until you obtain mules for your journey to Panama. *By no means attempt the Gorgona road in the rainy season.* Avoid hiring the miserable little horses, but get mules if possible—one for the baggage of each person, and one each to ride if in rainy season; but in dry season, on the Gorgona road, one mule will answer for two persons to "ride and tie," or if you prefer it, two mules for three of the party. To walk part of the way will be found a great relief; but in the *regular* rainy season it is a risk to health, even if you are able to accomplish it; and above all things, in that climate *avoid overfatigue*. Both on the Cruces and Gorgona roads, you will meet with houses of natives where rest and sometimes refreshment can be obtained, especially on the road from the former place; but I consider it far preferable to get an *early* start, and push through to Panama in one day, provided you find the fatigue endurable, which most persons in health can sustain. Let the pack-mules, attended by a native muleteer, *precede you*, and let one of the party always keep them in sight, or they will soon be turned off the road to some rancho in the mountains, involving a week's delay in their arrival at Panama, or the loss of baggage. Do not neglect to provide a small haversack, to contain provisions, a flask of best brandy, and a small *cocoa-nut* cup with a long twine attached, by which you can obtain water from the streams to quench your thirst, without dismounting. This cup you can buy of some of the natives at Chagres or other village on the river; but drink as little as possible, *especially* in the rainy season. In the contract for mules, stipulate to pay half the hire at your departure, and the remainder on arrival at your destination. If you should find prices very exorbitant, it may be better economy to purchase mules and sell them at the end of the journey; but in this case the risk of losing the animal is incurred, as many break down along the way. For the same reason, if a party of three or four travel in company, it is judicius to have an extra mule in your train.

Arrived at Panama, ascertain first when the steamer sails for San Francisco, registering your ticket at the same time; then obtain lodging at a hotel if you are to be detained only three or four days; but if for a week or more, get private lodgings, hiring a cook, and becoming your own caterers, or get meals at a restaurant. If hotels are established at Taboga, you will, of course, go to that island.

During detention at Panama, avoid midday sun, or exposure to rain, but take moderate exercise. If greatly fatigued, and not well, spunge the person with whiskey or spirits of some kind, bathe the feet in warm water, and retire to rest. *Do not resort to cold bath* when *fatigued*, or *during heat of the day*. During the rainy season mix with the water you drink a little brandy. It is best to *avoid all fruits entirely*; but if indulged in, let it be in moderation, and early in the morning. If you wish to *secure* the *immediate* payment of the amount insured to heirs or relatives on your life, eat freely of fruit and eggs *together*, and drink milk, or wash down plenty of fruit with brandy, or any kind of wine or liquor whtever. Three or four Peruvian bark pills every morning, are good preventives to fever, if predisposed to it. Take little medicine, and no advice from physicians not accustomed to practice in *tropical* climates. The following prescription is recorded by John H. Stephens, as having cured him of a violent attack of fever in Central America, vix.: "A decoction of the rind of the *sour orange*, flavored with cinnamon and lemon juice, a tumblerful warm every two hours, with copious draughts of tamarind water during the intervals." It was prescribed by a native.

On no account dispense with a flannel or merino undershirt; and if you never wore any, assume it now. Much of the foregoing may seem superfluous counsel, and to have emanated from a kind old ancestor of the female line; but it may, perhaps, enable some travellers by this route, to escape the doctors' hands, and forego the attention of a sexton—a difficult individual to discover in Panama even when wanted.

Lastly, I would advise any person to attempt to *swim* from Panama to San Francisco, rather than take passage in a *sailing* vessel. Get a *Pacific steamer's* ticket, before leaving New York, or do not attempt this route. For all your expenses on the Isthmus, *one hundred dollars* will be a safe estimate, though fifty may, perhaps, suffice. If there is no great crowd of travellers, and little detention at Panama. This sum should be in dimes, *eight* of which pass for a dollar in *all* payments to *natives*.

In conclusion, a steerage passenger from New York to San Francisco, by the Isthmus route, will require *three hundred dollars*, and a first-class cabin passenger *five hundred dollars*; unless the competition among the different lines should reduce prices materially, which, with the increasing emigration, is not to be anticipated.

Less sums than the above *may*, in some instances, suffice but I recommend no person make the experiment.

Panama is a regular old Spanish town, containing from six to eight thousand inhabitants, at least one-half residing outside the walls. We arrived there on the 21st of February, and were aroused from our slumbers at an early housr of the following morning by the firing of guns and pistols, and clangor of drums and trumpets, mingled with shouts, cheers and hurrahs.

Hastening out on the balcony to ascertain the cause, a strange, picturesque and animated scene presented itself. Below us in every direction appeared in close proximity the red, glazed, tiled roofs of the city, the houses of stone or brick, two and three stories in height, covered with a coat or plaster or whitewashed, and invariably srrounded on each story with a wide balcony floored with the large, flat, square brick, and protected from sun and rain, by the roofs of the houses extending over them.

Intersecting them at right angles, the strait and narrow streets were filled with natives selling fruit, or lazily strolling toward the scene of uproar. Away in the distance beneath the bright morning sun, shone the clear still surface of the bay, reflecting in dark contrast the shadows of its bold mountain isles, while the air was filled with thousands of buzzards on noiseless and almost motionless wing, or twittering martins restlessly flitting from ruined tower and wall.

In a few moments we heard the inspiring strains of Hail Columbia from a full military band, echoed from the rude pavement by the steady tramp of men; and the waving of the Star-spangled banner as the column passed the head of the street, assured us that our patriotic countrymen were appropriately celebrating the birthday of Washington. We had arrived too late on the previous evening to participate in the arrangements, and our fatigue had induced sleep till the morning was well advanced. The procession numbered three of four hundred Americans, and preceded by the Governor's band in full uniform, marched to his quarters and to the houses of the American and French Consuls, giving all in turn three cheers; after which our flag was unfurled, and saluted at the battery fronting the bay, and the festivities of the day were concluded by a dinner and grand concert at the American Hotel, in the evening.

The soldiers here are queer-looking specimens of the nucleus of an army. There are about seventy or at most a hundred, their uniform consisting of coarse, dirty, white linen pants, a shirt of the same, made *a la blouse* and worn outside, a blue cloth scull-cap, with red band in front, contrasting, *a la diable*, with their black faces; and bare feet with long toes complete the *tout ensemble*.

Shouldering their clumsy, condemned English muskets and bayonets—the latter suitable for a toad-sticker—they parade morning and evening in their barrack-yard, going through their evolutions with tolerable correctness, but still forcibly reminding one of the Jack Falstaff and his buckram warriors. These solders are employed as guards to the immense amounts of specie and bullion sent acros the Isthmus, and in various similar duties within the town.

After witnessing the celebration and parade of the morning, and partaking of our café, we sally forth to explore this ancient town and port.

Entering by the principal or Gorgona gate from the northwest, the traveller is struck both by the solidity and substantial character of the buildings, and the evidences of disuse and dilapidation everywhere presented. Immediately within the walls, and fronting the gateway, is the church of the blessed Virgin, extending to the next street, with the ruins of monastery or convent attached. The church itself is in tolerable repair; its yellow, stuccoed front adorned with antique-looking towers, and niches filed with images of saints. The principal entrance is at the side, from the street of la Merced, and at the corner fronting the gateway, is an open porch or shrine, with an altar and picture of the Virgin Mary, and jewelled cross, enclosed in glass. Here the tired *cargodores, vaqueros,* and *aguadores* are accustomed to offer their devotions; and after a brief rest upon their weary limbs, resume their incessant labors. None ever pass here without lifting their sombreros or crossing themselves.

Commencing here, the *Calle de la Merced,* or street of mercy, or the Virgin, extends directly through the plaza to the gate opening upon the shores of the bay—a distance of about a quarter of a mile; in width, twenty-five to thirty feet, with an old cobble pavement and narrow flag-stone sidewalks, much worn and broken, or covered with grease enough to afford good sliding. This, the principal street of Panama, is quite similar to all the others. Parallel, and next to it, is the street of *San Juan de Dios*, not so wide, but much neater in appearance, and attracting the notice of the stranger with its numerous and varied stores and shops.

With the exception of two or three warehouses of the more considerable merchants, who are chiefly located near the custom-house and mole, these shops are small, but filled with the greatest variety of wares, dry goods, hardware, and clothing, which is made by the industrious fingers of the *señoras* and *señoritas* who invariably waited on the counters. Some of them, who are creoles, bordering on the pure Castilian, have pretensions to beauty, but generally the dusky or sallow complexion quite naturalizes the effect of their jet-black hair and eyes. Besides these shops, every street has its wine-stores and fruit-stalls—the former lined with fancifully-painted shelves, and filled from floor to ceiling with glasses and chinaware, and bottles of wines, cordial, cogniac, or *aguardiente*. The strong drink is consumed chiefly by the laboring people; but all classes drink much of the light cordials and claret wines. Rows of dusty and empty bottles, however, and shelves long bereft of merchandise, evidence the poverty or want of industry of many.

On the street of la Merced, under the quarters of the French Consul, is the French café, and nigh to this the California and United States restaurants—the two latter established since the influx of American travel by this route. At all of them we obtained tolerable good meals. The French chocolate, prepared here from the nut, and the Sandwich Island coffee, were particularly fine. The only hotels were the Fonda Americana, Washington House, and Hotel

Française—the first and last tolerably well kept, considering all things; the other only a lodging-house. After tarrying all week at the former, we became tired of life at a hotel, and soon sought and obtained lodgings and a cook, at a respectable private house, becoming our own caterers.

We were so fortunate as to be received into the mansion of Señor Antonio Forns, a merchant of Havana, and of an ancient, wealthy, and highly-respectable Spanish family of Old Panama. To this gentleman's politeness and kind attentions, combined with his perfect knowledge of our language, were we especially indebted for many comforts and advantages while under his roof; and would advise our countrymen who are provided with proper credentials, to seek admission to his quarters, over the Jardin Italiano, in the street of la Merced.

The interior of the houses here are admirably adapted for comfort in this climate. They are mostly thirty to forty feet square, and often larger—the walls two or three feet thick, and provided with ornamental loop-holes to admit the external air—the floors of the upper stories composed of slabs of the bay-tree, or paved with brick laid on rafters of this tree, which is very strong and lasting. These stories are used as the residence of the family; and divided into large apartments, the partitions not reaching to the ceiling or roof, permit free ventilation, which is further aided by wide stairways and folding-doors, with windows cut in them opening on the balconies. Thus, with the impervious-tiled roof, as much comfort is ensured as is possible in a tropical climate. The ground-floor is occupied by a shop of some kind, and a wide, stone-paved hall, from whence the ample stone or mahogany staircase ascends to the family apartments. A wide courtyard, provided with well or cistern, and some few large trees, completes the description of a Panama house.

The *plaza*, or open common (for it is neither more not less) is worthy of notice only as a distinctive feature in a Spanish town, and is not to be named in comparison with any of the public squares of our large cities. Covered with sparse grass, it is a general playground for the children, who, instead of jeering and annoying poor cripples, or other pitiable objects of humanity, as in our own free country, are contented with the antics of a favorite dog, or to war with a belligerent goat.

Fronting on the plaza, is a seminary of learning, the old legislative hall, with its long row of short stone pillars, and New Grenadian coat-of-arms, and the great Cathedral.

The latter is an interesting relic of Panama in its palmy days; and though stripped by the old Spaniards of its principal paintings, jewels, and ornaments, in 1823, (the time of the revolution and triumph of Bolivar,) enough of the original structure yet remains to convey an idea of the superior energy of its founders. It is apparently one hundred and fifty feet in length, by fifty in breadth. The façade, though marred by the ravages of time, is venerable on that account, and quite imposing. Two massive square towers rear their solid structures from the foundation walls, terminating with conical spires, which are coated with stucco and spangled with large pearl shells, affording a most beautiful effect in the bright rays of the sun or mellow light of the moon. Surmounted each by a cross, and provided with a good clock, and chime of bells from cracked to musical, these towers are worthy objects of pride to all devout and good citizens. Between them, and over the great entrance, are figures in stone of Christ and the twelve apostles, rather the worse for wear from the floods of the rainy season, in spite of the niches provided for them. Below these are the three great doorways, the centre one being arched and highly ornamented, and all approached by a grand double flight of stone steps. There is, also, a wide doorway and similar ascent on the side, from the street of la Merced.

The architecture of the interior is, however, more effective. The central nave is apparently eighty feet high, with an open mahogany roof, and on each side a double row of thirty-two immense quadrangular columns, with arches between. The high altar is quite a fine affair, with saints innumerable, and over the crucifix a large silver stork presides with her young. There are also other altars and shrines to various saints, with pictures of the Crucifixion, Last Supper, Madonna, &c. Over one of these we saw what we supposed to be the figure of an Indian clinging to a tree, with an arrow transfixed through the heart, and one through each arm. Still above this appeared a figure like St. George standing over the dragon, with helmet, sword, and shield, but no steed. This we imagined to be "good ould Saint Patrick" killing the father of serpents, and the other some canonized Indian deity. If wrong in these surmises, we trust the good and indulgent *padres* will attribute it to the ignorance of depraved heretics, which, so far as their system is concerned, we acknowledge ourselves to be. Near the altar the pavement is covered with tombstones of *padres* and great folks. One, to the memory of a pious señora, we observed, was embellished with the figures of an angel opening the gate of heaven, and a lady weeping at the tomb; and another was of beautiful Parian marble, in the form of the cross, with an inscription. By the side of the principal entrance were also the usual white marble fonts of holy water, resorted to by all the faithful, and filled with the little insects dropped from the dirty sleeves of devotees. Two or three small and inferior organs supplied the music.

Outside the walls of the town and near the Gorgona gate is also the Church of Santa Anna. It is even larger than the Cathedral, and though of its great towers one only remains perfect, its appearance is quite grand and beautiful, especially when seen in bold relief against the evening sky, its gray walls and lonely tower gorgeous in the crimson light of the setting sun, while the deep notes of the vesper bell are returned in a plaintive echo from the neighboring hill.

There are many other inferior churches both within and without the walls, so that as usual in Roman Catholic countries the church bells are perpetually tolling, ringing or clanging; chiefly the latter, however, in Panama, as they are mostly rung by being pounded with a cobble stone and are thus often cracked. This abundance of churches also affords food and idleness to *padres* and priests innumerable, so that a large body of men are interested in extending the system as far as possible, and in the multiplication of ceremonies and observances.

The same plan is pursued among Protestants as well as Roman Catholics in our own land, where church edifices are built with money borrowed or begged. Debts are thus bequeathed to posterity, and the continual appeals from such sources for aid might put O'Connell to the blush.

The Sabbath is observed in Panama as in all Spanish cities. After attending early or morning mass, all classes turn out for amusements. The military and governor's band parade twice, the shops and billiard rooms are open, and it is the great day allowed by law for cock-fighting. We attended church service at the residence of the American consul, following the dictates of conscience or of home custom, as the case might be, which is exactly what most of the world do. Every Sunday morning, at two or three o'clock, the host is carried in procession through the streets. It was a strange sight to us, to behold the crucifix hung not only with the image of Christ but with cords and elegant tapestry; was it so on Calvary? Carried by priests in white robes, and followed by a band of musicians and many more priests all in white, chanting in full chorus and unearthly tones, the ghostly train swept by. From every door and window issued half-clad devotees to kneel and repeat their prayers in moonlight or shadow, while over all the impressive scene "the heavens declare the glory of God," and the eternal stars shed their bright ustre both "on the just and the unjust."

Processions are also frequent here on the days of the week. One evening we joined a crowd of our countrymen, and followed a procession bearing on a platform carried by four natives, a figure of Christ as large as life, dressed in a robe of purple velvet and crowned with thorns, bending under the weight of a large wooden cross. Tin lanterns, with six or eight tallow candles were stuck around it, and the top of the cross was adorned with a beautiful bouquet of flowers. There were few priests, but crowds of women and children followed close. As they neared the Cathedral door they all halted and gathered around, kneeling devoutly, while the priest with knees on the bare pavement selecting a clean place, repeated his prayers and invocations. Meantime we observed the fellows who carried the show had a talk and flirtation with the wenches nearest them. Resuming the march, we took off our hats and entered the Cathedral with them. Here they repeated the litany in a mixture of bad Latin and corrupt Spanish, the women and children, (the wicked men are too often absent on these occasions,) kneeling on the pavement of the church, joined with much fervor in the responses, elevating and extending their arms and outstretched hands towards the image. To their ignorant hearts it was true devotion, and side by side the rich and poor kneeled together, prevented neither by glittering robe nor tattered rag, by costly pew nor haughty pride; for "dust thou art, and unto dust thou shalt return," was not forgotten here.

Panama abounds with ruins of the most diversified and beautiful descripton. The most perfect of these is the Church of San Domingo. Siguated on one of the inferior streets near the bay, it frequently escapes the notice of strangers. Entering by a small opening, left in the wooden enclosure of the great doorway, we were at once in the body of the church. The walls appear almost entire, the mortar being hard as the stone itself, but no vestige of tower or roof remains. The arches are quite unbroken and perfect, stretching from side to side in bold and massive beauty. One of them especially attracted our admiration, being nearly level at the key-stone, and showing the intimate knowledge of its constructors with the principles of their art. At the east end were the remains of chancel, altar, and vestry, and the whole interior is filled with beautiful trees and shrubbery, with every variety of creeping vine, climbing gracefullly over arch and pillar, and mouldering wall. Near the west end hangs three antique-looking old bells on rude cross timbers. These are of different sizes and of various and most delicious tones. They bear date 1761, and the *inscription Francisco de Leon, N. del Rosario ora pro mobis.* Passing through a door opposite to the one by which we entered, we found ourselves in a quadrangular court overgrown with trees, and surrounded on three sides by the remains of a large monastery or nunnery. The inner walls remain, as also the pedestals of the columns in front of them. Adjoining the ruined church is a private stone staircase, leading to a small, square door in the wall of the convent, which perhaps could many a tale unfold. Strewed about the court were earthen vessels shaped like those in Eastern countries, and we obtained from one of them letters stamped in a circle, resembling the Arabic or Morish characters.

On our return here we found a beautiful little chapel of the convent, still preserved and in use called San Felipe, and adorned with massive silver-framed oil paintings of the Madonna and the Crucifixion, and large chandeliers also of solid silver.

We also visited the ruins of the College of Jesuits which cover a large extent. There was no perceptible mode of admission, but clambering to the top of the wall where it is lowest, we found the interior filled with trees and vines, and obtained some of the bolls of a wild cotton plant. Cocoa-trees and the palmetto were also displaying their grateful tops above the walls. This building it is said was never completed.

Standing immediately on the shores of the bay, are the remains of two old monasteries of immense size. Of these the walls and old bells only remain, but close at hand are the ruins of an old Spanish convent covering a whole square. A portion of the roof and the towers are yet to be seen, with the old bells swinging sentinels over all, where once their matin tones aroused the young and beautiful to prayer, now voiceless and hushed as they. Near this is the Convent of the Concepcion, where a few nuns yet reside. We visited it afterwards in company with an American lady, but were only admitted to the outer court. By the aid of a wooden wheel revolving horizontally, they supplied us with tumblers of pure and sparkling water, and a boquet of most rare, beautiful, and fragrant flowers. They refused any remuneration for their kindness, but seemed much delighted with the beauty of our fair companion, promising to admit her on a following day.

"But I won't be a nun, so I shan't be a nun,
"I'm so fond of pleasure that I cannot be a nun."

Seeing only the flash of their briliant black eyes through a knot hole in the wheel, we imagined ourselves transferred to the famed Alhambra, and were fain to enter there, but imitating the example of irresistible mother Eve, our "fair lady" drove us out of Paradise. A favorite walk with strangers, while tarrying in Panama, is on the East Battery fronting the bay. Stretching away to the south-east, some four hundred yards in length, forty feet in width and fifty feet above high-water mark, it presents a frowning battlement of solid masonry, in which are still remaining some fine old brass cannon of large calibre, bearing the arms of Hispaniola, and dated Seville, 1745 and 1777, also a brass mortar inscribed Barcelona, Phillip V. by the ruined watch tower on the wall, these relics of the olden time took out upon the sea, and like the once powerful nation whose arms they bear, behold the tide of commerce and civilization sweeping onward, bestowing wealth, power and refinement on a nation whose infancy was scarce inscribed in history, ere its republican fires destroyed the last remant of monarchical tyranny on both continents of the New World.

The view of the bay and town from this battery is remarkably fine. The gorgeous sunset of the tropics crowning the distant mountains with a blaze of glory and covering the green islands with a robe of crimson and orange; or after a brief interval, the gray light of the twinkling stars and bright effulgence of the rising moon, reflected from the gleaming waters at our feet, or falling with mellow light on spire, roof, and balcony, afford a scene which the heart of an artist might well delight in, but which his pencil can, ne'er portray.

At the barracks of the military hospital on the street of San Juan de Dios, we were encountered at the door by these rascals, with rusty muskets, crying *cigaros, cigaros, señores*, a few of which we bestowed, to their great delight. Ascending the ricketty stiars from a musty old courtyard, we were admitted by another sentry with a similar password into a large apartment, on a platform in the centre of which was a score or more of soldiers of all colors, from jet black, up to saffron-yellow, or white livered. They were employed in weaving straw hats, which they eagerly offered us for sale. Those denominated Panama hats by use are here called Guayaquil, and are made at Monte Cristo,

San Juan, and San Helano on that coast. We found these military hatters hard at a bargain and were proceeding to the further end of the room in quest of more liberal dealers, when they tried to stop us, crying *mucho infirmo, mucho infirmo, señor*. Taking this to be a mere ruse, we persevered, and there found sure enough several poor fellows yellow with Panama fever. We therefore beat a retreat, and as day after day, we saw the soldiers bearing a rude wooden coffin out of the Gorgona gate.

While musing over one of these scenes, we noticed a crowd of naives wending their way up a sort of causeway just within the walls, towards a small building half in ruins. As several of them carried their feathered champions under their arms, we knew directly that cock-fighting was the order of the day; and accordingly joined the rush. The interior is rudely fitted with seats against the old walls, rising in the form of an ampitheatre, a circular space of hard-beaten ground being left for the sport. The preliminary scenes here are of the most ludicrous description. A crowd of the fancy darkies and creoles shuffling and pushing about the ring, chattering like monkeys and gesticulating like ourang-outangs, discuss with the utmost rate and violence the merits of the different birds. Others are engaged in fixing on the murderous steel gaffs, while betting and hedging run high. At one side hangs a rusty old bell, which is used as a signal to clear the ring. After a long delay in completing the final arrangements, during which the woolly tribe often get into a fight in place of the feathered; the bell is struck impatiently, the enraged birds are placed opposite to each other, held by the several owners, while the one which is intended by the gambling knaves to win, has most of his tail feathers plucked violently out. Then comes a furious onset, the birds frequently leaping clear over one another, but in a few seconds blood spirts from second joint or neck, and the wounded hero falls. Screams, yells, and shouts of derision now burst forth; but in a moment all is still; for the floored combatant suddenly rises, and quick as lightning lays low his antagonist. When this happens, the excitement of the crowd becomes furious, and they watch with the greatest eagerness for the last gasp of either bird, the survivor being immediately declared the winner, but it more commonly happens that one or other of them is killed at the first onset. Then comes the payment of losses and preparation for another bout. This amusement appeared to us cruel, disgusting, and puerile, but is, nevertheless, the grand entertainment among these people. They also had, at the time of our visit, a circus company, which performed on Sunday evenings within the ruins of a fine old church adjoining the College of Jesuits. It was much frequented, but we did not go there.

Wandering one beautiful Sunday morning towards a favorite haunt amidst the lonely yet eloquent ruins, our attention was drawn to the attractive word *baths*, on a sign above an old gateway. Entering immediately, we found ourselves in a large court-yard, in which were three or four bamboo huts, or rather booths. Ushered into one of these, a coarse towel, comb, and soap were handed, and the curtain dropped. Within were three high oriental-shaped jars, containing each a half-barrel or more of water clear as crystal, and provided with wooden cover and calabash—the latter to be used in place of a shower-bath. There was a rough brick floor to stand upon with bare feet, and on one side a rude bench to receive clothing. Not relishing the rough floor, we succeeded in standing upright within the jar, though the bottom was so small as only to permit one foot to rest on the other. The soap used is made partly with a plant or root similar to that of California; and either its properties are extraordinary, or we had lost our power of comparison between ourselves and the dusky natives around us. While engaged in these delightful absolutions, we cast frequent glances through the bamboo sides of our modest retreat, fearing some young Señorita might linger in the grove to lave in turn her own fair form, or rather twilight skin. But in this, alas! we were not so fortunate or rather unfortunate as one of our *compañeros*, who on a prior occasion was forced to hasten from the garden, driven out by the impatient glances of one of these waiting daughters of Eve. This oriental style of bathing was afterwards much resorted to, and the attentive *hombe*, the proprietor, no doubt collected many riales.

The sea shore was a favorite walk in the cool of the morning and evening, but we did not often venture to bathe, as in these latitudes sharks are both numerous and daring. The tide, which rises and falls the extraordinary height of twenty-two feet; presented an imposing sight, when the flood making with a stiff breeze, the great combers came roaring and foaming up the beach with wonderful rapidity. The shore directlly in front of the city is flat, but composed of hard volcanic rock, while on either side it is a yellow or black sand beach. The tide when at full flood in stormy weather, dashes against the high wall of the east battery with great violence, throwing the spray far above it. In our strolls along the sandy beach, we gathered many small shells of great variety, and some quite beautiful. The best time for this amusement was on a rising tide, when intent on securing some attractive shell, we often got caught by the waves, and had a grand scramble to reach dry land.

We observed similar performances too, by the little land crabs, called soldier crabs, which bound on the shore, living in holes, and feeding on the animalculae of the tide. Some of these were quite large, and of a bright red color, from which with their belligerent attitude when approached they no doubt derive their name. The sand is marked all over with their claws, and when overtaken by the tide on the smooth rocks, they hold on with these until the wave recedes, when they scramble off as nimbly as possible.

Resting on the cool balcony after one of these rambles, we watched the evening shadows falling fast from tower and isle over city and bay, while busy memory was far away by the side of our own loved hearthstones in a wintry clime, when our attention was recalled by the sombre gloom settling gradually and strangely upon surrounding objects. Remembering at once the expected eclipse of the moon, we hurried forth to observe its effects among the ruins. Amidst the fading shadows of broken column and crumbling arch, the dim forms of tall and venerable trees seemed like the ghosts of old padre or stalwart knight, returned to gaze once more on the well-known scenes of a past century, their strong arms held aloft in deprecatory amazement, while the low night wind sighed the requiem of the olden time. Huge vines crept away over the dark and dismal walls, like the serpent of old deserting the desolation of the once bright abode. Silence disturbed only by the rustling leaf or flitting bat, reigned supreme, where once the vaulted roof or marble floor echoed with the sound of mailed foot or pealing organ. Altogether the scene was one not soon to be forgotton; and retiring to repose for the night, we were only aroused for a moment from our dreams by a serenade of the most delicious music under the balcony, when pleasant thoughts of far off homes rose up to blend with returning slumber.

Notwithstanding the many objects of interest in and about Panama, our delay there when en route for the El Dorado would have grown somewhat tedious, but for the new and agreeable scenes and incidents continually presenting themselves.

Imitating the enterprising example of our countrymen in Mexico, a small weekly newspaper called the Panama Star was early established to furnish information or amusement to our people sojourning here, as well as to those at home. This, we believe, was the first effort of the American press on the southern continent, but so great is the anxiety of the people of New Grenada to cultivate friendly relations with us, and acquire our language, that we hope an American newspaper will in due time be permanently established among them.

Of all American novelties, however, presented to the New Grenadians, none seemed to afford them more surprise and gratification than the arrival of some of our fair countrywomen. We had the pleasure of seeing two of these persevering and heroic ladies enter the Gorgona gate in health and safety, one of them mounted on a fine mule, holding her little boy before her, the other carried in a hammock *a la polanquin*. We received them with three hearty cheers, which they gracefully acknowledged. How little will the hardship and fatigue which they endured be appreciated by those who in a few years will be whirled across the Isthmus by railway in two or three hours.

Standing in the crowd of natives and Americans, we observed a tip top dandy, or regular Panama swell. He was dressed with loose gay linen pants, yellow leather or buckskin zapatos or shoes, Monte Cristo sombrero, and a curious-looking linen coat called a brusa, known among us under the soubriquet of bruiser. It is something between a shirt and a blouse, usually made of plaid linen, with ample sleeves, wristbands, and collar like a shirt, having wide band across the shoulders to which the full skirt is gathered, and open in front with pocket in each corner. Exceedingly comfortable in a hot climate, it is nevertheless quite comical in appearance.

The costume of the women of Panama especially attracted our attention. Although appropriate enough to the climate, it was rather different from our pre conceived ideas of modesty and propriety. A white petticoat, or with the better lasses, a black silk one, descends from the short waist; above this is a loose chemise ascends unwillingly, or rather hangs provokingly from the short-sleeved shoulder. Cut very low in the back, it is usually surrounded with common fringe, or sometimes rich, deep lace; this, with slipper down at the heel, or neat, black morocco shoe and white stockings completes the in-door attire. When dressed for mass or circus, the hair is neatly plaited and set off with pearls or rude golden ornaments; and the indispensable white lace mantilla, or *rebozo*, hangs gracefully from the back of the head, or is allowed to drop carelessly from the shoulder. This dress being universal we soon became accustomed to it. The style of dress among our fashionable bells we fear cannot plead adaptation to the climate, like that of Panama. What would the modestly-attired daughters of the Celestial Empire say to the beautiful barbarians of America. The well-worn motto of "boni soit qui mal y pense" we fear is too much relied on in these latter days.

Among the most conspicuous of the ornaments sometimes worn by the ladies of New Grenada are the celebrated Panama chains. Of the purest gold obtained in the country, and called Choco gold, these chains are made with combined delicacy and strength, frosted and colored with a peculiar yellow tinge, different from any other species of jewelry, and much admired. They are also adorned with a pendant of several large and beautiful pearls set in gold. These pearls are found in great abundance, and of large size, off the shores of the numerous islands in the bay of Panama, but the finest ones are obtained from the Isla del Rey, some thirty or forty miles out. Some are very perfect and of an egg or pear shape, and are often brought to the city by the poor divers who obtain them, and sold for a mere song. Many small and imperfect ones, or others partially cut from the shells in fanciful shapes, were disposed of for a few riales each. Cornelians and agates are also found here, and obtained very cheap of the different jewelers, whose shops, by the way, appear more like tinkers' shops and their instruments of labor of the rudest description. Among other curiosities which we saw, our polite host showed us a most curious pair of antique bracelets, made doubtless in Old Spain, more than three hundred years ago. He told us they had been in his family since the settlement of old Panama. They were of a rude net work, and weighed half a pound each of pure gold. We concluded it would neither be advisable nor safe, to allow one of our American ladies to box our ears with such a bracelet upon her wrist, as none but a steel-clad knight could withstand her.

Among the most important but not always agreeable of our occupations while in Panama, was mounting watch at the Gorgona gate, or Hotel Française, for the arrival of our different articles of baggage. Many ludicrous scenes, however, rewarded our patience, as the moment any poor cargadore or staggering mule made his appearance within the gate, there was a general rush to examine or claim the various packages. This would often bring a poor lean litle horse upon his knees, or induce a cargadore after a violent jabbering to consider his pilgrimage over and allow his heavy load to be deposited with the owner.

One of our party, like many others, had been anxiously watching nearly a week for a leather bag which contained numerous articles and papers of importance to him. To expedite its transmission and ensure its safety also, he had employed a fellow at Gorgona named Manuel Gomez. Paying him an extra price, and taking his receipt, he beheld him start for Panama, trotting off cheerily ahead of his mule. But, lo! This was the last of Master Manuel for many a day. Enquiring of every newly-arrived cargadore or muleteer, all knew Manuel Gomez; "Si, si, Señor mañana," meaning that he would arrive to-morrow, but though to-morrow surely came no Manuel came with it.

Thus mounting guard on the city walls one day "in quest of adventures," who should we espy in the midst of a crowd, but the identical Manuel Gomez himself; but unfortunatley for him he was not at that moment in *propria persona*, being a Bacchante, or in vulgar parlance gloriously drunk. Mingling at once in the circle of his admirers, the blackamoor's conscience at sight of us did cause his vagabond senses to return to the aid of his now trembling limbs. With the dread of the police before his eyes he begged for mercy, and explained that having confided the bag to another *hombre*, who was out at the old stone bridge, he could not recover it from him without more *riales*, of which himself was minus. A true and ready friend from the land of the claymore and kilt, volunteered to accompany the slippery Manuel and obtain the property or thrash the rogue, on behalf of the owner who was suffering with severe indisposition. Arriving at the bridge, sure enough, there was the darkey, bag and all. Paying him the four riales demanded, the rascally Manuel made a grab at the funds, and obtaining part both held on to the bag. Whereupon *auld reekie* tappit them on their crowns, producing immediate resignation. Now Master Manuel offered to carry the bag to the hotel in the town for *dos riales*, which was accordingly promised him, but when the "shrewd operator" arrived at his final destination, he had the audacity to demand twelve riales more, which the party interested immediatelly settled by whacking the scamp from top to bottom of the stairs. Thus vanished the redoubtable Manuel pale as a ghost to the land of *spirits*, where no doubt he quickly forgot the world and its troubles. Similar rows with the natives were not unusual, when their pockets were well-filled with the riales of the Americans, and their heads proportionately stored with aguardiente.

 We saw another instance of this kind one day in

the street of La Merced. One of our people who had been on a hunting and shooting expedition, in quest of the small red deer, which are numerous, or of the wild pigeons which abound in the neighboring mountains, being unsuccessful in obtaining the former, had purchased a young fawn of a native who killed it, and employed him to carry it to his lodgings. Some one, however, offered the fellow a higher price than he obtained, where he at once claimed the game as his own property, and throwing it down in the street, refused to proceed farther. Our Yankee friend drew his bowie-knife to intimidate him; but he was too cunning for that, and retorted by handling his own knife, where at the American quietly replaced his in his belt, and then deliberately knocked our belligerent *hombre* down, aiding his rapid rise by a kick. The *argumentum ad hominem* he perfectly understood, and nimbly picking up the game, trotted off in the required direction.

The natives, however, are generally honest, as the smallest thefts are punished with long imprisonment; and although some trunks were lost or rifled on the Isthmus, yet, among the vast number transported in safety, this was not surprising, especially considering also the carelessness of the owners.

Other and higher crimes are of rare occurrence, and are punished by placing the criminals in chain gangs. We saw some forty or fifty of these in all, going about the streets, carrying garbage and mending pavement. They are linked two and two by the leg and ankle, with strong iron chains, which are not very heavy. They are always accompanied by sentinels to make them work and preclude escape: their arms and hands are free, and they appeared to walk without great difficulty. At first, the continual clank,

clank, of their chains conveyed unpleasant feelings; but when we compare their easy existence in the free air of heaven, and in sight of their families, it is far less painful than the solitary confinement of our penitentiaries. The ignominy, no doubt, constitutes the chief punishment; for we never saw any of the natives notice or speak to them.

Passing, in one of our walks, a large house which had apparently been the residence in palmier days of an old Spanish grandee, we heard a loud buzz of voices, and looking in beheld row after row of small and mischievous-looking boys busily engaged at their studies and tricks. The sight was a pleasant one, as well as comical, and had the good effect to induce us forthwith to obtain a Spanish primer, and commence the study of the language. This we found to be the best mode to obtain a perfect idea of the pronunciation, and of course, the orthography; and brief as was our *schooling*, we were impressed with the opinion, that the best way to acquire any foreign language, is to learn it as we learn our own—from *alphabet* and the *primer*—and not by plunging at once into the grammar, though we are also quite ready to confess our general imperfect knowledge of the latter.

Early one morning we wended our way to the market, which is situated immediately upon the mole. Here we found a noisy, jabbering, and dirty crowd of black women, and creoles of both sexes—the former not so notable for their rotundity as those of our more favored land. They had the usual immense variety of tropical fruits, especially bananas, mangoes, tamarinds, and yams—the latter a very fine vegetable, and the potato of this climate, though, in our opinion, quite superior to that watery and common esculent. The yam seems to be almost pure farina, and served up in the style of American cookery would be a universal favorite, making with the addition of a little flour, the finest bread. We saw, also, a great variety of fish, some very fine; and a species of salmon, weighing fifteen pounds, we had on our table. They showed us some very large oysters, which, when cooked, tasted and looked more like our long clams; and we obtained some of a species of minute and beautiful shell-fish, not larger than one's finger-nail, which were very delicious.

The countrywomen gather a species of herb, which they dry and prepare a tea from, which they call *agua marba*, very agreeable to the taste, and quite a good substitute for our Chinese beverage.

Much to our horror and surprise, we found, too, that the natives eat monkeys, and are very fond of them. A roast monkey was set before some of our people, who had curiosity enough to taste it; but we had been too often in a menagerie for that, and felt that in this case *ignorance was bliss*.

Returning to our lodgings after these excursions, well laden with sundry good things of this life, we indulged our appetites *a la Americano*, calling lustily on our lazy cook, Manuella, for coffee to begin with. But this extraordinary procedure bewildered her for a whole day; and we were almost ready, in despair, to conform to her Panama modes and customs, of coffee at seven o'clock, breakfast at ten, and dinner at four, having but one dish before us at a time, and coffee always last.

Our lodgings were remarkably comfortable, being provided with chairs, tables, sofas, and glass chandeliers, all of which, barring the chairs, were extra luxuries in Panama. Our nightly bivouac upon the boards, was a funny scene. First, *shaking up* the boards, we spread out our tents, and rolling up in our camp blankets, lay out in rows, provided with boots and pilot coats for pillows. Then, sure that we could not fall out of bed, and that the curtains would not cause us to oversleep, we forgot the matter-of-fact world in dreams of El Dorado, till the sound of the matin-bell calling the faithful to prayer, aroused us to turn out, stow hammocks, and clear the decks for breakfast.

History informs us that New Grenada was conquered, and annexed to the crown of Spain, by Gonzala de Ximenes, in 1536, who overthrew Bogota, the native king, a redoubtable cheiftain, in honor of whom the capital of that name is called.

Seven miles from the existing city of Panama are the ruins of Old Panama. Founded by the Spaniards in the early part of the sixteenth century, and famous as the port from which Pizarro sailed in 1525, on his first epedition to Peru; it was sacked and burned by bucaniers in 1670, under a famous chieftain named Mogan. From this calamity it never recovered; and there is now only to be seen the remains of crumbling walls overgrown with trees, and a few houses of the natives.

Returning to the present city, we are impressed with the resources, munificence, and enterprise of its founders.

Its massive and high walls, its fortifications and defences, numerous large churches and other public buildings, as well as substantial private edifices, erected from a species of stone brought from a long distance: all attest the truth of the foregoing observations.

As long as Mexico, New Grenada, and other

South American states remained subject to the crown of Spain, the whole of their commerce in obedience to her enactments, passed by the way of the Isthmus to the mother country and the world. Thus Panama became the principal commerical port of the Pacific, and the mart of the whole west coast of South America and Mexico. But her glory departed the moment that trade and commerce left to their natural channels, attained a comparative degree of freedom, and flowed into immediate and direct communication with other countries.

While under this state of things, one generation has passed away—a new and longer day of prosperity is now apparently dawning on the next. The hope and expectation of the whole civilized world, long directed to the Isthmus route as the great highway of nations, are, at length, soon to be gratified. And with just pride and exaltation do we point to its final accomplishment, by the enterprise and energy of the people of our Great Western Republic; thus adding another bright and enduring record to the volume of American history. Though both the Isthmus of Panama and that of Darien had been surveyed many years ago by the English, French, and Spanish governments or capitalists, and the route by the former Isthmus ascertained to be entirely feasible for a railroad, and although especially England and the English eternally boast that theirs is the strongest government and wealthiest nation on earth, yet has it remained for their more powerful political and commercial rival to open new portals to her Indian empire and China trade.

Thus by our superior enterprise, as well as by our *peaceful annexation* of Texas in the West, compared with her forcible and *bloody annexation* of the Punjaub in the East, let us assure the world, that we have not only outstripped our Anglo-Saxon parentage in the race of civilization, but that if the "sun never sets" on England's boasted possessions, neither will it every again rise upon her commercial or political supremacy.

Crossing the Isthmus, both during the progress of the American survey and after its completion, we had every opportunity of observing the route selected for the proposed railroad and cannot doubt its certain and speedy construction. The chief difficulty to contend with will be the floods of the rainy season, and their effect upon the viaducts and embankments; competent engineers will, however, overcome this.

This great undertaking once accomplished, Panama must not only resume her former position, but become one of the chief commercial cities of the western hemisphere. Her magnificent bay, salubrious climate, and fertile surrounding country, afford her every desired advantage. Capital, it is true, must and will be freely employed, in the construction of docks rendered necessary by the great rise and fall of the tides, but this improvement may, with others of similar importance, be accomplished with comparative ease. The smooth stone beach on the most accessible front of the city, will afford a solid foundation for the work, while abundance of the best material may be obtained from the old walls and numerous ruins.

There is also every facility for the establishment of large commercial houses. Fine substantial buldings, suitable for warehouses, many of them entirely fire-proof, and now quite unoccupied, may be obtained at extremely low prices. Much of this species of property, and especially of the old ruins, belongs to the Roman Catholic Church; but as their poverty is, notwithstanding, great, moderate prices would be gladly accepted by them. As an instance, however, of the effect of the American imigration upon the value of real estage, a large and fine building is now occupied as a hotel at an annual rent of three hundred dollars, which could have been purchased a few months ago for one thousand dollars. A corresponding advance on property in general has, nevertheless, not taken place.

As to the climate of Panama, and the coutry immediately surrounding it, there can be none in the world more delightful than it is in the dry season. The morning is always beautiful and clear, with a fine air from the sea, the thermometer during the hottest part of the day 80 to 85 degrees of Fahrenheit, relieved by a refreshing land breeze, which usually sets in about noon, continuing till sunset, followed by nights cool and comfortable. This continues about four months from the beginning of the year, when the rainy season approaches and sets in very gradually, attaining its height only during the latter four months of the year. Its intensity here is not near as considerable as on the other side of the Isthmus; and although it rains every day for at least four months, yet the afternoons are usually clear and pleasant. The atmosphere is of course sultry during this season, but to preserve the health, it is only necessary to keep the feet and person dry, ad avoid too much fruit at all seasons.

The much-talked-of Panama fever is simply a common form of billions fever, brought on generally by over-fatigue, or too great exposure to sun or rain. Dysentery also results from imprudence in diet, as in any other tropical climate. The yellow fever, or *black vomito*, never prevails, and the Asiatic cholera as an epidemic was unknown there until the present year; which is likewise the fact with all, or nearly all, the seaports on the Pacific. True the native physicians denominate the Panama fever as yellow fever, but to our inquiries on the subject, replied that they never knew a case of the *black vomito*. Sporadic cases of cholera have occurred; but it generally avoided the Pacific coast during its epidemical prevalence in 1832. No better proof of the healthfulness of the climate can be given, than the general exemption from illness of the 5000 Americans who have already tarried there, in the wet and the dry season.

In addition to the salubrious and healthy climate, the surrounding country is literally a paradise and indeed the whole extent of the Isthmus affords abundant evidence of wonderful natural resources. Covered with a magnificent growth of forest trees, much of which is suitable for ship building as well as for other purposes, the soil is also exuberant for every species of cultivation. We saw, besides, the greatest abundance of every kind of fruit, Indian corn many feet high in the stalk, and sugar cane growing spontaneously from year to year, without exhausting the soil. Hemp, cotton and tobacco, may also be grown in the greatest luxuriance, the planter dreading no frost, and having reference only to the wet and dry seasons, while the marshes of the Chagres and Rio Grande rivers would produce the finest rice. Gold is also found in great purity in parts of New Granada, while recent discoveries in Veragua, the adjoining province of Panama, have disclosed large depositos of excellent coal. These great resources in wood and coal will be found to be of incalculable advantage in the construction of the railroad, and supply of fuel to our locomotives and steamships. In short, this is the real El Dorado, which so many of our countryment have undertaken a voyage of 17,000 miles to behold in California.

For the invaluable treaty with New Grenada, entered into and confirmed during the administration of the late President Polk, the American people are chiefly indebted to our late lamented Charge des Affaires to that country, the Hon. Benjamin A. Bidlack, of Pennsylvania. Gifted with diplomatic talents the most eminent, he also combined a noble and generous disposition with a distinguished person and pleasing address, securing a paramount influence with the government to which he was accredited, and the highest popularity with the people among whom he resided. These qualifications, together with the well-known friendly and liberal sentiments of his government, enabled him to secure from the government of New Grenada that important and memorable treaty, and this, too, at a period when the ministers both of England and France were exerting their talents and influence to the utmost, to secure a similar treaty on behalf of their respective governments. The preceding narrative of facts, partially gleaned while in New Grenada, was extended and confirmed on our voyage home from Carthagena, by a highly-respectable American gentleman, who was very intimate with Mr. Bidlack, conversant with the whole history of the negotiation of the treaty, and placed in charge of the Legation immediately after his mournful decease. Thus, has our country acquired one of the most important treaties negotiated in the history of the world, while she has one of her most patriotic and eminent citizens. Peaceful be his repose and ever green his laurels.

As an evidence of the complete establishment of friendly relations with the people of New Grenada, we received, in common with most of our countrymen, the utmost attention and kindness from the natives and residents of the Isthmus, and especially of Panama, as well as from Señor Don Mariano Arossemena, the intendente of that department.

Having remained just a month among the New Granadians, we now prepared for our departure, filled with many pleasant recollections.

> 1849-Nov.10 News Items from the "Panama Star"
> 1849-Chagres-The peculiarities of its inhabitants—This little village is situated at the mouth of the Chagres River, on a low flat piece of ground, but little above tide water. The town itself is a miserable place with houses covered with a species of long leaf and without floors or chimnies. The old Spanish fort is the only object worthy of notice and it stands immediately between the town and the ocean. Its bold battlements frown upon the dark and briny waters that lash unceasingly its rocky base.

The citizens of Chagres are a very rude, innocent and uncultivated people who have but little to eat and less to wear. One American lady would absolutely wear more clothes to church than would supply the women of the whole town. Notwithstanding this they all seem gay and happy.

1851-Oct.28-Account received from

Chagres after a riot there on the 23rd: The boatmen's Club of Chagres have for some time claimed the exclusive privilege, not recognized by the inhabitants, of taking passengers to and from American steamers. A short time ago an outrage was committed on some natives who had infringed upon the clubs arbitrary laws and a few of the principals were arrested and given up to the Alcalde. This time when the Californians came down the river, a number of blacks principally from Santo Domingo and Jamaica armed themselves and crossed over to our side.

They marched down on the town and shot a man opposite the Consuls office. The Consul attempted to arrest the blacks and when he was fired upon he retired to his office for safety. The invaders stayed about an hour before retiring back to the other side. The Alcalde claimed he was not sufficiently manned to solve the situation so he authorized the people on our side to arrest the principals when they could.

The next day the rioters returned and a gun battle began with the rioters then manning the guns on the fort. A few of them were picked off by rifle balls but they did not stop firing untill we got two cannon from an American steamer. When the natives saw the two cannon were manned and ready they came to terms. By the time the hostilities had ceased some twenty-five natives had been killed and one American killed and one wounded.

Violence and killings persisted still for some days and the Americans were in an uproar over having to claim they were English or French to safely move about. Also American mail and specie shipments had to be moved out of Chagres being carried by the help of English ships and personnel to the outrage of Americans who felt it should have been under the Stars and Stripes or else.

1850 = Daniel Horn

Among the many Americans who journeyed to California in the 1850's was Daniel A. Horn a young man from Cheraw, S.C. Like others Horn went west for economic reasons but was motivated by a desire to see the world and cut loose, at least temporarily, from family ties. Horn was an intelligent observer and recorded his impressions in narrative letters to his family.

>Panama, New Granada, June, 1850
>
>My dear Sisters and Mother;
>
>We arrived at the anchorage of Chagres on Sunday morning, May 12, but did not land until after three o'clock, as the steamer could not get within a mile of the town. It was very tedious landing the passengers and baggage as we had to be transferred to the steamer Orus to be taken to the city and you never saw such a scramble to get ashore. The passengers all anxious with each

thinking if he were first ashore he could hire boats to go up the river on better terms. I found out the Orus would not go up until all the passengers were aboard so I made myself easy and waited till the rush was over but some more impatient hired small boats to take them to the town paying one dollar each for their passage. We had to go from one steamer to the other in an open boat and just as I got on board there came up a tremendous rain and a number in the small boat got a thorough ducking and had some of their baggage greatly damaged.

Chagres is situated at the mouth of a river of the same name which is here about 150 yards wide. The old Spanish ,or native town , is on the south side of the river and a miserable looking place it is. I did not go over there as it rained nearly all afternoon and there is nothing to be seen but an old Spanish fort now intirely in ruins. That did not look as if it would repay for the trouble of crossing the river and walking up a steep and muddy hill to see it. The houses are only hovels that, in the States, would not even do for Negro quarters or even for a respectable cow house. The whole town does not look near so well as the quarters on a Southern plantation. They are built by planting four posts in the ground, about 10 feet high for the corners, with the rafters made of cane or bamboo. Forming a very steep roof covered with cocoa or palm leaves. Though when properly put on they make a very tight roof but do not last probubly more than a few years. Many of them are not enclosed at all at the sides and those that are have only cane put upright and daubed with mud.

The houses are filled with filth, have no beds, but the occupants either sleep in hammocks or have cow hides on the ground. They have no tables or chairs and the only cooking utensil I could see was an earthen jar in the shape of a pot in which they cooked their food. They have no dishes, forks, and a shell for a spoon.

The natives are, perhaps a majority of them, full blooded negroes, one-third Indians, the balance mixed, with here and there a Spaniard. Their language is a mongrel Spanish and their appearance not as respectable as our negroes. They dress very slovenly, in fact, with few exceptions their dress in the States would not be decent. The females dress rather better than the men and are fond of gaudy laces and ornaments without any taste in their dress show they are littles better than savages so far as civilization is concerned.

Their food is jerked beef, which is prepared by cutting small strips several yards long and half drying it in the sun, plantain, coconuts, yams and rice, all of which they can raise with scarcely any trouble or labor. There is not a framed house on the native side of the river and the above descriptions apply to the natives and houses all over the Isthmus.

The American town is on the opposite side of the river where there are a few rough frame houses but the best would not be a respectable warehouse in South Carolina and there are a good many huts as on the other side. The Americans there are men whose only object is to make money at any cost and they are far more dishonest than the natives. I find this to be the case all over the Isthmus with scarcely an exception. Many of them will no doubt make fortunes but I would not have the greatest fortune if

I had to make it that way with utter disregard of the Sabbath and all rules of justice or honesty. The hotels which have assumed the names of crack houses in New York such as Irving House and United States Hotel are perfect hog holes that are hardly fit for a dog to eat at with furniture, food and everything filthy. It went very hard to eat such stuff as I have had to and to pay 75c for a meal and 25c to 50c for a cot to sleep on with a straw pillow, no blanket and only a dirty calico spread.

Everything looked so filthy at Chagres that myself and several others, with the consent of the Captain of the Orus, took our blankets and slept on benches on board. We stayed there until 9 o'clock the next morning and were not in a hurry to get off as we knew we would be detained at Panama waiting for the steamer that we had tickets on.

Myself and five others hired a large canoe and three natives for $12 each to take us up to Cruces a distance of about 50 miles. We had expected to make the trip in three days but were disappointed as it took us nearly five days. Our boat was all open except for five feet in the middle which had a piece of canvas over it on hoops to protect our baggage from the rains now set in.

The next morning we went 10 miles to a native village where we found an American who had a shelter, kept coffee, ship biscuit and made pies of musty apples. It was the best fare we had since leaving the the steamer and poor enough at that and we paid 10c for a cup of coffee and 25c for a pie about as large as a large saucer. After resting a while we left the village and went about 8 miles further to a ranch or native settlement where we also found an American. He had a large shelter made mostly of cloth stretched on poles and he had an eating house. He had bunks made one above the other like shelves and charged 50c a night to sleep on them. I wanted a cup of coffee but could not get it without eating the supper for 75c so I made out with the bread and cheese which we had with us and with three others slept on the boat on our luggage and slept very well.

For the next two days we lived on crackers, cheese, and bologna sausage with an occasional cup of coffee we got from the natives and it was coffee only in name. We had a good boiled ham but alas lost it. The second night I slept on the boat again ; the next on my blanket in the open air and the next under the shelter of an old Indian who tended cattle on the hills. At noon on the 4th day we got to Gorgona where several Americans were living and one kept a passable tavern and we got a tolerable dinner. Gorgona is, in the dry season, the head of navigation for canoes and is a village of 5 or 600 inhabitants who live in perhaps 50 huts and one or two frame houses in which the Americans live, but they are only rough makeshifts. At this place when the river is low persons crossing the Isthmus have to hire mules and natives to take them and their baggage over the mountains to Panama.

The Americans were all for moving up to Cruces which for the next month will be the place to stop and get mules. The price of mules for the trip to Panama is from $14 to $20 and only takes three days there and back, Almost every hut there, as everywhere else, keeps a few bottles of poor liquors, wines and native segars which are very good. Every village has an alcalde or magistrate whose word is law and whose decisions are submitted to without appeal. They have a small church and priest and the churches are built of rough stone. The priests all wear black hats covered with silk with a brim about 12inches wide and drawn to meet on the top. Long black gowns, slippers or low shoes, black stockings and knee britches. Altogether they make a rather singular appearance and, as in all Catholic countries, their influence is supreme.

We left Gorgona at 3 o'clock expecting to get to Cruces by night but the current was so strong that we did not get more than half the distance. Ran several risks of upsetting, had to lodge with the Indians and had nothing to eat but bread and cheese. A little after daylight we started and by hard pushing got to Cruces by 11 o'clock where we were to leave the boat and take mules for the 22 miles to Panama.

Cruces is a village of 4 to 500 inhabitants and their huts are as I have described. There was an old stone church with three old broken bells, hanging on a gallows at the side, which are rattled several times a day and make a horrible din. I stayed there until the next day and got good coffee and light bread which was the first I had seen. I put up in a hut kept by an American and paid 50c to sleep on my own blanket on the ground under the tent and paid $2 for supper and breakfast. I had bargained for two mules to be ready by 7 o'clock so as to make the passge by night but the fellow disappointed us and before I could get the mules all my company had left. The most of them left their baggage in the hands of a transportation agent to be forwarded the next day. But they did not get it for some days and then some in a damaged state with some of the trunks opened and robbed. I finally came across an Irishman and we hired two mules and a guide for $28. One mule to ride and one to carry the baggage and we were to ride turn about. There is no danger of being lost as there is but one road.

All along the banks of the river at Gorgona and Cruces I saw native women washing and they charge a dime apiece to wash and two when ironed and starched and all smoke segars, men, women and children. The children commonly wear no clothing or only a short loose shirt; the laboring men wear a pair of pants at work and at other times a clean white shirt and pants. There was a fandango at Cruces and it is a kind of dance of the Isthmus and the greatest amusement of the natives.

All of the inhabitants of the Isthmus are Catholics but have no idea of religion. Their worship consists in dipping the finger in holy water, making the cross on the forehead and breast, bowing, getting on their knees before the altar, muttering something, counting their beads and, I suppose, confessing occasionally.

The scenery was in some places, very grand along the river, but did not come up to the glowing descriptions I have frequently read about and were it not for the novelty would be a most irksome trip. I did not see many pretty flowers as this is not the time for them to be in bloom for a months hence the whole face of the earth will be covered with them. The birds are most beautiful and some of them had the sweetest notes I ever heard and our Captain said they sold for a doubloon when tamed. Saw numerous parrots and paroquettes as well as iguanas that are eaten by the natives. Saw many cattle along the river banks and bought a bottle of milk from a native woman but could not drink it as it tasted of the weeds. I saw canoes made out of single trees that were 50 feet long, 6 feet wide, and 4 feet deep. I saw no ironware except a large knife that is two or three feet long and very heavy.

Coconuts grow all over the country and are exactly like the picture you see of them and they are full of fruit. The plantain is also very abundant and if fried or roasted like potatoes are very good. In fact all the tropical fruits either grow spontaneously or are cultivated. The natives raise a good many fowls but it is hard to get them on the road. In Panama they are tolerable plenty, but very high, about $1.00 each but eggs are plentiful at 20c a dozen. I saw an Indian plaiting a Panama hat, it was very pretty, priced at $20 but in stores they sell from $3 to $50. Many of the women wear them but I have not seen a single bonnet except on Americans on the Isthmus.

The native women make fancy lace with thread wound on spools and they kind of plait it. At almost every hut they have two or three fine fat pigs but they sell very high. Generally they go where they please in or about the house and in fact are about as great favorites as the children. Not withstanding it is almost impossible to get some to eat for travel is so great that all is sold faster than they can raise it.

The mules that are used are rather small and poorly fed and it is surprising what burdens they take, 200-300 lbs. tied across their backs, and go up and down hills where it is difficult for a man to go. The mule I got to ride was about as poor a specimen of a pony, for it turned out to be a horse, as you ever saw. But it was a fine saddle animal and as sure footed as a cat and would go up or down the steepest hills in perfect safety. It was a rough trip I assure you but better than I had expected. I walked about two-thirds leaving my companion with the horse to keep up with the baggage. You would have laughed heartily to see me mounted on the bob-tailed pony, my coat tied up by the sleeves over my shoulders, my hat cocked up, pants rolled up to my knees, boots all covered with mud and my bossom open but I was cheerful and borne up with hope.

About sundown we got to a ranch or hut where the mules and baggage were to stay all night. They not being able to make the trip in a day unless they get a very early start which they seldom do as they take their time and cannot be hurried. They told me that it was only three miles to the city and that the road was very good. As I was very anxious to get there I left my companion, to take care of the baggage, and pushed on afoot thinking I would get in by dark and get a good supper and bed but I was greatly disappointed. We pushed on but did not get to the suburbs until 8 o'clock and we had found the road very rough and muddy and not less than six or seven miles.

When we got in the neighborhood we met some Americans who told us of an outbreak between the natives and the Americans and that the gates of the city were shut so we could not get in. The soldiers were all out and that in the fray 6 or 8 whites and as many natives were killed. I was now in a bad fix with my friends all in the city and my blankets behind me with the baggage and nowhere to stay the night. However I got the privilege of sitting in a brokrn chair all night for which I paid a dime. I made my supper on a piece of ginger cake and a glass of beer and of course did not spend a very pleasant night. In a foreign land with another outbreak expected and with no person that I had known more than a few hours, no arms, not knowing where to go or what to do in case of danger but though it may seem strange I did not feel the least alarmed.

In the morning early I came into the city and found all perfectly quiet and after a tolerable breakfast I felt greatly relieved as well as refreshed. A negro had stolen a trunk with several hundred dollars in it from an American. The American and his friends took him to the place from which he had taken the trunk and I suppose either used violence or threatened it unless he confessed or delivered the trunk. The natives got wind of it, raised a mob and attacked the office with stones, breaking out all the bars from the windows, and released the boy and then killed one man and wounded several others. The mob then passed through the city, out the gate, into the part where they live in great numbers yelling and threatening. The Governor and American Consul went out and made speeches to quiet them but as they were returning to their homes some American fired a gun into the crowd from the wall and shot down a native. That of course roused them worse than ever and another American was killed and several badly wounded and it was thought several natives were also killed.

I have but little doubt that the Americans were wholly to blame as the riot was brought on by their own high handed measures, contrary to law, in a way that could not be submitted to in any civilized country. The last fray was outside of the gate and some of those who were in my party, but had left me at Cruces, had very narrow escapes as they were just coming into the city when the mob was rushing out. All has been quiet ever since and I have no doubt if the Americans mind their own business and let the natives alone there will be no further difficulty for they are disposed to be friendly.

I got the offer of accommodations in a tent on the Island of Taboga, 12 miles south of the city, where vessels in this port get their water and fire up for going to sea. The place is perfectly healthy and the steamship companies have there a depot for coal and stores and spend several days fitting out before starting on a voyage. When in Panama only a few hours I went over there but was greatly disppointed in the place. Accommodations were very bad, living worse and altogether it was a most lonesome, tiresome place. There is a native village of 3 to 400 inhabitants who are more orderly and of better appearnce than in the villages on the Isthmus. I went up on the hills, which are several hundred feet high, in search of fruit and found several large patches of pineapples. By far the finest I ever saw and helped myself to what I wanted to eat and took several to the tent. I walked all about the beach looking for shells but did not find any worth preserving for they had all been picked over by the great crowds of travellers. I found the island so lonesome I could not stand it and after a stay of four days I returned to the city where I expect to remain until I embark for California.

Panama is an old Spanish town at the head of the bay of the same name and is on a narrow tongue of land surrounded by water on three sides and has 5 to 6000 inhabitants. A part of the city is surrounded by a high stone wall now partly in ruins. The better class reside within the wall and the business is transacted there. The harbor is very poor and vessels have to anchor from 1 to 2 miles off and discharge their freight in small boats and canoes. The city had been founded some 200 years and before the tide of immigration to California was greatly on the decline but is now in rather more flourishing condition As soon as the travel is turned another way , which I truly hope will be soon, the city will go to the dogs with railroad speed as it has no commerce or trade to support it. If the people would make good use of their opportunities they could make their fortunes, but the majority know not its value, spending their money as fast as they make it, thinking that the present prosperity will continue forever

There are a dozen or more old churches, several nunneries and Jesuit colleges but all mostly in ruins, though several of the churches are in a sufficient state of preservation to be used. If I had all the silver that is in the churches here I would not go to California but would back track at once to home. I went into the Cathedral one day after service and one of the boys that waits on the altar showed me all over the building for which I paid him a sixpence. I should think there were at least 25 priests about here, some of them quite goodlooking men and all inveterate smokers. I attended a service and all the priests were in full dress, saw the confirmation of the wafer, which was carried through the church and city in procession. It was held up on high by an old priest who walked under a silk canopy covered in gold and held up by six gentlemen who, I suppose, were the grandees of the city. During the ceremony the priest took something that appeared to be a miniture likeness, kissed it, then took it to the six bearers of the canopy and each bowing to the other also kissed it.

There were about 100 candles burning all over the house and when the procession was about to start a large number of candles were handed around the congregation and a majority of those who joined the procession took one. The music went first, then the priests with large silver staves, then the priest under the canopy with the wafer, and then the people followed by the soldiers. As they passed all the spectators took off their hats and some got devoutly on their knees till they passed. From what I could learn it is what the Catholics call Corpus Christi, and from what I could see, for I could not understand a word that was said, they paid the same homage to the wafer as should be paid to the Savior. For it is their doctrine that after consecration it is his real body. All during the ceremony the bells of the city, and they are legion, were ringing and the canon firing. There was a great deal of bowing, kneeling, and burning incense on and around the altar. All the churches have a small image of Christ on the cross on the altar in front and the Virgin Mary over it. Both are objects of worship and I cannot see the difference of their worship and rank idolatry.

The soldiers, of whom there are about 100 in the city, are all Indians and Negroes, and a pretty set they are. When not on duty they may be seen passing about barefooted, with course round white jackets, a rusty cartoche box about their waist and an old red cap with a black band on the head but on parade they make a tolerable appearance. I would take them to be a worthless and inefficient set although their officers are of Spanish descent and make a more respectable appearance.

All the hotels are kept by Americans, except one, and that by a Negro that was once a servant in a hotel in New York and he keeps the best hotel in the place. But they are all miserable poor affairs, poor food, badly cooked, no beds, eight to twelve dirty cots in a room and everything else to match. The board is from eight to twelve dollars a week and sometimes I could not stand it and would leave the table with not half enough to eat. I bore it a week and then left taking a room in the best part of the city. I now have a good clean cot with clean sheets, water, etc., furnished me and pay four dimes a day. I eat at the restaurants and pay only for what I eat with expenses being about $1.25 a day and I am as comfortable as could be expected in this country. My room is on the third floor just opposite the only land entrance to the city where I see all that goes in or out of the city. At the back of the house I have a fair view of the bay and beach for miles out toward the Pacific. There is in the same house a dozen who came on with me and most are waiting for the same vessel that I am.

I often sit in the gallery and watch the immigrants as they come into the city, some on mules, some on foot, muddy, weary, some dejected and homesick, and some occasionally swung in a hammock borne on the shoulders of two natives when they are sick and unable to ride. Most of them seem borne up with the prospect of the golden reward thinking, no doubt, that their troubles on the Isthmus are ended and that they will speedily embark on some swift gliding steamer for the Eldorado. But alas many have to wait weeks before they can get away. The agents in New York represent to all that they will not be here more than one or two weeks at the most. Yet many do not get away for 8 or 10 weeks and then perhaps sell their tickets at a sacrifice on steamers that they found out too late will not be here for weeks and buy tickets on other steamers at enormous prices or go on sailing vessels with the prospect of being at sea 75 to 90 days.

I often feel for the poor mules as they come into the city overloaded and panting for breath while frequently they give out on the way and drop dead. Some of the natives will bring a trunk on their backs weighing from 150 to 200 lbs. for 6 or 8 dollars. Every steamer now brings some females and many of them are bad characters. Frequently the females, for convenience in crossing the mountains, put on men's clothes . A day or two ago I saw a lady dressed in man's clothing astradle a mule, a child in front, and her husband and another child walking. She seemed quite cheerful and I thought was quite amused at her own appearance and the notice she attracted.

All the drinking water is brought from springs in the country, in jars, on mules and it is not clear or very good but we soon get used to it. The jars hold about five gallons and sell for a dime. All the wood used is also brought in on mules or bullocks. The climate is so warm that no fire is wanted except to boil the pot or do their cooking on a small furnace and it is done by the side of a wall indoors or out.

The houses in the city are stone covered with tiles with some plastered and white washed. All have a gallery in front projecting over the street, no windows, but large doors with a small opening in the middle with a small shutter. There is much less furniture wanted or used here than in the States and cots or hammocks are almost entirely used to sleep on. I have not seen but two or three bedsteads in this country, not a glass window or blind, no carriages or wagons and only two or three carts. The face of the country is such that it is impossible to use any kind of carriage without great expense in making roads which the natives have not the energy or ability to do. But there is an American company at work on a railroad from Navy Bay, south of Chagres to this place. If completed would make this a choice spot but they have not done much and from present appearances never will.

The streets are all very narrow and in some of them two carriages could not pass each other. The galleries in front of the houses, projecting over the streets, make them appear much narrower and the sun shines between them only for a short time in the middle of the day. The streets are paved with round stones as in New York, but the sidewalks are very narrow, not more than two or three feet wide, making walking them very unpleasant. All around the walls and in many parts of the city the filth is suffered to collect in great quantities and if it were not for the constant fresh breeze would breed pestilence and death. There are but a few cities of the same size in the United States that are more healthy and with a little trouble this could be made one of the most pleasant and healthy in the world.

There are no large fine stores here, but a great many small shops mostly kept by women, some of them quite neat, but most of them have their shelves disgraced with wine and liquor bottles. Everything sells very high with shirts that I bought in New York for 37c & 75c selling for $1.00 to $1.50. Shoes worth 50c in New York sell for $1.25 to $1.50. Lard, butter, and hams all 40c to 50c. Eggs 25c to 37c a dozen, fresh meats not so high and washing and ironing 15c to 20c apiece.

Everybody, man, woman and child smokes segars and drinks wine or liquors, but seldom is a native seen drunk, but it is quite common to see a drunken foreigner.

There is a Presbyterian minister here on his way

to California as a missionary. He preaches every Sunday in some private room and does not have very large congregations but they are solemn and attentive. Most of the Americans appear to have thrown aside all restraint and give loose rein to evil practices. I have lost a great deal of the high respect I always have had for the American character. All, with scarcely one exception, appear to be actuated by no other principle than selfishness or passion.

The city has a half finished, dilapidated appearance, but if prosperity should continue to hang over it, it will soon change as there is already considerable appearance of improvement. The scenery all around is most beautiful and about a mile west of the gate is a mountain from 6 to 800 feet high. This country if in the hands of an industrious, enterprising people like the Americans would be the finest in the world. But it is not now a paradise for the people are indolent, sloven, with nothing showing of prosperity or comfort and scarcely any of the convenience of civilization.

The number of persons here waiting for passage is very great with at times at least two thousand. Many instead of waiting for steamers on which they have tickets take sailing vessels. They buy tickets in New York on steamers that are on their way around Cape Horn and so when they arrive here they find they will have to wait for weeks so they sell their tickets and take sailing vessels. The agents in New York misrepresent when the steamers will arrive here. I myself was told I would not have to wait more than 10 or 15 days but I will be here about two months before I get away. Many of those here are very imprudent in their habits, expose themselves a great deal to the weather, eat much fruit, cake, beer and lodge in badly ventilated rooms or filthy parts of the city. So as a matter of course they get sick and die or get discouraged and return home.

A young man who came in the same vessel with me from New York died with delirium tremens and I assisted to bury him and God grant I may never have to assist at another such one. He formed an intimacy on the vessel with a New York gambler who was the main cause of his ruin. The gambler took the management of the funeral and had the coffin made. It was made of rough boards, perfectly square, except a little broader at the head than foot. It was so slightly made that when lowering it into the grave part of the bottom fell out. The grave was not more than two feet deep but there is little respect for the dead here.

There is very great complaint at the wrong done to passengers by owners of steamers in New York in sending them on here when they know they will be detained for weeks, endangering their lives, and at heavy expense. Many a poor fellow has fallen victim to the rapacity of those worse than robbers and their bones lie mouldering in a foreign land. A short time ago an agent of one of the lines stuck up a notice that a number of tickets would be sold the next day on a steamer to start in a few days for California, at New York prices of $150 for steerage and $300 for cabin. The tickets were to be sold at nine o'clock and first come first served. Many to be sure and get tickets at that price took their stand at the door at one o'clock in the morning and by seven o'clock there were several hundred all crowding and pushing each other. Then they did not get them for there was not one ticket for every fifth man. The tickets we have bought are for steamers that will not be here for 4 to

6 weeks so the tickets of course are worth but little more if any than what they were sold for in New York. While tickets are low speculators buy them and hold on until the steamer comes in and then sell them for one or two hundred percent which puts them out of the power of a large majority to buy.

You would hardly think that here in 8 degrees of latitude we sleep at night in closed rooms under sheets or heavy counterpanes. But it is winter here and is the rainy season when the air at night is cool and damp. So damp that all woolen or leather goods have to be frequently aired or they are ruined with mold. I greased my boots yesterday and threw them under my bed and they are moulding already.

June 20th—Today attended the funeral of a lady who, with her husband, came here four months ago on their way to California. She was taken sick and was unable to get away again. She left a child not quite a year old. There was to be buried at the same time a man who was an agent for vessels here. The processions met in the street, formed into one, and went to the graveyard together. The Episcopal service was read over the body of the man and the Prebyterian missionary conducted the services over the lady. It was a solemn time and how hard it seemed to die and be buried in a foreign land.

Sunday, 23rd—Spent all week mostly in the house, took one excursion into the country, but did not see a thing of importance. Some of the ranches have the appearance of having once been under a high state of cultivation but are all nearly in ruin now. Another day I took an excursion for several miles on the beach which extends on both sides of the city. When the tide is out and the weather good it is a pleasant walk indeed. It is clean, white sand, covered with shells and after being confined in the city it is a great relief to breathe the fine seabreeze and scratch about picking up shells.

Sunday, 30th—Another steamer will leave tomorrow for California but not the one I have a ticket on which is now daily expected and I confidently hope to get away some time next week.

July 2—Myself and a roomate took our dirty clothes to a creek and had quite a frolic awashing. I had shirts, pants, and coat etc., and assure you they were decently washed. I calculate to do most of my washing while gone.

July 4th—We spied a steamer coming up the bay and hoped it was our long looked for steamer but it turned out to be a steamer that had been on the way from New York for nearly eight months. A sad disappointment for us but we have had several such before. The Americans had quite a time of it in the city. The Stars and Stripes were hoisted on a high pole in the main plaza and there was a procession and orations with authorities and foreign officers joining in and the natives enjoyed it quite well. They took as much pleasure in shooting crackers as the little boys at home. All passed off well without any disturbances of which I was afraid would happen.

July 5th—This morning a steamer came in from California and reports my vessel, the Sarah Sands, will be in in a day or two probubly. It does not matter with me now as I have bought a ticket on the steamer that is now in and certain to get off in a few days. I will lose considerable as I have paid a high price and will take a loss on my other ticket.

Today myself and three roomates took an excursion on a high mountain a mile west of the this city. The mountain is about 800 feet high and the view was the most magnificent I ever saw.

Sunday 7th—Heard the Baptist missionary preach in the house of a Frenchman who offered the use of it to the Americans whenever desired. He is a merchant and his home was fixed quite in style for this place. In the afternoon the Prebyterian missionary preached on the Battery to quite a large congregation. There were a good many natives there, but they did not pay much attention, as they could not understand what was said. I think this would be a first rate place for a missionary that could preach in Spanish to be stationed and I have no doubt a great good could be done.

July 8th—This morning I had an opportunity of sending a letter to New York and wrote to my mother inclosing some seed that an Indian woman had given me saying that they used the seed to put among clothes to give them a good smell.

July 14th—This morning I heard a Baptist missionary, on his way to California, preach in the house of the Frenchman to quite a large congregation of mostly Americans and in the afternoon the Prebyterian missionary preached on the Battery to a very large congregation, There was a petition circulated to the President of New Granada to appropriate one of the many unoccupied churches in the city for the use by the Americans as place of worship and I hope it will be granted.

The priests here are a most unworthy set and exercise no good influence on the morals of the people. There has been quite a perceptable change in the conduct of foreigners here in the last few weeks no doubt owing to the efforts made by the American Protestants in having regular worship on the Sabbath and preaching against their immoral conduct.

The Sarah Sands has not yet made her appearance but I will no longer wait for her. I have to pay more for my ticket on the Columbus which will leave here on the 16th. I expect to go aboard tomorrow and without any accident will be in California when you receive this. With my expenses here for my long detention, the extra price for the ticket on the Columbus, loss on my Sarah Sands ticket, my expenses in all will be from two hundred to two hundred and fifty dollars more than I expected when I left home.

When I left home I had no doubt that I would be in California by the 1st. of July but I have been in this city eight weeks this morning and will always regard it as the most unpleasant of my life. Quite a number got disheartened and returned home but after starting and getting this far I could never do that. For the last three or four weeks I have been a good deal low spirited but I have been blessed by a kind Providence with good health and taking all into consideration have done better than could be expected. But I hope it will all turn out for the best and that Providence will yet favor me so that before a great while I may return with enough to settle with my friends and spend the balance of my days in their company. It is my greatest fear that my mother or some member of the family may be taken away before I return home.

I have no doubt but you are heartily tired of this long epistle and I am afraid you will not be able to make a great deal of it. I will not trouble you with such a letter again as I have written a good deal of this from time to time to amuse myself and make my time pass off less heavily. I am getting exceedingly anxious to get to San Francisco.

Coat of Arms of the Old City of Panama

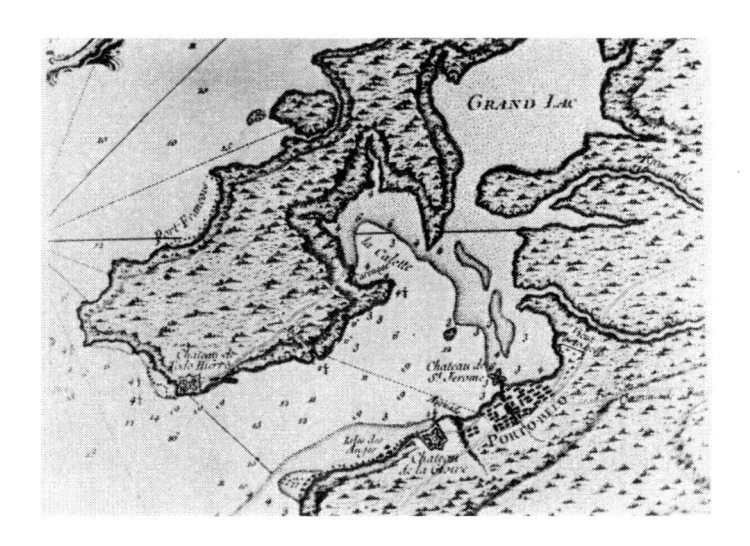

Map of Porto Bello

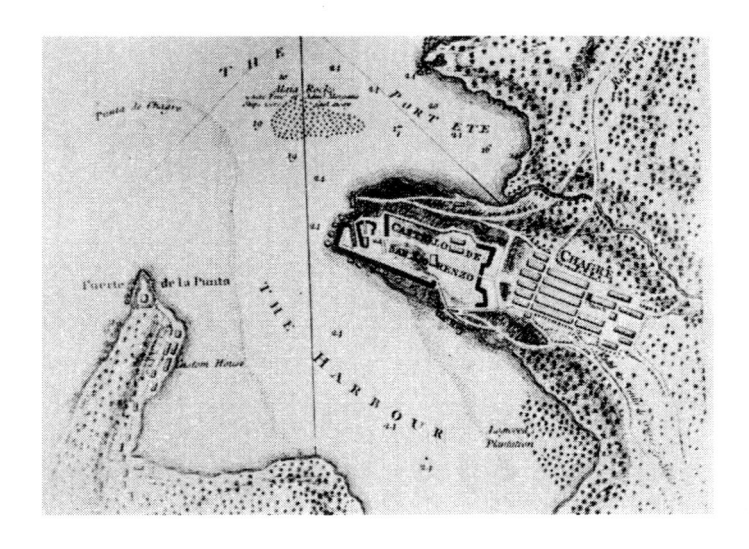

Map of Chagres, Yankee Chagres was on the west side of
the harbor and river

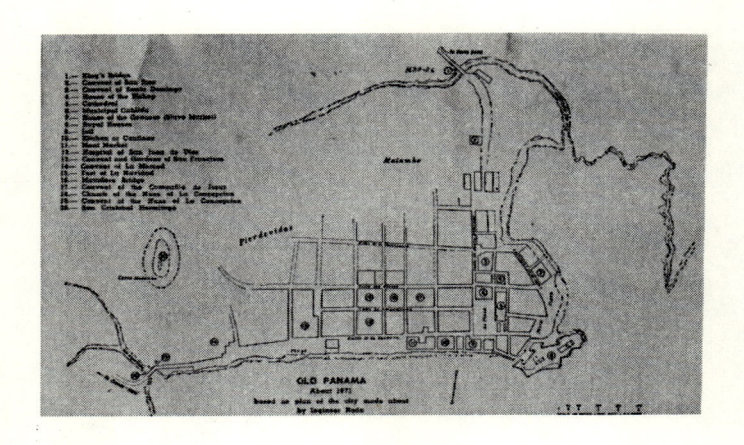

Map of Old Panama about 1671

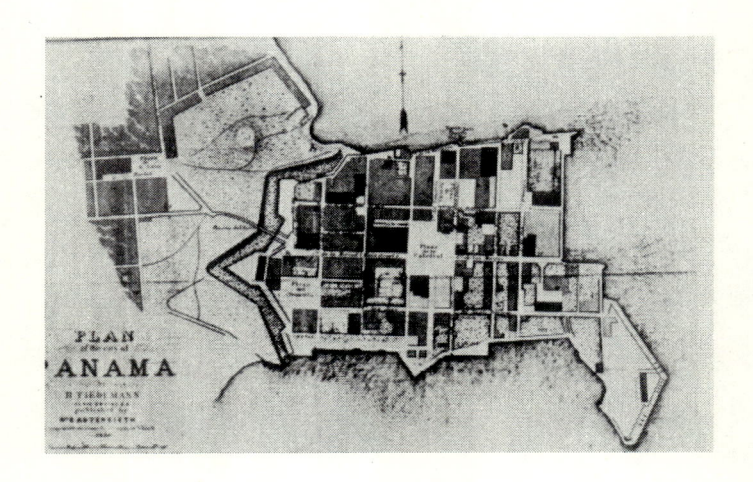

Plan of the New city of Panama

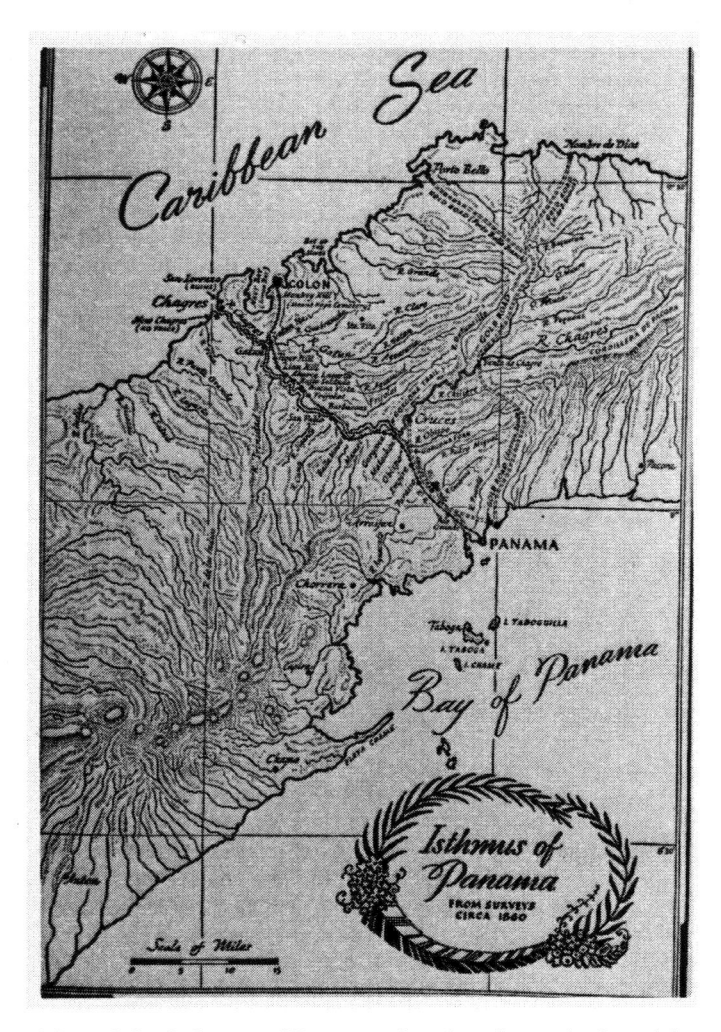

Map of the Isthmus of Panama showing the main Spanish Trails and the new Panama Railroad

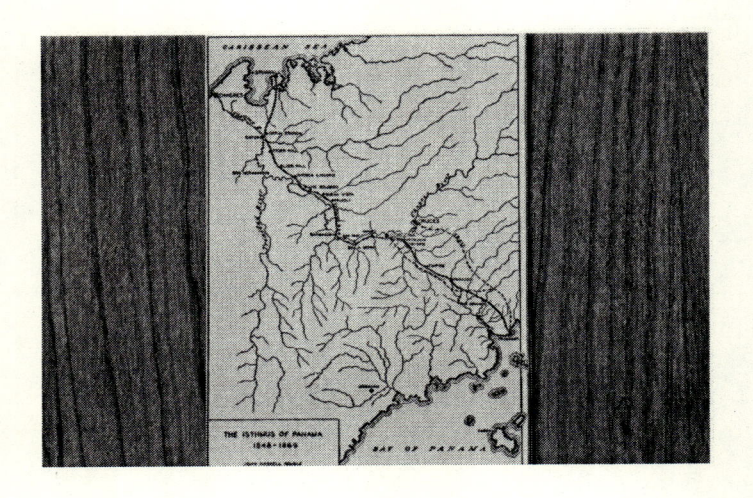

Map of the Isthmus of Panama showing the Gorgona and Cruces Trails and the Panama Railroad

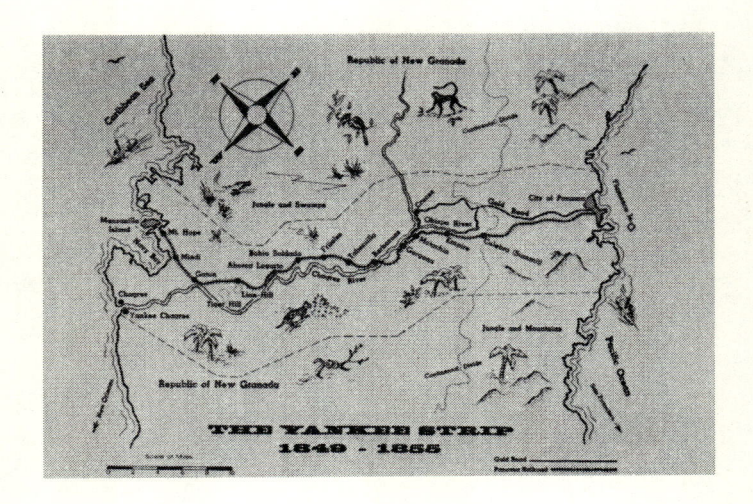

Map of the first Panama Railroad line

Section of the original Camino Real as it exists today

Photograph of the SS Ancon in Gatun Locks on it's 25th Anniversary

Carl Meyers=1850

Now, I too had set foot on this tropical rim of the earth and looked with astonishment around me. Behind the rocky foothill, crowned by the castle of St. Laurent, at the edge of a slope bounded by jungle, lies the town of Chagres in which various palm trees shade with their canopies the bamboo huts of the natives. Both shores of the quiet river, which separates the town from the landing place of the ships, were thick with boats or *cayucas*. Several sailboats rocked on their anchor chains in the middle of the bay, which was 250 minutes broad. Several others lay wrecked on the rocky coast as proofs of the violent and dangerous storms which often assail these shores. A steamer which did duty as both hotel and hospital, was continually engaged in towing ships in or out.

On the landing places the colorful crowd of emigrants increased hourly. Tents were scattered over the place and hammocks hung between the trees were filled with tired or ailing returning gold seekers. Several groups of quite strange adventurers, who could find no lodging either in the American log inn or in any tent, lay about in the shade of the palm trees. Happiness and sorrow, joy and misery were in evidence on every side. The hot sun made the air sultrily oppressive and the climate dangerous in this narrow gulf. Time was valuable—one by one the *cayucas* disappeared upstream and with them the crowd of emigrants. Finally the sailboats, freighted with those tired of California, were launched, and Chagres returned for several hours to its original state of desertion.

It was four o'clock in the evening when three German passengers and I from the *Sea Lark* pushed off from shore in a *cayuca* managed by two natives, father and son. February is one of the most beautiful summer months here and we had glorious days suitable to crossing the isthmus which had been described as so difficult. The boat pushed on by the splashing oar, glided gently towards the interior of the majestic tropical forest, and soon, surrounded by the most varied forms, the enchanted eye was delighted by the ingenious disorder of the exotic scenery.

Of course it requires a certain composure not to be overcome by childish feelings of joy when after a somewhat long sea voyage one places his uncertain feet with felicity on firm land; but double strength and self-denial is required to suppress this urge if soon thereafter he finds himself in a joyous tropical region where everything charms the soul with its newness and rarity. Upon my arrival in Chagres I did not rejoice aloud, but stood quietly aside to observe and to obtain a quick conception of the strange customs and manners of the new land. Here, however, on the river in the midst of this indescribably beautiful plant world I opened my full heart and the admiration which could not be formed in words expressed itself in a chain of exclamations: "Man sighs and groans with Ah! and Oh! to give vent to his happiest feelings."

The shores of the Chagres are at first low and flat. The jungle here consists solely of tall slim palms, from the *Palma real* to the *Palmito* with its grape-like fruit. Where these do not shade the damp earth, grasses and lilies of the monocotyledons fill out the spaces. The swordlike aloe and the oar shaped leafed banana, which shows the peculiar tropical leaf-green in all its nuances, grow down to the edge of the river where, bending their inclined leaf points in a slight arch, they dip into the blue wetness. Water lilies gently opened their soft buds and some of the flowers looked shyly at us through the narrow slits of their green flower covering while others had already opened wide and offered their honey-scented chalices to the fickle greedy ones, the small insects. They reminded me of young girls, who, hardly cognizant of their fate, smile at the boys.

The farther we came from the gloomy negro village the more densely the sap-green growth crowded together. The dainty, slim silver heron dipped down into the midst of this jungle appearing to the admirer in a poetic mood as the only bearer of light in a tropical land.

As the river banks rise the trees of the forest become more varied. The different groups of *Myrtaceae*, begonias and *Melastomacae* change off with acacias, *Mimosas*, and *Lauraceae*. Everywhere are varied forms of trunk, leaf, and blossom. *Cappees*, begonias, and *Aristolochiaceae* entwine and unite it all to a wall which daylight can hardly penetrate. One would like to enter that queer tangle but a thorny net bars the first step. Everything that has roots grows wild over the ground, tree-trunks, branches, and tree-tops. There is no end to the creepers and tangles, and thoughts whirl about as the vines weave in and out. The enormous *Ceiba* seems to succumb to the weight of the agavas, orchids, *Anthurium* and giant ferns and is like a swelled-up grass-giant; but the sun makes countless colored blossoms on its branches and changes the giant into a Christmas tree. Vanilla, and other vines, have spun a network over the trees along the banks, a thick green veil which covers them from crown to trunk and where in places they are pulled together they form the oddest forest creatures. A great variety of blossoming twigs force their way towards the sunlight, balsam scents are wafted from the banks and the golden fruits of the lemon, of the guava and the papaya shimmer through the dark foliage of the smaller trees. The tall bamboo covers the bank varying with other trees.

> And so it continues; it makes one wild !
> The air, the water and the earth
> Produce a thousand seeds
> In dryness, wetness, warm and cold !

The first day of our trip will soon be done and the forest has lost its monotonous quiet. The peculiar voices of the woodpecker and *Blechschläger* can be heard; strident swarms of parrots from the *Aras* to the parokeet, followed by the Todd, the wonder parrot, fly to their night quarters; soon the *Tukan* pecks his peppercorn supper, and the monkey groans his night call. We glide around a bend; Gatun or Philippi, a small Indian village, with its poor but carefree inhabitants, lies before us. A large fire burns in its center around which joyous young women dance the *Zamakunka,* a New Year's dance which requires not a little moral and muscular flexibility and originated truly in the jungle. It consists of wrestling and writhing as though the participants would jump out of their skin and one can say of it:

> *Sans souci,* is what these joyous creatures are called
> They cannot stand any longer on their feet
> So now they stand on their heads.

These Philippes seem not have had their Paulus yet; and one would hardly dare to enter their group around the night fire, which burns high with bright tongues of flame as an excellent symbol of the flaming passion and pleasure lust of the half-wild dancers.

We, too, burned a night fire here on the banks, and prepared some of the travel rations which are probably adapted to satisfy a healthy appetite but do not deserve a description. A refreshing bath in the Chagres substituted for the refreshment of dessert. Hardly, however, had we begun to enjoy this pleasure when a weird looking alligator drove us back to shore. The poor animal was just as surprised as we were, and swam fearfully away from our neighborhood. After we had gone to bed in the narrow boat, the Prokrustes bed of the brown boatman, my neighbor dreamed about the tropical *Lagarto,* the alligator, and fleeing from it he jumped overboard into the water, thus freeing himself from both fear and dream.

Although sleeping out in the open is unpleasant in many respects, and only healthy constitutions can stand it, it has also a certain effect which dispels all disadvantages for travelers who avoid no adventurous situations. Thoughts are busy with the strange surroundings and lose themselves in all kinds of combinations. A sound which suddenly quavers through the stillness of the night makes the senses intensely alert, but it dissolves again into quietness and this creates new exhilarating sensations. We tire from this frequent change of thought and stimulation of the senses and will, that rudder of our soul,. steers us finally to Morpheus. Sleep out of doors is the great temple sleep in which the Voice of God speaks to our soul.

We continued our voyage up the Chagres in the pale twilight of a late daybreak which, however, only gradually awakened tropical nature from its torpor. Damp with dew, leaves and twigs hung slackly above the wooded shores, and the blossoms on vines and trees were still half closed. No sound could be heard in wood or vale; but we had hardly rowed for a mile, when we heard the varied voices of feathered forest dwellers, whereby I became convinced that even the voice of the *ferrador*, the woodpecker, which often almost splits the ear drums during the day is much softer and more modulated in the morning. Perhaps it is the dampness of the morning air which affects the glottis, perhaps it is the magic of the early hour, which even urges the tropical birds to more melodious outpourings of their hearts and entices them to unite in a chorus. Finally the sun's rays shone forwards the forest thickets, and everything that was bent, bowed, and hung down raised itself up for the day's life. The forest awoke from its morning dream which had spread perspiration over its limbs in pearling dew, and the song of the forest died out in the distance, drowned out by the German songs with which we expressed our happiness.

The river for several miles below Gatun shows no marked current and tastes salty until it reaches the village, but about ten miles above that place swelled by the high tide of the Gulf stream, it becomes very difficult for the passage of boats, with a strong current, sandbanks, and snags of planters. It is necessary for the boatman to push his canoe with his *Balanka,* or to pull it along himself in the water. It is dangerous, however, only during the rainy season when there is such water, or if, as is often the case, one is too much in a hurry. The distance from Chagres to Panama is ninety miles; my companions and I covered this in six days in order that we might all obtain the full enjoyment of the tropical trip at our leisure.

The Riviera, the country along the river banks now stretched out in large grassy meadows dotted with small Indian settlements or with scattered wooded hills, at whose feet shady, inviting paths paralleled the river. Much in evidence here are the many nests of a sort of wood ant, or *comaje.* These nests are made of a bark substance pasted together in balls of honey-comb structure two or three feet in diameter, and are attached either to the base of a tree or to branches and shrubs. Neat ant paths lead from one to the other which intersect in many places and thus resemble the network of roads in a civilized state. The procession of ants moves on these paths, eager to satisfy their greed and lust for murder on the bush leaf-lice, tiny creatures of the "lord of Creation". The industry of these animals is untiring, they strongly remind one of the marvelous gold-digging ants of the Ethiopians, in a country which today is flooded by gold seekers of all nations. One could spend many hours observing the activity of these beasts of prey, and again one would always see evidence of new movement and new communication in the swarm which seems to be ruled by an animal mind of high order. The second part of Vogt's *Thierstaaten* gives more detailed information about this. Often they wrathfully pursue the one who steps carelessly on the banks of the Chagres and pitilessly sting him. The sand wasp differs from the *comajes* only by its poisonous stinger, and in that at times it loses its wings, while the *comajes* retain theirs in old age. Producing all kinds of metamorphoses and abnormalities is one of the most marvelous games of Nature, who below the Tropics is pleased to show her unlimited sway of all kinds of creatures, animals and plants. It seems intentional under paradisiacal skies that not even during the day should we be able to guess at "ever ruling nature's" effects, which so stimulate our thoughts.

> Where deformities rule over abnormalities
> And illegality rules legally.

To prove this one need only recall the *Gia-wasp*, who carries a plant twig on its body; the duckbill; the cashew nut, so well liked for its edible flower-base and the simultaneous appearance of blossoms and green and ripe fruits on one and the same twig. The grape palm is destined to be a blade of grass, and bears fruit as heavy as a ton which when ripe produces an enormous conglomerate of nuts with an oily seed, and when immature produces a sour drink. The liane vine creeps at first then grows onto a tree, and by means of its entwining power is able to choke the strongest trunks; its ends which hang down as twigs serve as ropes for the natives, or they cut them and quench their thirst with the watery, thin juices which flow out. And thus the oddest formations of the tropics seem to have been created for usefulness to the native who from birth is dependent on his immediate surroundings.

Other remarkable phenomena in Chagres are the many iguanas which are disgusting to us because of their salamander-like appearance, but which are in high favor with the natives because of their tasty flesh. If the iguana is roasted over the fire in the customary way, peeled and cooked with rice, the meat can hardly be excelled by that of a carefully fattened hen. Its soft-shelled eggs, which contain much yolk, are equally tasty and nutritious whether boiled in salt water or strung on strings and dried in the sun. It is not rare to see a native provided with rations for a whole day's trip of such a string of eggs around his neck, a piece of sugar cane in his hand and several ounces of boiled rice in banana leaves in his apron. The iguana eggs are one of the favorite foods of the woods dwellers of the tropics, and they must never be missing in the pantry of the housewife if she would have her kitchen well stocked, and like you, pretty dwellers of the antipodes, without egg yolks she cannot make that popular rice pudding and dessert. She knows nothing, naturally, of gastronomical studies and her kitchen which, incidentally is the only room under the leafy roof, is as simple as her whole house. Right at the entrance of it is the mortar made of a block of wood in which corn or *maniok* is crushed to flour, a work with which the father of the house would certainly earn his bread by the sweat of his brow, even if the sun did not beat down on his naked back. This bread is nothing but an unseasoned dry mass, which has hardly any taste at all and which must often be ground up on the *metate*, the grinding stone, before one can venture one's teeth on it. Nothing is more noticeable in the interior of the room than the altar with its colorful picture of the Virgin, surrounded by all kinds of household articles, before which the housewife comfortably prepares the meal. Thick clouds of steam soon rise from the earthenware pot in which she has put, one after the other, water, rice, several *platanos* and the much praised iguana, pleasantly filing the nostrils of the hungry members of the family returning from the forest. While they settle down on the *banquetas*, the wood blocks which serve as chairs and are placed on the *manzas de guangocha*, or seaweed mat which is spread in front of the hut, the magic pot is placed in their midst. The banana leaf is lifted from it and the witches' brew and bony remains of the cooked iguana are distributed into the *calabasses*. "*A su disposicion* !" is the friendly invitation extended the stranger by his naked hostess, reduced to a living mummy by ten years of a marriage very rich in children. She feels hurt if he does not join or if he refuses the drink which she offers him from a cocoanut shell, after she has first drunk from it with her thick, withered lips. His answer must be "*Me gusta mui bien*," as soon as he has forced down the first bite and I would be telling an untruth if I found fault with the dish. The drinks made from a variety of juice fruits are, however, more pleasing. Besides *chicha*, the well known tropical wine and *frangollo* punch, the extract prepared from the cream-like contents of the *cherymoya*, is the most remarkable drink. It is fine refreshment for the thirsty, especially when it is proffered in a delicately carved *hiccora* from the hand of a virgin *muchacha*, whose life seems not be measured by years for she will appear aged before her twentieth year like my able hostess. In short, regardless of the limitations of their kitchen and the little knowledge of what is tasty, much is found on the table of the tropical native that tastes well to the foreigner; food and drink to which he can soon become accustomed without prejudice. For instance, it happened to me that after being lost for a half day I joined an Indian and forever overcame all disgust of a dish of monkey meat he placed before me. My being lost is worth mentioning because so many who crossed the Isthmus of Panama had a similar experience.

It happened in this manner. In order to cut off a large bend of the Chagres, three miles below the town of Gorgona, my companions and I took to the shore and followed the shady path which, according to the information of the boatman, would lead us in one mile to a landing place, the goal of our river journey. It was the hottest hour of midday, so we took off our upper garments, and naked and barefooted were only too glad to go into the cool forest. The beautiful forest, alive with monkeys and parrots, afforded us such pleasant continuous entertainment that we did not realize we had already walked for an hour. The path, which at first was like a *prado*, became stony and finally ended altogether, like the paths of the ants and their consorts at the top of a nearby tree, reminding one of the deceiving finish of philosophical systems. At the foot of this tree there lay some gnawed off monkey bones near some still glowing embers, which almost made us think that a Robinson [Crusoe] episode or an adventure with anthrophages had happened here. Annoyed by our own awkwardness and worried about losing too much time in returning we rushed, like Hans Klavenstaken, "straight through". The pain in our hands and feet caused by the thorns of the cactus and aloe plants served only to spur us on so that we penetrated deeper and deeper into the forest where there was not a single ray of sunlight to help us find our way. Frequently climbing over fallen and decaying tree trunks, we followed a narrow forest stream flowing between steep cliffs and rocks, which should have led us to the Chagres. From time to time pieces of wood were shaken down from the branches as we laboriously made our way through the thickets. Now and then a huge eagle, fearful and curious, dipped down and suddenly the jaws of a monstrous snake gaped at us from the bushes. Prepared for the worst, we threw stones at the horror and it proved to be a vine which our excited fantasy had made into a boa constrictor. Not until late in the evening did we finally leave the forest. Arriving at a meadow we surmised the nearness of the river from the sandy bed of the stream and the timid, sensitive mimosas (*Mimosa pudica* and *M. sensitiva*) which bowed shyly at our footsteps. We finally reached the river below the place where we had stepped on land before getting lost. The forest stream instead of helping our progress had led us back in a circle. Exhausted, we met an Indian whose hospitality we enjoyed. We stayed the night in his hut and the next morning he accompanied us to Gorgona.

The most dangerous part of getting lost like this is the frightening and adventurous things one imagines, especially towards nightfall. Steps are doubly hastened and with the same energy a disregard for all obstacles is increased. Physical injury is regarded less and less and the results of the exertion are felt only after the return of composure. We certainly realized this on our rest day in Gorgona; but a bath in the Chagres helped us and a sweet sleep in the shade of a banana field took away the last trace of our fatigue. Gorgona was full of California emigrants; a truly Gorgonian confusion existed in which the Gorgonians of the village played the leading role in doing everything in their power to make the stay of the travelers as pleasant as possible. "*Las Gente de razon*" did not prove to be "dilettanti" but hurried away for the ocean steamer awaiting them in Panama. Soon I too was riding along with a large group on my way to the Pacific Ocean.

Although the trip over the mountains between Gorgona and Panama may be said to be difficult, it offers so many novel and interesting sights that one is completely repaid for the exertion expended. The scenery changes constantly from wooded heights to valleys with springs and brooks; soon we come to a shady passage through which our jolly crowd passes; then again, narrow rocky passes warn us to be careful. The naked burden bearers lead the way disturbing the quiet of the forest by their peculiar groaning which is caused by the heat and their burdens. They carry the boxes and goods of the travelers on light hurdles made of bamboo and reed which rest on their neck and tower high above their head, and as they are able to balance the weight skillfully up hill and down dale they hurry on so as soon to be relieved of their burden. They earn from six to twelve dollars, a pay which makes the native who formerly earned only *reales,* believe that his land is an Eldorado in which he would like to earn as much daily. This, however, is not possible as to carry so much would kill him.

The colorful emigrant band follows behind these leaders. The men wear red woolen shirts and broad straw hats and carry weapons and saddles at their sides. The women wear bloomers which prove their practical worth nowhere better than here.

Now this crowd of riders rejoices with shrieks and cries ! The mules walk briskly with their lady riders swaying, the men laugh and tell jokes, and the *muleros* strike the animals with the flat blade of their *machettas*, reminding the American of his "Time is Money". Soon the procession has reached the *Half-way-House* and rested there. Refreshment is taken and we move on. Another valley and another mountain are crossed and then we reach a height corresponding to that of Sierra de Quarequa from where Balboa first saw the South Sea and with raised hands thanked the heavens for his discovery from which his rival, Pedrarias, profited. Glittering like silver the Pacific Ocean lies before the delighted wanderer; but in vain he looks for the Caribbean Sea from this high wall which separates the two great oceans. We stay here only a short while, the *muleros* call "*Adelante* !" and applying their *machettas* again to the hides of the pack animals, the caravan moves on down the mountain towards the city of Panama.

The plain is reached; above it rise the towers of the cathedrals of the city in which Pizarro received the Host before he brought to the Incas the decline and destruction of their empire. First, there is a suburb of half-ruined houses, witness of a former prosperity, in which the poorer classes have now settled. In the center of this is a stone, pyramid-shaped monument from the time of Pedraria Davila, governor of Castillo del Oro. A road toll which I charged here would make an unknowing person believe that it is the memorial of a road-gang overseer. We have soon passed through the suburb to an empty square covered with weeds and growth and passing through a ruined arch we arrive on the uneven pavement of the old city.

> Gray walls, musty halls
> Deserted and gloomy to view
> Into pieces it all falls
> Will the future build it anew?

The stranger must ask himself this when he makes a tour of the streets of the "Fish rich," of the City of Panama. Everywhere he sees piles of rubbish and wreckage, sad monuments of the time when Panama also succumbed to her efforts for independence. A ray of revival and of new creation shines in the heart of the city. On Main Street, which has already lost its original Spanish name, the damp, cellar-like ground-floor rooms have been made over into modern shops and an active pursuit of earning money shows that a new destiny is in store for the old city. That great nation which seems destined to elevate lands and nations from their decay and lethargy has also achieved astonishing results here in a short time. The citizens of the United States have been able to make a new stopping place in Panama for the world of commerce and trade and have made a way for making easier commerce and trade with the Pacific Ocean.

Since the time of the Revolution Panama has sunk more and more into oblivion and it is characteristic that as far back as the present generation can remember no new house has been built In the first year of the California migration the city consisted of barely 7000 inhabitants, 800 houses and five churches of which only four were open. In 1850 there was already a population increase of several thousands. The Creoles who had retired to Bogota and the blacks and colored folk who scattered through the country, returned gradually to the coast. The empty dwellings were soon crowded by people of all colors and characteristics, so that it became more and more difficult for strangers to find shelter. Ships from all parts of the world came into the harbor. Surveyor's markers for the cutting of the railway through the isthmus were raised in the jungle and in two short years the shrill whistle of the locomotive was heard where only the whistling of the monkeys had been. *"Quien no cae, no se levanta"* (Who does not fall does not rise). The city of Panama at the terminal of the railroad from Navy Bay will flourish again like her old demolished predecessor, only it is not the Castillian but the Yankee who assures her progress.

I stayed in Panama for two months and when I left I was still not satiated. The enjoyment of the varied charms in the forest and on the forever new Savanna and the continual change of population in the stream of migration made the place a greater Théâtre des Variétés. Although it is very difficult to discover the true character of an American in his native land, it is much easier in a strange country where the sun and shadow of his nature break through his composure and are more easily discernible. Panama brought me new knowledge of this nature.

There are picturesque ruins of churches and monasteries in the this city which is built on a rocky dam projecting into the ocean. Thick agave covered walls with great cracks, in which the loafing lizard and poisonous *geko* breed, surrounded one place where a ruined altar stands and a pair of bells, damaged by the falling of the tower, are hung on decaying beams showing to what purpose the place served formerly. Neglected palms are rooted in the rubbish and spread their branches towards the sunlight through the cracks in the wall; vines creep on the walls and across the place, here and there forming a loop in which the observer sits swinging, and quietly surrenders himself to his astonishment and dreams.

The eye marks a thick cactus hedge growing above a portal in which stands a vase covered with vines reminiscent of the Greek myth of the Acanthus leaves and the basket, while a haggard man comes through the portal towards the bells of "Santa Maria." The people of the neighborhood can hear the muffled sound of the bells of the ruin which soon harmonizes with the bells of the city. The striker of the bell stops, raises his hat, prays an "Ave Maria," bows before the "Sacred One" and, quietly as he came, goes away.

A similar ruin serves as Municipal Theater; wild nature couples herself here with raw art. The room has no ceiling, chairs are scattered about and the stage is decorated at the top with twigs and vines. Creoles, Americans, colored people and negroes *e tutti quanti* spend their idle evenings staring here. Usually they amuse themselves with those Spanish folk plays in which every scene is distinguished by certain degree of triviality. Intriguers, robbers, drunkards or *Fanfarones* are the heroes of the plays, or farces are presented in which the most foolish smutty jokes of Signor Pantalone, Arlechino, Tartaglia etc, are improvised. We are horrified when we think of the remark made by the philosopher who said "to learn about a people it is only necessary to observe their dramas". We laugh and applaud and when the jubilation has reached its highest point the American does not hesitate any longer to express his irony at it all. It commences to rain and the play is over.

Next to the theatre is the garrison and the prison. A number of colored people serve both as soldiers and policemen. The drollness of the West Indian soldiery is also found here; while the barefooted, half-naked privates are content with either straw hat or policeman's cap, sword or *machetta* gun or spear, their superiors are distinguished by many colored strange decorations; silver cords, tombak buttons and gold epaulettes being much in evidence also. The soldiers are used once a month to escort the West Indian mail and the great silver and gold transport from Peru across the isthmus and once in a while are also sent out to capture bandits. Then the company, weighted down by beds, cooking utensils and all kinds of weapons, resembles a band of Indians who are getting ready to move their wigwams.

The Americans have often clashed with this military. Once they even stormed the garrison and got control of all the weapons. As there was no general interest in the revolt they contented themselves with showing the government how little they respected it. I still remember how a chief of one of the squads vainly urged his frightened soldiers to attack a group of Americans and how the whole soldiery then made a *tabula rasa* under a hail of stones. All Panama was in the grip of a panic of fear at that time and the creoles were ready to leave the city.

When the governor heard this bad news be issued a proclamation in which he gave friendly warning to the Americans to keep the peace, and declared himself prepared to do everything possible for the upholding of their rights. By this, however, he only showed his own futility and the American Consul was still the most important person in Panama.

The life of the market place is varied and different; it is located in the southeastern part of the city on the shores of the bay. Early in the morning many pirogues loaded with all kinds of forest and field fruits arrive. The tide falls and the market, flooded with people and products, extends far out into the sea. Boatmen with their brown apprentices attempt to dispose of the most varied and different smelling goods in pots and kettles, moving up and down the long aisle of crouching market women who offer for sale in *calebasses* and *batras* the delicate fruits of the *cherymoya*, guava, tuna, pomegranate and sapodilla, together with other wares. The people buy and sell, then with the return of high tide the market is at its ebb. Two merchants still stand near a pile of oranges, however, who cannot agree on a price. Their animated gestures show the great difference in their opinions. Then they finally divide the *medio* about which they quarreled for almost a half an hour, part contentedly; one in his pirogue goes across the bay, the other to the shopkeeper in the city and soon thereafter to the gambling table, where he will lose the whole sum of his profits on one card of Monte.

Gambling halls spring up as a matter of course wherever returning Californians stay for any length of time. The rooms of the one to which the merchant went were formerly part of a nunnery and are always crowded now with people about whom the pious sisters and priests spoke their anathema. The gambling halls of Panama are on Main Street which therefore is not dedicated any more to church processions, the main reason being that the high clergy does not wish to unfold its magnificence in a street almost entirely populated by Americans. Such church processions occur frequently in Panama. Palm Sunday is the most exalted occasion and worthy of mention. An hour before sunset the people gather in the Church of Mary in the suburbs. After several of the customary ceremonies have been performed in the interior of the church a long procession moves towards the city. Striding at the head of this in black robes are the church laity. In their midst is a young female donkey, especially trained, bearing on her back a somewhat shoddy paper-mâché crucifix with Christ clothed in silk and decorated richly with gold and pearls. She is followed by the ecclesiastics in full vestment, surrounded by a group of sacristans; then come white-robed virgins, youths; and finally the entire population of the city, all bearing palm, aloe, and myrtle twigs and reciting the "*ora pro nobis*".

> On Palm Sunday in the Vatican
> They use genuine palms
> The cardinals all bow down
> And sing genuine psalms.

The gates are closed once a year on this evening. On and near them stand men, women and children so as to be the first to shout joyously to the approaching crucifix. This scene of the long procession at whose sides the inquisitive Americans play the role of the Pharisees, lacks nothing to give a true presentation of the gospels Matthew 21. It makes one think that here Dubufe painted from life his picture of "The entry of Jerusalem". The gates are opened after a pause and the laity has told the purpose of entry. As soon as the donkey enters there is a general rejoicing. Twigs and flowers are thrown in her path from all sides; women spread their dresses and young girls go so far in their joy as to disrobe entirely to permit the donkey to step on their calico coverings. The cry "Jesus el Nazereno-Hosanna !" resounds through the whole city while the procession moves on to the convent of the Sisters of Mercy and fragrant perfumes are poured on it from the balconies of the houses so that for once in Panama, on Palm Sunday, one can breathe pleasantly.

From all this it can be seen how diligently and with what cordiality the *Curas*, the clergy, attempt to gratify the national urge of the Castillian people. A look into the crumbling cathedral of Panama, covered from base to towers by dense growth, but filled with an abundance of riches; its silver altar, silver candelabra, and gold *vasa sacra*, shows what impresses the people from a religious standpoint. The natives crawl on their knees around this church treasure, which is said to be only a small part of what the clergy saved from the revolution,, while the other less richly furnished churches are usually empty. Even at the funeral processions this mania for ostentation and decoration is evident, more or less limited, however, by the means of the dead person. Single persons are borne to the grave in an open coffin. A virgin is dressed in her best as if for her wedding, with a wreath on her forehead, flowers on her breast and her pale cheeks are even rouged. So, with pompous escorts the corpse, like a flourishing creature, arrives at an *estafo* in a niche of the cemetery wall.

Such funeral ceremonies seem less tragic; how different it is in the case of a foreigner who is buried without pomp or decoration, even without ordinary decency. The corpse of a foreigner is not permitted in the burial in the *patio* of the city. The bodies of foreigners, who often succumb quickly to the epidemic diseases, are put hardly a foot deep under the hot earth, at times without a coffin, in a place covered with jungle growths. The grim hatred of the *Curas* against everyone belonging to a different church and the crass superstition of the people have designated this barren forest of graves as the place of sinners and heretics. There dark ghosts of these unpardoned unfortunates still wander years after the decay of all earthy remains as the church has arranged for no priestly intercession for them. Such a ghost sprang on my breast once when I lifted a coffin lid to look at its mummified contents. After my first surprise I convinced myself, however, that it was a small sand-rabbit, friend of death. San Juan de Dios, the grave digger, who had just arrived with a new corpse maintained, however, that it was the restless soul of a dead person. Another time when I happened to meet him in the forest of the dead and drew his attention to a grave from which extended the bloody mangled hand of a corpse buried the day before, he maintained that the dead person's burden of sin was so great that he probably found it necessary to wave for aid to poor Lazarus in heaven. I suspected strongly, however, that the unfortunate one must have been buried while unconscious and, struggling against death after burial, had pushed his hand up through the earth ! Such suspicions are really justified when one has seen so often for himself with what superficiality and indifference the emigrant who has fallen ill with violent Panama fever is treated by both the doctor and his family or nurses. This illness, which begins usually with dysentery, robs the patient of all strength and he sinks into a coma, accompanied by frightful fainting spells which are easily mistaken for death by ignorant people. If the weakened patient lies there with corpse-like stillness it is easily possible that the grave digger is called instead of the doctor as there is fear of decay infection which is always close at hand in a tropical country, and the traveling companion, if there is one, hurries away from the place which threatens him with the same fate. If the body is not cold and stiff enough for the grave digger he understands his expensive business as well as did the *matadores* theirs, who, in the role of Sisters of Mercy, made death easier for their patients by giving them a few sturdy nudges with their elbow.

A great American evil in such sickness is the exaggerated and immediate consumption of mercury and quinine. The American never takes a trip without a suitable supply of popular patent medicine in which quicksilver and poisonous alkaloide play the main role. Every American is such a living dispensary, and has a box crammed with "drugs and medicine". If he feels "feverish" or not quite fit he immediately swallows enormous doses of medicines and so decides whether it will be life or death. In the hot regions large doses of radical curatives are sometimes necessary but one should have more than a little medical knowledge to observe the rapid course of the illness or to check it. Every untrained person who acts officiously in such illness is certainly a murderous meddler with human life.

If, while making a sightseeing tour of Panama, you cross the patio and go farther, you come to a narrow path which leads to a spring in a wall from which all Panama obtains its water. This water has caused the death of many an un-acclimated foreigner. Pregnant with vegetable stuffs and filth, it is often drunk in heat and then causes diarrhea or fever. It is customary, however, to let this water go stale before using it. Poor Indians, called Aguaderos, bring it into the city in large stone crocks, *cachocols*, and the buyer pours it into smaller antique-shaped clay vessels in which he allows it to stale, while at the same time the evaporating process cools it off. On all the balconies of the city, increasing the exotic appearance of the houses, stand long rows or groups of these water vessels in the process of making the cool drink which seems the most delicious refreshment beneath the hot heavens. The Panamanians cool their wine in a similar way by drawing a small dampened net cover over each bottle and putting it out in the night air.

The mountain of Ancon towers above the only spring of Panama and offers a pleasant place of sojourn with its refreshing, constant land and sea breezes and an extensive view of the gulf dotted with islands. At the foot of this mountain are several deserted sugar plantations and the ruins of demolished refineries. The great size of a copper kettle taken from a hearth there still bears witness to the once enormous volume of this former industry.

A rum distillery is yet in operation. Sugar is mostly brought here as *peloncillo* from the interior of the country and is sold cheaply. It is dissolved, poured into earthenware crocks and put in a cool place to ferment. This process begins after twenty-four hours, but is purposely delayed by the evaporation of the matter in the porous vessels. The fermentation is thus more penetrating and more complete and seems to increase the aroma and the butyric acid-ether taste. A distillery apparatus in which neither the principle of wood saving or that of hastened distillation is observed produces daily a few gallons of fine-tasting rum, which by reason of its excellence is quickly disposed of. The ingredients of anisette are grown here and it is produced in the same quantity and quality. It would be well to enlarge this business and to organize it better.

This is the only trace of industry in Panama and the only place where one sees uninterrupted work. The colored people are more lazy than diligent. Their one ambition is to earn a few *pesos* as quickly as possible and then to gradually spend them at leisure. These colored people carry on commerce in the city with calico goods, reed mats, fruit and all kinds of tinsel wares. At times Nuremberg products are sold in the narrow shop, the *pulperia*, in which a brown Panamanian woman also prepares and sells native drinks and sweet pastry, the popular *Cocadillo de Coco*. She earns many a real from the secret business of hawking the fine-tasting *Cigarillos de Panama*. These are made of cigar butts gathered up on the streets, chopped up and turned on a machine, which perhaps because of their maceration equal the best Havanas. The pursuit of pleasure and adventure is the colored person's main object in life. He directs most of his attention to his clothing. White trousers, a dazzling white *Jaceti*, a vest of the most beautiful primrose yellow, a sash of poppy red, vari-colored light leather slippers and an elegant sombrero make him such a dandy that no *Donna* can refuse a "date" with him. This finery makes him feel happier than the aristocratic Creole living the life of a retired business man. Even the naked Indian feels the pride of a Roman or of a Hidalgo, when he possesses a calico shirt and wears his hat tipped over one eye. After he has eaten his meal, which either forest or two hours of paid labor produced for him, he is free to stroll at will in this city. If the situation is too "damned tedious" he lies down in a hammock and smokes a goodly number of *cigarillos*.

The Creoles are the heirs to rich estates and restrict their activity to commerce of gold, precious stones and pearls. They are hesitant about giving any appearance of working. "*Todo Blanco es Caballero,*" is the watchword and Caballeros do not work, for work is a sign of poverty and that is a disgrace. Behind the cool walls they wait half-dressed for the evening, quenching their thirst diligently. They hardly understand the spirit of enterprise in the California travelers. They live well here, although the kitchen seems a miserable place, with its low stone-flanked hearth in which glows a coal fire surrounded by earthenware pots and bowls. A colored charwoman, who learned her culinary art in a *Cura* kitchen and paid for it with the most beautiful years of her youth, blows dense clouds of smoke from her *cigarillo* while she plays the rôle of an excellent *Cura* cook. With a piece of wood she energetically stirs the mixture in the earthenware pots and from time to time adds new ingredients, or after tasting, takes some away. The many courses selected for the evening meal, which from eggs to fruit resembles an old Roman feast, taste excellent, and the Panamanian like the

Roman consumes them in quantity especially if his favorite dish of turkey is not lacking, without which it seems hardly possible to digest a meal in all Spanish-America.

The main occupation of the Creole woman is to go to church. Early in the morning she goes to Mass, accompanied by a young *cholo* who carries her footstool and carpet. During the day she lies in her hammock, the cradle of Hilaris, enjoying the life rich in "Love and idleness" for which she has been destined from birth. In the evening she promenades with one of her family on the Bataria, the harbor terrace of the city where she enjoys the fresh sea air and the glorious view at sunset.

The Bataria [Bateria] takes the place of a *Paseo*. The sea rages at the foot of its high wall; frequent earthquakes have made in it many great cracks and crevices which give it a rather threatening appearance. Bombs and piles of cannon balls lie around everywhere and an old garrison with a spacious deserted courtyard still commemorates a sad event. This is the pleasure and recreation ground of the Panamanians. The muzzles of several large cannon, on their weathered gun carriages, project over the parapet of the Bataria out towards the sea. These pieces are not only valuable for their quality but have also historical worth, and have been the objects of British envy for a long time. Large sums have already offered for their purchase but the government shows no desire to dispose of them. In the meantime Brother John's [Uncle Sam's] sons scratch or file their names on them and will continue to do so until they are completely Americanized and finally come under their starry banner.

Ships anchor two or three miles from the Bataria;

the twelve foot ebb and many rocky banks in the harbor do not permit them to come closer." Boats and pirogues travel continually between it and the landing place where natives are at work, in the water up to their arm pits, carrying goods and passengers to shore, running the risk while doing so of becoming a tidbit for the sharks, as has sometimes happened.

Another of the evening recreations of the Panamanian is riding towards the savanna. Hardly has the sun disappeared behind the islands when the Caballeros are seen everywhere, dressed in the colorful linen mantles, *Mangas*, on lively ponies loping through the streets; nothing seems able to hinder their course except the sound of the people praying the Ave Maria coming to them through the open portals of the church. Doffing their hats the *Caballeros* join in the prayer and then rush away across the peak of the mountain of Ancon, where in the blue evening air they appear for a moment like giants, and then vanish. The stranger sees it and he too feels a strong desire to join them. Then he sees a crowd of people moving towards the *rempart* [rampart] of the city. The arena is located there in which cock fights are staged. Everyone goes to the arena.

Two fighting cocks are chosen for the battle. Their owners take sharp and narrow scythe-shaped blades, three inches long, from leather cases. These are bound to the legs of the fighting cocks below the spurs and a call is made for bets which is the real purpose of a cock fight. "*Quien quiece [quiere] dos, seis, dies, pesos*!" is heard on all sides and he who does not wish to bet is considered cowardly. All is quiet; the cocks are held opposite each other; they bristle with mutual hate and anger and strive to be let loose to fight for victory or death. Several rushes are made, whereby each vainly attempts to thrust his sharp spur weapon into the breast of the other. Then the owners pluck a few feathers which incites new battle lust in them. Finally one gets a bloody head but his owner does not find the wound dangerous; he licks away the blood with his tongue and sets the fighter free again.

It frequently takes an hour before one of the cocks succumbs. Usually they tire themselves out so that they fall down gasping and wheezing. Then the cocks are worth nothing, absolutely nothing—not the least thing—*nadita*. A new pair makes those betting more impatient or excited. The crowd is very restless and rarely agrees with the decision. A skillful cock is filled with the lust to battle and makes use of every opening to attack his opponent and like a flash pierces his heart or veins.

Such cock fights are customary on Sundays in Panama and are then extremely well patronized. The cocks are well cared for and are usually tied to the entrance of the house where they appear as a symbol of bravery and anticipated victory. A paladin who is of importance in the eyes of the Panamanians enjoys being with cocks, horses, and wild steers and usually lives in the house where such a cock stands.

The Corren el Toren is as familiar and popular an Isthmian game for the inhabitants of Panama as a bull fight, and as pleasurable. A wild steer rushes bellowing through the streets of the city attacking every one he meets with his horns. A crowd of young people pursue him, attempting to catch him or throw him. Whoever is able to do this single-handed receives a distinction at the *Vandango* that evening.

> When the Faun extends his paw
> The belle cannot with ease withdraw.

The most beautiful women and girls in the city take part in such balls. Here, over and over again, an opportunity is afforded to realize that the women of Panama possess everything that makes the female of the tropics charming. The Panamanians all claim to be descendants of the last Ynca daughters, and are really so, at least in regard to their beauty and incomparable gentleness which makes the foreigner admire them. They are always thinking about and imitating Rava Ruska and often they include the unforgettable daughter of the last Ynca king in their prayer when they kneel before the brown Madonna or the Ynca picture of San Bastian in front of the church.

The Panamanian woman increases the charms of her physical beauty by the thick folds of her hip skirt, the *enagua*, light *manto*, and the ever present Panama hat. The Panama hat and the heavy gold Panama chain are the only objects manufactured in the country for which one must praise the skill of the colored people. The former is indestructible, withstanding years of sun and rain, and surely worth the high price at which it is sold, even in this country. A Panama hat should be of Creole tint, waterproof and flexible; it should be possible to fold it to any size and it must be able to stand the most horrible abuse without showing any signs of wear. Every year it should be bleached with lime and here it finally serves as decoration for an Indian, who paints it with white lead or covers it with red or brimstone colored oil-cloth. The horse reins plaited of the same fibre (*palo de laghetto*) and the handkerchiefs woven of *pita*, which are equally as fine as the Chinese ones made of Filkgrass, are just as durable. The finest Panama hats are those made in Panama itself, not those made in Guayaquill. The work of such a hat takes much time and patience; therefore it is a fitting occupation for the hands of the prisoners who busy themselves with this for the duration of their sentence. Thus the sweat of the prisoners sticks often to the most valuable article of clothing of the Panamanians but the Panama hat is not disgraced by this any more than it would be if it were the needlework over which the Panamanian woman at times "transpires". This transpiration which occurs even during idleness is a sign of health and therefore honorable. Whoever does not sweat in the tropics is close to illness. That is why the tropic dweller consumes so many of the spices which stimulate the skin secretions. An organism which adapts itself readily to all the demands of warmth will soon flourish here and will swell up rich in strength and juice like a fruit ripening in the sun's blaze. Easy digestion and great appetite are the results. Healthy men of the northern countries who lacked corpulence will be bothered by it here. The lazier the soul the more active the body. The spirit is depressed but the sleepless night with which the thinker of the north is often tortured is unknown here. Here on the isthmus one finds people of very great age. I knew a Castillian matron who was 121 years old. She lived with her grandchildren between the *Half-way-House* and Panama, was still vigorous and with her *cigarillo* in her mouth, still swung in her hammock as comfortably and with as much pleasure as she had a hundred years before. Her memory was still vivid and she had a living source of her country's history from which additional humorous ideas purled like the sweat which stood on her lips.

Under the tropical heavens everyone must live the days of his life in the sweat of his brow. The thought that life is passed here in a paradise in the midst of the greatest glory and beauty of generous nature is embittered by the drop of sweat which is always present.
>
> Thinking of places you have left
> Of Paradise you feel bereft.

During the last days of my stay in Panama there was a great change in the weather. The west wind blew over the city; the barometer fell several degrees; the swarms of poisonous *tabanos* flies disappeared from house and street; the weather indicator *alacran* (scorpion) withdrew into his hiding place; the crickets made their nests near the city foretelling by this the time when their scissor-sharpening sound would be dampened; and finally the rain fell in streams. On the glowing savanna the earth crevices closed up tight giving forth a peculiar "greening" or earth smell and the earth disappeared quickly under a green-grass carpet on which the emaciated cattle soon recuperated while the diligent *savannaro* cut the tall guiana grass and sold it in the city.

The return of the rainy period brought with it again the feared epidemic into the walls of Panama; everyone who could get away fled and filled the ships in the harbor of the city. These ships called also to me with their gleaming sails and so I left the glorious green of the tropical country to embark on the celestial blue of the sea.

Bayard Taylor—1850

The hour of departure at length arrived. The levee opposite our anchorage, in Lafayette City, was thronged with a noisy multitude congregated to witness the embarkation of a hundred and fifty additional passengers. Our deck became populous with tall, gaunt Mississippians and Arkansans, Missouri squatters who had pulled up their stakes yet another time, and an ominous number of professed gamblers. All were going to seek their fortunes in California, but very few had any definite idea of the country or the voyage to be made before reaching it. There were among them some new varieties of the American—long, loosely-jointed men, with large hands and feet and limbs which would still be awkward, whatever the fashion of their clothes. Their faces were lengthened, deeply sallow, overhung by straggling locks of straight black hair, and wore an expression of settled melancholy. The corners of their mouths curved downwards, the upper lip drawn slightly over the under one, giving to the lower part of the face that cast of destructiveness peculiar to the Indian. These men chewed tobacco at a ruinous rate, and spent their time either in dozing at full length on the deck or going into the fore-cabin for "drinks." Each one of them carried arms enough for a small company and breathed defiance to all foreigners.

We had a voyage of seven days, devoid of incident, to the Isthmus. During the fourth night we passed between Cuba and Yucatán. Then, after crossing the mouth of the Gulf of Honduras, where we met the southeastern trades, and running the gauntlet of a cluster of coral keys, for the navigation of which no chart can be positively depended upon, we came into the deep water of the Caribbean Sea. The waves ran high under a dull rain and raw wind, more like Newfoundland weather than the tropics. On the morning of the eighth day, we approached land. All hands gathered on deck, peering into the mist for the first glimpse of the Isthmus. Suddenly a heavy rain-cloud lifted, and we saw, about five miles distant, the headland of Porto Bello—a bold, rocky promontory, fringed with vegetation and washed at its foot by a line of snowy breakers. The range of the Andes of Darien towered high behind the coast, the further summits lost in the rain. Turning to the southwest, we followed the magnificent sweep of hills toward Chagres, passing Navy Bay, the Atlantic terminus of the Panama Railroad. The entrance is narrow between two bold bluffs, opening into a fine landlocked harbor, surrounded by hills.

Chagres lies about eight miles to the west of this bay, but the mouth of the river is so narrow that the place is not seen till you run close upon it. The eastern shore is high and steep, cloven with ravines which roll their floods of tropical vegetation down to the sea. The old Castle of San Lorenzo crowns the point, occupying a position somewhat similar to the Morro Castle at Havana, and equally impregnable. Its brown battlements and embrasures have many a dark and stirring recollection. Morgan and his buccaneers scaled its walls, took and leveled it, after a fight in which all but thirty-three out of three hundred and fourteen defenders were slain, some of them leaping madly from the precipice into the sea. Strong as it is by nature, and would be in the hands of an enterprising people, it now looks harmless enough with a few old cannon lying lazily on its ramparts. The other side of the river is flat and marshy, and from our place of anchorage we could only see the tops of some huts among the trees.

We came to anchor about half past four. The deck was already covered with luggage and everybody was anxious to leave first. Our captain, clerk, and a bearer of dispatches were pulled ashore in the steamer's boat, and in the meantime the passengers formed themselves into small companies for the journey up the river. An immense canoe, or "dug-out," manned by half-naked natives, shortly came out, and the most of the companies managed to get agents on board to secure canoes for them. The clerk, on his return, was assailed by such a storm of questions—the passengers leaning half-way over the bulwarks in their eagerness for news—that for a few minutes he could not make himself heard. When the clamor subsided, he told us that the Pacific steamer would sail from Panama on the 1st of August, and that the only canoes to be had that night were already taken by Captain Hartstein, who was then making his way up the Rio Chagres, in rain and thick darkness. The trunks and blankets were therefore taken below again and we resigned ourselves to another night on board, with a bare change of sleep in the disordered staterooms and among the piles of luggage. A heavy cloud on the sea broke out momently into broad scarlet flashes of lighting, surpassing any celestial pyrotechnics I ever witnessed. The dark walls of San Lorenzo, the brilliant clusters of palms on the shore, and the green, rolling hills of the interior leaped at intervals out of the gloom, as vividly seen as under the noonday sun.

I left the *Falcon* at daybreak in the ship's boat. We rounded the high bluff on which the castle stands and found beyond it a shallow little bay, on the eastern side of which, on low ground, stand the cane huts of Chagres. Piling up our luggage on the shore, each one set about searching for the canoes which had been engaged the night previous, but, without a single exception, the natives were not to be found, or when found, had broken their bargains. Everybody ran hither and thither in great excitement, anxious to be off before everybody else, and hurrying the naked boatmen, all to no purpose. The canoes were beached on the mud, and their owners engaged in re-thatching their covers with split leaves of palm. The doors of the huts were filled with men and women, each in a single cotton garment, composedly smoking their cigars, while numbers of children, in Nature's own clothing, tumbled about in the sun. Having started without breakfast, I went to the "Crescent City" Hotel, a hut with a floor to it, but could get nothing. Some of my friends had fared better at one of the native huts, and I sat down to the remains of their meal, which was spread on a hen-coop beside the door. The pigs of the vicinity and several lean dogs surrounded me to offer their services, but maintained a respectful silence, which is more than could be said of pigs at home. Some pieces of pork fat, with fresh bread and a draught of sweet spring water from a coco shell, made me a delicious repast.

A returning Californian had just reached the place, with a box containing $22,000 in gold dust, and a four-pound lump in one hand. The impatience and excitement of the passengers, already at a high pitch, was greatly increased by his appearance. Life and death were small matters compared with immediate departure from Chagres. Men ran up and down the beach, shouting, gesticulating, and getting feverishly impatient at the deliberate habits of the natives; as if their arrival in California would thereby be at all hastened. The boatmen, knowing very well that two more steamers were due the next day, remained provokingly cool and unconcerned. They had not seen six months of emigration without learning something of the American habit of going at full speed. The word of starting in use on the Chagres River is "go ahead!" Captain C-and Mr. M—, of Baltimore, and myself were obliged to pay $15 each, for a canoe to Cruces. We chose a broad, trimly-cut craft, which the boatmen were covering with fresh thatch. We stayed with them until all was ready, and they had pushed it through the mud and shoal water to the bank before Ramos's house. Our luggage was stowed away, we took our seats and raised our umbrellas, but the men had gone off for provisions and were not to be found. All the other canoes were equally in limbo. The sun blazed down on the swampy shores, and visions of yellow fever came into the minds of the more timid travelers. The native boys brought to use bottles of fresh water, biscuits, and fruit, presenting them with the words: "bit!"

"picayune!" "Your bread is not good," I said to one of the shirtless traders "*Sí, señor!*" was his decided answer, while he tossed back his childish head with a look of offended dignity which charmed me. While sitting patiently in our craft, I was much diverted by seeing one of our passengers issue from a hut with a native on each arm, and march them resolutely down to the river. Our own men appeared towards noon, with a bag of rice and dried pork, and an armful of sugar-cane. A few strokes of their broad paddles took us from the excitement and noise of the landing-place to the seclusion and beauty of the river scenery.

Our chief boatman, named Ambrosio Mendez, was of the mixed Indian and Spanish race. The second, Juan Crispin Bega, belonged to the lowest class, almost entirely of Negro blood. He was a strong, jovial fellow, and took such good care of some of our small articles as to relieve us from all further trouble about them. This propensity is common to all of his caste on the Isthmus. In addition to these, a third man was given to us, with the assurance that he would work his passage; but just as we were leaving, we learned that he was a runaway soldier, who had been taken up for theft and was released on paying some sub-alcalde three bottles of liquor, promising to quit the place at once. We were scarcely out of sight of the town before he demanded five dollars a day for his labor. We refused, and he stopped working. Upon our threatening to set him ashore in the jungle, he took up the paddle, but used it so awkwardly and perversely that our other men lost all patience. We were obliged, however, to wait until we could reach Gatun, ten miles distant, before settling matters. Juan struck up "Oh Susanna!: which he sang to a most ludicrous imitation of the words, and I lay back under the palm leaves, looking out of the stern of the canoe on the forests of the Chagres River.

There is nothing in the world comparable to these forests. No description that I have ever read conveys an idea of the splendid overplus of vegetable life within the tropics. The river, broad, and with a swift current of the sweetest water I ever drank, winds between walls of foliage that rise from its very surface. All the gorgeous growths of an eternal summer are so mingled in one impenetrable mass that the eye is bewildered. From the rank jungle of canes and gigantic lilies, and the thickets of strange shrubs that line the water, rise the trunks of the mango, the ceiba, the coco, the sycamore, and the superb palm. Plantains take root in the banks, hiding the soil with their leaves, shaken and split into immense plumes by the wind and rain. The zapote, with a fruit the size of a man's head, the gourd tree, and other vegetable wonders, attract the eye on all sides. Blossoms of crimson, purple, and yellow, of a form and magnitude unknown in the north, are mingled with the leaves, and flocks of paroquets and brilliant butterflies circle through the air like blossoms blown away. Sometimes a spike of scarlet flowers is thrust forth like the tongue of a serpent from the heart of some convolution of unfolding leaves, and often the creepers and parasites drop trails and streamers of fragrance from boughs that shoot half-way across the river. Every turn of the stream only disclosed another and more magnificent vista of leaf, bough, and blossom. All outline of the landscape is lost under this deluge of vegetation. No trace of the soil is to be seen; lowland and highland are the same; a mountain is but a higher swell of the mass of verdure. As on the ocean, you have a sense rather than a perception of beauty. The sharp, clear lines of our scenery at home are here wanting. What shape the land would be cleared, you cannot tell. You gaze upon the scene before you with a never-sated delight, till your brain aches with the sensation, and you close your eyes, overwhelmed with the thought that all these wonders have been from the beginning—that year after year takes away no leaf or blossom that is not replaced, but the sublime mystery of growth and decay is renewed forever.

In the afternoon we reached Gatun, a small village of bamboo huts, thatched with palm leaves, on the right bank of the river. The canoes which preceded us had already stopped, and the boatmen, who have a mutual understanding, had decided to remain all night. We ejected our worthless passenger on landing, notwithstanding his passive resistance, and engaged a new boatman in his place, at $8. I shall never forget the forlorn look of the man as he sat on the bank beside his bag of rice, as the rain began to fall. Ambrosio took us to one of the huts and engaged hammocks for the night. Two wooden drums, beaten by boys, in another part of the village, gave signs of a coming fandango, and, as it was Sunday night, all the natives were out in their best dresses. They are a very cleanly people, bathing daily, and changing their dresses as often as they are soiled. The children have their heads shaved from the crown to the neck, and as they go about naked, with abdomens unnaturally distended, from an exclusive vegetable diet, are odd figures enough. They have bright eyes, and are quick and intelligent in their speech and motions.

The inside of our hut was but a single room, in which all the household operations were carried on.

A notched pole, serving as a ladder, led to a sleeping-loft, under the pyramidal roof of thatch. Here a number of the emigrants who arrived late were stowed away on a rattling floor of cane, covered with hides. After a supper of pork and coffee, I made my day's notes by the light of a miserable starveling candle, stuck in an empty bottle, but had not written far before my paper was covered with fleas. The owner of the hut swung my hammock meanwhile, and I turned in, to secure it for the night. To lie there was one thing, to sleep another. A dozen natives crowded round the table, drinking their aguardiente and disputing vehemently; the cooking fire was on one side of me, and everyone that passed to and fro was sure to give me a thump, while my weight swung the hammock so low that all the dogs on the premises were constantly rubbing their backs under me. I was just sinking into a doze when my head was so violently agitated that I started up in some alarm. It was but a quarrel about payment between the Señora and a boatman, one standing on either side. From their angry gestures, my own head and not the reckoning seemed the subject of contention.

Our men were to have started at midnight, but it was two hours later before we could rouse and muster them together. We went silently and rapidly up the river till sunrise, when we reached a cluster of huts called Dos Hermanos (Two Brothers). Here we overtook two canoes, which, in their anxiety to get ahead, had been all night on the river. There had been only a slight shower since we started; but the clouds began to gather heavily, and by the time we had gained the ranch of Palo Matida a sudden cold wind came over the forests, and the air was at once darkened. We sprang ashore and barely reached the hut, a few paces off, when the rain broke over us, as if the sky had caved in. A dozen lines of white electric heat ran down from the zenith, followed by crashes of thunder, which I could feel throbbing in the earth under my feet. The rain drove into one side of the cabin and out the other, but we wrapped ourselves in India-rubber cloth and kept out the wet and chilling air. During the whole day the river rose rapidly and we were obliged to hug the bank closely, running under the boughs of trees and drawing ourselves up the rapids by those that hung low.

I crept out of the snug nest where we were all stowed as closely as three unfledged sparrows, and took my seat between Juan and Ambrosio, protected from the rain by an India-rubber poncho. The clothing of our men was likewise waterproof, but without seam or fold. It gave no hindrance to the free play of their muscles, as they deftly and rapidly plied the broad paddles. Juan kept time to the Ethiopian melodies he had picked up from the emigrants, looking round from time to time with a grin of satisfaction at his skill. I preferred, however, hearing the native songs, which the boatmen sing with a melancholy drawl on the final syllable of every line, giving the music a peculiar but not unpleasant effect, when heard at a little distance. There was one, in particular, which he sang with some expression, the refrain running thus:

> Ten piedad, piedad de mis penas,
> Ten piedad, piedad de mi amor!
> (Have pity on my sufferings—have pity on
> my love!)

Singing begets thirst, and perhaps Juan sang the

more that he might have a more frequent claim on the brandy. The bottle was then produced and each swallowed a mouthful, after which he dipped his coco shell in the river and took a long draught. This is a universal custom among the boatmen, and the traveler is obliged to supply them. As a class, they are faithful, hard-working, and grateful for kindness. They have faults, the worst of which are tardiness, and a propensity to filch small articles; but good treatment wins upon them in almost every case. Juan said to me in the beginning: "Soy tu amigo yo" (Americanicé: I am thy friend, *well* I am), but when he asked me, in turn, for every article of clothing I wore, I began to think his friendship not the most disinterested. Ambrosio told me that they would serve no one well who treated them badly. "If the Americans are good, we are good; if they abuse us, we are bad. We are black, but *muchos caballeros*" (very much of gentlemen), said he. Many blustering fellows, with their belts stuck full of pistols and bowie-knives, which they draw on all occasions, but take good care not to use, have brought reproach on the country by their silly conduct. It is no bravery to put a revolver to the head of an unarmed and ignorant native, and the boatmen have sense enough to be no longer terrified by it.

We stopped the second night at Peña Blanca (the White Rock), where I slept in the loft of a hut, on the floor, in the midst of the family and six other travelers. We started at sunrise, hoping to reach Gorgona the same night, but ran upon a sunken log and were detained some time. Ambrosio finally released us by jumping into the river and swimming ashore with a rope in his teeth. The stream was very high, running at least five miles an hour, and we could only stem it with great labor. We passed the ranches of Agua Salud, Varro Colorado, and Palanquilla, and shortly after were overtaken by a storm on the river. We could hear the rush and roar of the rain, as it came towards us like the trampling of myriad feet on the leaves. Shooting under a broad sycamore we made fast to the boughs, covered ourselves with India-rubber, and lay under our cool, rustling thatch of palm until the storm had passed over.

The character of the scenery changed somewhat as we advanced. The air was purer, and the banks more bold and steep. The country showed more signs of cultivation, and in many places the forest had been lopped away to make room for fields of maize, plantain, and rice. But the vegetation was still that of the tropics and many were the long and lonely reaches of the river, where we glided between piled masses of bloom and greenery. I remember one spot where, from the crest of a steep hill to the edge of the water, descended a flood, a torrent of vegetation. Trees were rolled upon trees, woven into a sheet by parasitic vines that leaped into the air like spray, from the topmost boughs. When a wind slightly agitated the sea of leaves, and the vines were flung like a green foam on the surface of the river, it was almost impossible not to feel that the flood was about rushing down to overwhelm us.

We stopped four hours short of Gorgona, at the hacienda of San Pablo, the residence of Padre Dutaris, curé of all the interior. Ambrosio took us to his house by a path across a rolling, open savanna, dotted by palms and acacias of immense size. Herds of cattle and horses were grazing on the short, thick-leaved grass, and appeared to be in excellent condition. The padre owns a large tract of land, with a thousand head of stock, and his ranch commands a beautiful view up and down the river. Ambrosio was acquainted with his wife, and by recommending us as *buenos caballeros,* procured us a splendid supper of fowls, eggs, rice boiled in coco milk, and chocolate, with baked plantains for bread. Those who came after us had difficulty in getting anything. The padre had been frequently cheated by Americans and was therefore cautious. He was absent at the time, but his Felipe, a boy of twelve years old, assisted in doing the honors with wonderful grace and self-possession. His tawny skin was as soft as velvet, and his black eyes sparkled like jewels. He is almost the only living model of the Apollino that I ever saw. He sat in the hammock with me, leaning over my shoulder as I noted down the day's doings, and when I had done, wrote his name in my book, in an elegant hand. I slept soundly in the midst of an uproar, and only awoke at four o'clock next morning, to hurry our men in leaving for Gorgona.

The current was very strong in some places it was almost impossible to make headway. Our boatmen worked hard, and by dint of strong poling managed to jump through most difficult places. Their naked, sinewy forms, bathed in sweat, shone like polished bronze. Ambrosio was soon exhausted, and lay down; but Miguel, our *corps de reserve,* put his agile spirit into the work and flung himself upon the pole with such vigor that all the muscles of his body quivered as the boat shot ahead and relaxed them. About halfway to Gorgona we rounded the foot of Monte Carabali, a bold peak clothed with forests and crowned with a single splendid palm. This hill is the only one in the province from which both oceans may be seen at once.

As we neared Gorgona, our men began repeating the ominous words: "*Cruces—mucha cólera.*" We had, in fact, already heard of the prevalence of cholera there, but doubted, none the less, their wish to shorten the journey. On climbing the bank to the village, I called immediately at the store of Mr. Miller, the only American resident, who informed me that several passengers by the *Falcon* had already left for Panama, the route being reported passable. In the door of the Alcalde's house, near at hand, I met Mr. Powers, who had left New York a short time previous to my departure and was about starting for Panama on foot, mules being very scarce. While we were deliberating whether to go on to Cruces, Ambrosio beckoned me into an adjoining hut. The owner, a very venerable and dignified native, received me swinging in his hammock. He had six horses which he would furnish us the next morning, at $10 the head for riding animals, and $6 for each 100 lbs. of freight. The bargain was instantly concluded.

Now came the settlement with our boatmen. In addition to the fare, half of which was paid in Chagres, we had promised them a *gratificación*, provided they made the voyage in three days. The contract was not exactly fulfilled, but we though it best to part friends and so gave them each a dollar. Their antics of delight were most laughable. They grinned, laughed, danced, caught us by the hands, vowed eternal friendship, and would have embraced us outright, had we given them the least encouragement. Half an hour afterwards I met Juan, in a clean shirt and white pantaloons. There was a heat in his eye and a ruddiness under his black skin, which readily explained a little incoherence in his speech. "*Mi amigo!*" he cried, "*mi buen amigo*! Give me a bottle of beer!" I refused. "But," said he, "we are friends; surely you will give your dear friend a bottle of beer." "I don't like my dear friends to drink too much," I answered. Finding I would not humor him, as a last resort he placed both hands on his breast, and with an imploring look sang:

> "Ten piedad, piedad de mis penas,
> Ten piedad, piedad de mi amor!"

I burst into a laugh at this comical appeal, and he retreated, satisfied that he had at least done a smart thing.

During the afternoon a number of canoes arrived, and as it grew dark the sound of the wooden drums proclaimed a fandango. The aristocracy of Gorgona met in the Alcalde's house; the *plebs* on a level sward before one of the huts. The dances were the same, but there was some attempt at style by the former class. The ladies were dressed in white and pink, with flowers in their hair, and waltzed with a slow grace to the music of violins and guitars. The Alcalde's daughters were rather pretty, and at once became favorites of the Americans, some of whom joined in the fandango, and went through its voluptuous mazes at the first trial, to the great delight of the natives. The Señora Catalina, a rich widow, of pure Andalusian blood, danced charmingly. Her little head was leaned coquettishly on one side, while with one hand she held aloft the fringed end of a crimson scarf, which rested lightly on the opposite shoulder. The dance over, she took a guitar and sang, the subject of her song being "*los amigos Americanos.*"

There was less sentiment, but more jollity, at the dances on the grass. The only accompaniment to the wooden drums was the "*ña, ña, ña,*" of the women, a nasal monotone, which few ears have nerve to endure. Those who danced longest and with the most voluptuous spirit had the hats of all the others piled upon them, in token of applause. These half-barbaric orgies were fully seen in the pure and splendid light poured upon the landscape from a vertical moon.

Next morning at daybreak our horses—tough little mustangs, which I could almost step over—were at the door. We started off with a guide, trusting our baggage to the honesty of our host, who promised to send it the same day. A servant of the Alcalde escorted us out of the village, cut us each a good stick, pocketed a real, and then left us to plunge into the forests. The path at the outset was bad enough, but as the wood grew deeper and darker and the tough clay soil held the rains which had fallen, it became finally a narrow gully, filled with mud nearly to our horses' bellies. Descending the steep sides of the hills, they would step or slide down almost precipitous passes, bringing up all straight at the bottom, and climbing the opposite sides like cats. So strong is their mutual confidence that they invariably step in each other's tracks, and a great part of the road is thus worn into holes three feet deep and filled with water and soft mud, which spirits upward as they go, coating the rider from head to foot.

The mountain range in the interior is broken and irregular. The road passes over the lower ridges and projecting spurs of the main chain, covered nearly the whole distance to Panama by dense forests. Above us spread a roof of transparent green, through which few rays of the sunlight fell. The only sounds in that leafy wilderness were the chattering of monkeys as they cracked the palm nuts, and the scream of parrots, flying from tree to tree. In the deepest ravines spent mules frequently lay dead, and high above them, on the large boughs, the bald vultures waited silently for us to pass. We overtook many trains of luggage, packed on the backs of bulls and horses, tied head-to-tail in long files. At intervals on the road we saw a solitary ranch, with a cleared space about it, but all the natives could furnish us was a cup of thick, black coffee.

After ascending for a considerable distance in the first half of our journey, we came to a level tableland, covered with palms, with a higher ridge beyond it. Our horses climbed it with some labor, went down the other side through clefts and gullies which seemed impassable, and bought us to a stream of milky blue water, which, on ascertaining its course with a compass, I found to be a tributary of the Rio Grande, flowing into the Pacific at Panama. We now hoped the worst part of our route was over, but this was a terrible deception. Scrambling up ravines of slippery clay, we went for miles through swamps and thickets, urging forward our jaded beasts by shouting and beating. Going down a precipitous bank, washed soft by the rains, my horse slipped and made a descent of 10 feet, landing on one bank and I on another. He rose quietly, disengaged his head from the mud, and stood, flank-deep, waiting till I stepped across his back and went forward, my legs lifted to his neck. This same adventure happened several times to each of us on the passage across

As we were leaving Gorgona, our party was joined by a long Mississippian, whose face struck me at the first glance as being peculiarly cadaverous. He attached himself to us without the least ceremony, leaving his own party behind. We had not ridden far before he told us he had felt symptoms of cholera during the night, and was growing worse. We insisted on his returning to Gorgona at once, but he refused, saying he was "bound to go through." At the first ranch on the road we found another traveler, lying on the ground in a state of entire prostration. He was attended by a friend, who seemed on the point of taking the epidemic, from his very fears. The sight of this case no doubt operated on the Mississippian, for he soon became so racked with pain as to keep his seat with great difficulty. We were alarmed; it was impossible to stop in the swampy, forest, and equally impossible to leave him, now that all his dependence was on us. The only thing resembling medicine in our possession was a bottle of claret. It was an unusual remedy for cholera, but he insisted on drinking it.

After urging forward our weary beasts till late in the afternoon, we were told that Panama was four hours further. We pitied the poor horses, but ourselves more, and determined to push ahead. After a repetition of all our worst experience, we finally struck the remains of the paved road constructed by the buccaneers when they held Panama. I now looked eagerly forward for the Pacific, but every ridge showed another in advance, and it grew dark with a rain coming up. Our horses avoided the hard pavement and took bypaths through thickets higher than our heads. The cholera-stricken emigrant, nothing helped by the claret he drank, implored us, amid his groans, to hasten forward. Leaning over the horse's neck, he writhed on his saddle in an agony of pain, and seemed on the point of falling at every step. We were far in advance of our Indian guide and lost the way more than once in the darkness. At last he overtook us, washed his feet in a muddle, and put on a pair of pantaloons. This was a welcome sign to us, and in fact we soon after smelt the salt air of the Pacific, and could distinguish huts on either side of the road. These gave place to stone houses and massive ruined edifices, overgrown with vegetation. We passed a plaza and magnificent church, rode down an open space fronting the bay, under a heavy gateway, across another plaza and through two or three narrow streets, hailed by Americans all the way with "Are you the *Falcon's* passengers?" "From Gorgona?" "From Cruces?" till our guide brought us up at the Hotel American.

Thus terminated my five days' journey across the Isthmus—decidedly more novel, grotesque, and adventurous than any trip of similar length in the world. It was rough enough, but had nothing that I could exactly call hardship, so much was the fatigue balanced by the enjoyment of unsurpassed scenery and a continual sensation of novelty. In spite of the many dolorous accounts which have been sent from the Isthmus, there is nothing, at the worst season, to deter anyone from the journey.

I saw less of Panama than I could have wished. A few hasty rambles through its ruined convents and colleges and grass-grown plazas—a stroll on its massive battlements, lumbered with idle canon, of the splendid bronze of Barcelona—were all that I could accomplish in the short stay of a day and a half. Its situation at the base of a broad, green mountain, with the sea washing three sides of the narrow promontory on which it is built, is highly picturesque, yet some other parts of the bay seem better fitted for the purposes of commerce. Vessels of heavy draught cannot anchor within a mile and a half of the city, and there is but one point where embarkation, even in the shallow "dug-outs" of the natives, is practicable. The bottom of the bay is a bed of rock, which at low tide lies bare far out beyond the ramparts. The southeastern shore of the bay belongs to the South American continent, and range of lofty mountains behind it is constantly wreathed with light clouds, or shrouded from view by the storms which it attracts. To the west the green islands of Taboga, and others, rise behind one another, interrupting the blue curve of the watery horizon. The city was already half American. The native boys whistled "Yankee Doodle" through the streets, and señoritas of the pure Castilian blood sang the Ethiopian melodies of Virginia to their guitars. Nearly half the faces seen were American, and the signs on shops of all kinds appeared in our language. On the morning after I arrived, I heard a sudden rumbling in the streets, and observing a general rush to the windows, followed the crowd in time to see the first cart made in Panama—the work of a Yankee mechanic, detained for want of money to get further.

We found the hotels doing a thriving business, though the fare and attendance were alike indifferent. We went to bed immediately after reaching the Hotel Americano, that our clothes might be washed before morning, as our luggage had not arrived. Nearly all the passengers were in a similar predicament. Some ladies who had ridden over from Cruces in male attire, a short time previous, were obliged to sport their jackets and pantaloons several days before receiving their dresses. Our trust in the venerable native at Gorgona was not disappointed;

the next morning his mule was at the door, laden with our trunks and valises. Some of the passengers, however, were obliged to remain in Panama another month, since, notwithstanding the formal contract of the Alcalde of Gorgona, their luggage did not arrive before the sailing of the steamer.

The next day nearly all of our passengers came in. There had been a heavy rain during the night, and the Gorgona road, already next to impassable, became actually perilous. A lady from Maine, who made the journey alone, was obliged to ford a torrent of water above her waist, with a native on each side, to prevent her from being carried away. A French lady who crossed was washed from her mule, and only got over by the united exertions of seven men.

The roads from Cruces and Gorgona enter on the eastern side of the city, as well as the line of the railroad survey. The latter, after leaving Limon Bay, runs on the north side of the Chagres River till it reaches Gorgona, continuing thence to Panama in the same general course as the mule route. It will probably be extended down the bay to some point opposite the island of Taboga, which is marked out by Nature as the future anchorage ground and depot of all the lines touching at Panama. The engineers of the survey accomplished a great work in fixing the route within so short a space of time. The obstacles to be overcome can scarcely be conceived by one who has never seen tropical vegetation or felt tropical rains. The greatest difficulty in constructing the road is the want of stone, though this is in some degree supplied by abundance of lignum-vitae and other durable wood. The torrents of rain during the summer season will require the side-hill cuttings to be made of unusual strength. The estimated cost of the road appears small, especially when the value of labor is taken into consideration. The natives are not to be depended on, and there is some risk in taking men from the United States half-way to California.

Panama is one of the most picturesque cities on the American continent. Its ruins—if those could be called ruins which were never completed edifices—and the seaward view from its ramparts, on a bright morning, would ravish the eye of an artist. Although small in limit, old and terribly dilapidated, its situation and surroundings are of unsurpassable beauty. There is one angle of the walls where you can look out of a cracked watchtower on the sparkling swells of the Pacific, ridden by flocks of snow-white pelicans and the rolling canoes of the natives—where your vision, following the entire curve of the Gulf, takes in on either side nearly a hundred miles of shore. The ruins of the Jesuit Church of San Felipe, through which I was piloted by my friend Lieutenant Beale, reminded me of the Baths of Caracalla. The majestic arches spanning the nave are laden with a wilderness of shrubbery and wild vines which fall like a fringe to the very floor. The building is roofless, but daylight can scarcely steal in through the embowering leaves. Several ells, of a sweet, silvery ring, are propped up by beams, in a dark corner, but from the look of the place, ages seem to have passed since they called the crafty brotherhood to the ocarina. A splendid college, left incomplete many years ago, fronts on one of the plazas. Its Corinthian pillars and pilasters of red sandstone are broken and crumbling, and from the crevices at their base spring luxuriant bananas, shooting their large leaves through the windows and folding them around the columns of the gateway.

There were about seven hundred emigrants

waiting for passage when I reached Panama. All the tickets the steamer could possibly receive had been issued and so great was the anxiety to get on, that double price, $600, was frequently paid for a ticket to San Francisco. A few days before we came, there was a most violent excitement on the subject, and as the only way to terminate the dispute, it was finally agreed to dispose by lot of all the tickets for sale. The emigrants were all numbered, and those with tickets for sailing vessels or other steamers excluded. The remainder then drew, there being fifty-two tickets to near three hundred passengers. This quieted the excitement for the time, though there was still a continual undercurrent of speculation and intrigue which was curious to observe. The disappointed candidates, for the most part, took passage in sailing vessels, with a prospect of seventy days' voyage before them. A few months previous, when three thousand persons were waiting on the Isthmus, several small companies started in the log canoes of the natives, thinking to reach San Francisco in them! After a voyage of forty days, during which they went no further than the island of Quibo, at the mouth of the Gulf, nearly all of them returned; the rest have not since been heard of.

The passengers were engaged in embarking all the afternoon of the second day after my arrival. The steamer came up to within a mile and a half of the town, and numbers of canoes plied between her and the sea-gateway. Native porters crowded about the hotels, clamoring for luggage, which they carried down to the shore under so fervent a heat that I was obliged to hoist my umbrella. One of the boatmen lifted me over the swells for the sake of a *medio,* and I was soon gliding out along the edge of the breakers, startling the pelicans that flew in long lines over the water. I was well satisfied to leave Panama at the time; the cholera, which had already carried off one fourth of the native population, was making havoc among the Americans, and several of the *Falcon's* passengers lay at the point of death.

Mrs. D. B. Bates—1851

Upon arriving in the harbor of Panama, we came to an anchor about two miles from the city. Ships scarcely ever go nearer on account of rocks. It is not a very good harbor for vessels to lie in with safety, it is so open. At anchor close by us was the ship Marianna, of San Francisco, Captain Rossiter. He recognized my husband as an old acquaintance, invited us on board his ship, where he was enjoying the society of his wife and an interesting little child.

Captain Rossiter informed us he was going to take his ship down to Taboga, an island which lies about ten miles from Panama. The P.M.S.S. Co. have a depot there. All the steamers, when in port, lie there. The shipping frequent this place to get a supply of water, which gushes in clear rivulets down the sides of the mountains. A little steamer plies constantly between Taboga and Panama for the accommodation of passengers, who are constantly flocking from the miasma-infected city of Panama, to inhale the health-breathing zephyrs of this island retreat.

The shore is very bold. Ships of the largest tonnage lie within a stone's throw of the shore. Nearly all the washing is carried from the city, and here cleansed in the running streams by the native women, and spread upon the bushes to dry. At this time there were three hotels there, and quite a number of native populace. Since the time I allude to, they have been visited by a destructive fire. It has been rebuilt, however. We spent one happy week here.

Daily Mrs. Rossiter and myself wandered up and down the mountain's side, protected from the sun's rays by the umbrageous foliage which formed a complete net-work above our heads. Here grew the cocoa-nut and pine-apple. The monkeys chattered and swung from branch to branch above our heads. The parrot and paroquet screamed at us from their leafy habitations. Birds of beautiful plumage were carolling their sweetest notes, giving to these sylvan mountain-slopes a truly vivifying appearance. Here, thought I, in company with loved ones, could I dream away a happy existence. The impersonations of romance and solitude could scarcely find a more congenial abode than this beautiful and sequestered isle.

At the expiration of this memory-treasured week, which was, indeed, an oasis in the waste over which I had been wafted, we returned to an anchor at Panama. That night I was suddenly and severely attacked with what was conceded to be, by all, Panama fever of the most malignant kind. The next day I was carried on shore, through the city, to a house outside the city gates, owned by a gentleman from New Orleans. For the use of one furnished room and board, the sum of forty dollars per week was required.

It was a large, barn-like dwelling. Nearly all the

rooms were rented to Spaniards. The partitions which divided the house into apartments only extended to a height sufficient to conceal the occupants from one another, without in the least obviating the noise and disturbance naturally occurring from so many living under one roof. Even this tenement, rough as it was, far exceeded, in point of cleanliness and healthy location, the crowded, and at that time filthy, hotels of the city.

Ours was a corner room in the second story, fronting the street. Large doors, very much resembling barn-doors, opened from two sides of the room upon a balcony, that indispensable appendage to all the dwellings situated in tropical climes. Every breath of air which fanned my burning brow seemed wafted from a heated furnace. For days I lay a victim to that consuming fever, part of the time in blissful unconsciousness. I say blissful, because my thoughts wandered to my distant home, and I was relieved, for the time being, from the agonizing thoughts that in intervals of reason obtruded themselves upon me. I was attended by no physician. Captain Rossiter administered dose after dose of calomel, until my system was completely prostrated.

Well was it for me that my knowledge of the Spanish language was so limited; otherwise I might have been shocked by the language of some of the inmates of the house. Every footfall, every loud word, echoed and reverberated through that hollow building, sending, at each recurrence, a pang of agony through my burning brain. Fear, too, would assert her sway when left alone, as I oftentimes was. For nearly two weeks the fever raged incessantly; after which time, I gradually convalesced. When raised by pillows in my bed, I had a view of the street leading to the rear gates of the city, and day after day could I see the silent dead borne to their last resting-place.

At that time, Panama was crowded with Americans waiting to be conveyed to the gold-studded placers of California. Alas! many of the number never reached to the goal they so ardently desired, and for which they had sacrificed their own happiness, and that of those dearer to them than aught else except gold, the yellow dust of temptation. Truly it may be said to be "the root of all evil," when it allures thousands from their peaceful homes, to meet an untimely death. Reflections such as these had a decided tendency to depress still more my already despondent heart. My recovery, at times, was considered doubtful. It was too sickly to entertain the idea of remaining there longer than was absolutely necessary. I was too weak to attempt to cross the Isthmus; therefore, all hope of returning home was abandoned.

It was decided to take passage at once for San Francisco. We remained one month at Panama. During the last two or three days of our stay, I walked a short distance each day. One of our walks we extended as far as the burying-ground. What a shunned and desolate spot was that American burial-ground at Panama,—a mere necessary receptacle of lifeless flesh and crumbling bones,—not even a stone raised to mark the last resting-place of the many loved friends who had breathed their last sigh in a strange land, and by strangers been consigned to mother earth! A little piece of board was sometimes reared, with the name, age, and place of residence, marked thereon; but often this little mark of respect and affection had been displaced by mules, numbers of which are constantly grazing among the graves. No inclosure protects these often nameless mounds; straggling bushes struggle with rank and choking weeds that overtop them. The whole place bears a deserted, forsaken aspect—untrodden by the feet of memory and love. It is within sight of the bay, whose waters, as they eternally dash against the shore, seem to be chanting a requiem for the departed.

The evening before we left Panama, our attention was attracted by what we conceived to be a torchlight procession, issuing from the city gate. Upon a nearer approach, it proved to be a funeral cortege. First came several horsemen bearing torches; these were followed by a band of music, playing very lively, heart-stirring strains; then came an open bier, carried by natives, upon which was borne the lifeless remains of a sweet little cherub, a lovely Spanish child—lovely even in death. It seemed to be in a sitting posture. In each hand was placed a wax candle; wreaths of flowers entwined its angelic brow, and were strewn in rich profusion upon the bier. Innumerable wax tapers were inserted around the outer edge of the bier, which shed an ethereal halo upon the little form of clay, which had so recently been the pride and joy of fond parents. Then followed another company of equestrians and pedestrians. It had the appearance of some joyous festive scene rather than a funeral procession. And, truly,

> "Why should we mourn for the child early called
> From the sin and suffering of this darkened world?
> Though ties of affection may early be riven,
> Why wish back on earth the dear loved one in heaven?"

Oh, how I suffered, while at Panama, for a draught of cold water, to allay that feverish, burning thirst which seemed to be consuming the very life-blood in my veins! By the time they could get the clear, cool water from the gurgling rivulets of Taboga to Panama, it would be tepid, and I would turn from it in disgust. Often, in my hours of delirium, would I fancy myself at home, travelling again the little school path. I would arrive at the running brook which wandered through green meadows, and was spanned by a rustic bridge, over which, for twelve happy years, our little feet had skipped each day, on the way to and from school. Then I would fancy myself leaning far over the grassy brink—so far, I could touch my lips to the transparent surface, and imbibe draught after draught of the sparkling liquid. Pleasing hallucination! too quickly dispelled by returning reason. In my lucid moments, I was ever thinking of the old well at home, and wishing *one* drink from the "moss-covered bucket." I felt it would save my life, when all else should prove abortive. One who has never been prostrated by fever in a burning tropical clime, when it was utterly impossible to obtain ice or cool water, can scarcely conceive of the torture and agony endured. Every breath of air is a simoom to the sufferer. My principal sustenance was the banana and plantain.

We took passage in the steamer Republic for San Francisco. The price of our tickets at that time were six hundred dollars. The Republic was commanded by Captain William Hudson, a son of the commander of the sloop-of-war Vincennes. He was a lieutenant in the navy, but was then enjoying a furlough of four years, which he improved by taking charge of the Republic.

I saw nothing of the city of Panama except what met the eye in passing through its narrow streets,—more properly, lands,—bounded on either side by high, prison-looking buildings, which iron bars in lieu of window-sashes. Plenty of naked natives, all eager to carry us on board in their bungoes (boats),—a noisy, wrangling set they were,—assembled there upon the beach. Immediately upon reaching the steamer, I repaired, to my state-room, and, in an exhausted state, was assisted into my berth. I remained in this situation through all the hurry and bustle incident to the departure of an ocean steamer, but then was fated to be disturbed in a manner I little dreamed of. A lady came to the state-room, and very unceremoniously demanded my berth, saying her ticket, which she had purchased in New York, called for it. Here was a dilemma! The ticket calling for that berth had been sold twice. Captain Hudson was called to the rescue. He decided I should not be removed. He had previously been informed of the series of accidents that had befallen us on our eventful voyage, and declared, laughingly, that, unless routed by fire, I should not be molested. He offered to provide the lady from New York with another room; which she obstinately refused to occupy, vehemently averring that she would lie upon the cabin-floor, and prosecute the company for practising such duplicity. This threat she put in execution upon her arrival at San Francisco, and received compensation to the amount of several thousand dollars.

Upon getting out to sea, my recovery was visibly accelerated by the invigorating sea-breezes and cheerful companionship of our fellow-voyagers. I made many pleasant acquaintances, and formed friendships which have endured to the present,—

not the fashionable friendship of an hour, which dishonor the name, but attachments that have stood the test of adversity and misfortunes. The steamer Republic had on board four hundred passengers. Thirty out of this number were ladies,—the largest number which, at that time, had been taken on board any one steamer to San Francisco. There were but very few of them accompanied by their husbands; the remainder were going to meet their liege lords, from whom they had been separated.

THE RETURN—1854

After twelve days and some hours' sail from San Francisco, the old, walled city of Panama rose to view. The steamer's gun was fired; she dropped her anchor; and a fleet of boats and bungoes were seen approaching. They neared and surrounded the ship. Most or all of them were manned by swarthy-visaged, half-naked Carthaginians, and a mongrel race of natives, whose appearance and gestures were equally as repulsive.

Such a perfect Babel as that steamer's deck presented! Some running to and fro, looking for baggage, some bargaining and bantering with the boatmen, boatmen fighting with one another for a berth next the gangways, ladies screaming at the top of their voices, children bawling in unison, and parrots joining in the chorus! Curses and oaths, singing and shouting, filled up the intervals of this hurly-burly scene. I stood agape with astonishment at witnessing the haste and recklessness with which they rushed, helter-skelter, down the gangways, and tumbled (some of them headlong) into the boats. More than one individual I saw floundering in the water; and carpet-bags and valises were floating about quite merrily.

The hideous-looking boatmen kept up a continual jargon and fighting with one another; and perhaps, just as some person was going to step into a boat, some native would give it a shove away, and the person, pressed hard from behind, if not remarkably nimble, would get a ducking.

I was determined to wait until the last, rather than go with such a rush; and I did wait, until the coast was clear. Then our party, which consisted of four or five ladies and gentlemen, secured seats in a boat, and bade good bye to the Uncle Sam. We had gone but a short distance from the ship, when we heard the report of a gun booming over the water. The steamer Panama, which left in company with us, had arrived. She had about five hundred passengers on board; and, with the eight hundred who had just left the Uncle Sam, the hotels in Panama would be likely to be rather crowded. It behooved us to hasten, in order to secure a place on the floor, if nowhere else.

As we neared the shore, the water was full of natives, who waded off almost up to their necks, surrounded the boat, and arrested its progress. The boatmen are agreed with the natives on the shore to manage thus, in order to secure as many pieces of money as possible. No entreaties or threats could induce the boatmen to budge one inch nearer to the shore. There was no alternative but to place ourselves upon the backs of these natives, and (as the expression is) ride post-back to the shore. Before placing ourselves in this rather unladylike position, there was much screaming and laughing, and crying, and scolding; but it all terminated in one general post-back ride to the shore. The natives being so submerged, one could not judge well of their muscular developments; and some of the more corpulent ladies were afraid to trust their immense proportions on the back of a slender native, for fear of being dropped. This accident did happen to some of them, and it was ever accompanied with much laughing and joking at the sufferer's expense. Finally, we were all landed,—some in one shape, and some in another. More than a dozen natives surrounded me, all holding their hands for a bit, (ten cents,) each claiming the honor of having carried me on his back to the shore. They all bore such a striking resemblance to one another, and having on no garments by which they could be distinguished, I was sorely troubled to know to whom I was indebted for my novel ride. It was settled, however, to their satisfaction.

The natives took our trunks upon their backs, (not us, this time,) and our party started for the Louisiana Hotel. When we arrived there, it was literally jammed full; but, knowing we should fare no better by going elsewhere, we crowded ourselves in with the multitude.

This was in the afternoon, and our appetites were considerably sharpened by the rather scantily furnished tables which had been spread on board the steamer for one or two days previous to our arrival.

Six or seven of us ladies were shown to a room on the second floor, which overlooked the courtyard in the centre of the range of buildings. Each story was surrounded by a balcony. Our room had no windows, but two very extensive doors, which opened like folding-doors on to the balcony. The partitions all through the house only ran two thirds of the height to the ceiling; so there was plenty of ventilation and plenty of noise circulating through the house. There was not a particle of paint or paper in the whole building. The walls and partitions were of rough boards, and these were all whitewashed. The great vaulted passages leading through the house, and the great wide, worn staircases, presented a cheerless and gloomy aspect. In our room were six or seven cots, over which were thrown two sheets and a straw pillow to each cot. This constituted the entire stock of furniture, if we except two old rickety chairs and our trunks.

From the balcony opposite our door we could watch the proceedings in the cook-room; and it was amusing to watch those half-naked natives knock over the fowl, of which there were numbers in the back yard, about half-divest them of their feathers, hurry them into a kettle, and by the time they were well heated through, run with them to the tables, if they were not met on the way there by the half-famished passengers, who would snatch the half-cooked viands from their hands, and beat a hasty retreat to their rooms.

In vain we waited to be summoned to supper. Finally, one of our party made a descent upon the cooks, and procured the wherewith to appease, in a measure, our hunger.

The Uncle Sam's passengers had intended to get mules, and start that night from Panama to cross the isthmus; and this could have been accomplished, had not the natives been so shrewd. When they saw the steamer Panama coming in directly after the Uncle Sam, they rightly conjectured, that, if they kept their mules out of sight until all from both steamers were landed, there would be such a demand for mules they could get any price they saw fit to ask. Therefore, when mules were called for by those of the passengers who reached the shore first, there were none to be found. No entreaty or persuasion could induce them to bring one forward; but we were told there would be plenty on the morrow. That afternoon a party of us took a stroll around the city, visited the oldest and largest cathedral in the place, walked upon the battlements which surround this ancient and once flourishing city, but now, in many places, wearing the aspect of decay and ruin. Some portions of the wall were falling into ruins; but in some places it was sufficiently wide for two carriages to drive abreast; but there were no vehicles there then. There were the sentry-boxes, built at short intervals along the battlements, which, in days gone by, had sheltered the wearied sentinel during his nightly patrol.

I saw in some places the ruins of old churches and convents. Some portions of the high stone walls would be standing, out of the sides of which were growing bushes and small trees. The sight of those trees growing out of high stone walls at once attracted my attention. For how many ages must those old walls have been exposed to burning suns and deluging rains, to have thus afforded sustenance for those scraggy shrubs and trees! The stones were all moss-grown, and rank vines were running in great profusion over the decaying ruins. An air of silent desertion seemed to pervade those ruinous remains, which gave rise to melancholy reflections. They forcibly reminded one of the mutability of all things earthly. Just as the setting sun was casting its red beams upon the high and narrow stained-glass windows of the rich old cathedral, we were wandering under its vaulted roof, feasting our astonished senses with a sight of the massive gold and silver ornaments which were displayed in such rich profusion upon the walls. What an air of mystery and gloom seemed to surround us! How our voices echoed and reverberated in the far-off niches and recesses of this gloomy-looking edifice. Several times I was startled by the appearance of some old monk, with his cowl closely drawn, who would start from some niche in the wall, where he had remained unperceived, and, without uttering a word, hold out a silver plate, whereupon you were expected to deposit a piece of money. When once more in the open air, I experienced a sense of freedom from the feelings of mystery and gloom, which unavoidably cluster around one while traversing those silent cathedrals.

We then repaired to the vestibule of a convent, not with the expectation of gaining admittance, however. There was a wooden frame which turned in the wall, after the manner of those yard-gates which turn upon a pivot, and on which stood a pitcher of water and a glass. After drinking, a person is expected to leave a piece of money beside the pitcher. Every few moments, this frame is turned by an unseen hand; but, when the pitcher and glass appear again, the money, if there had been any beside it, had disappeared.

It being a moonlight evening, several of us ladies, accompanied by one gentleman, started to prosecute our walk through some other parts of the city. We passed through several streets, or, as they appeared to me, lanes; but they looked *so* gloomy! And, then, those old ruins seemed such grand lurking places for the revengeful Spaniard, with his murderous stiletto, that we all frightened ourselves by such imaginings, and ran back again to the hotel as quickly as possible.

What a night was that at Panama! So many returning Californians, and some such wild ones, too! They seemed determined to make the night hideous with their singing and shouting. There was little sleep for any one in Panama that night.

As soon as daylight dawned, the natives began to swarm in the streets with their mules, opposite to the hotels, and the people commenced bargaining for the use of them.

The railroad was completed from Aspinwall to within eighteen miles of Panama. Eighteen miles! When we came to traverse the route, it seemed thirty, at least. As the rains had commenced, we were advised to travel the Cruces route, as the Gorgona route would be impassable on account of the mud.

Some of the passengers who had before traversed the Cruces route advised all the ladies to dispense with the side-saddle altogether, as it would be utterly impossible for them to retain their seats, unless upon the gentleman's Spanish saddle. Most of us were provided with India-rubber boots, and pants, and a large sombrero, as a protection for our heads.

The natives asked twenty dollars for the use of a good, plump-looking mule, to take us to Obispo, at which place was the terminus of the railroad; but one could get a miserable-looking animal, which, in all probability, would die on the way, and leave you to prosecute the remainder of your journey on foot, for twelve and fifteen dollars. For my mule I paid twenty; and, many times during the journey, I had occasion to congratulate myself for having secured such a gentle, kind, serviceable little animal. I really became so attached to him during the journey, that

I parted from him with regret. Generally, the natives from whom you hire your mules, and pay for them in advance, trot along with the company, and are ready, upon your arrival, to take the animal.

There was great frolicking and laughing with the ladies while fixing away on the mules. I shall never forget *my* feelings when I found myself seated astride my mule, arrayed in boots and pants, with my feet firmly planted in the stirrups, ready for any emergency.

About five o'clock in the morning, I left the hotel, in company with thirty or more of the passengers. They all travelled in parties of thirty and forty together. Most of the children were carried across by the natives. They were seated astride their necks, with their little hands clasped across the natives' foreheads; while they have hold of the children's legs in front. Those who have infants generally get some gentleman to take them in front of him on the saddle.

One of our passengers (a widow lady, with two little children) was very sick indeed when she arrived in Panama. She was advised to remain there for the present; but, although she felt convinced that her days on earth were numbered, she preferred to go on with the company. She was placed in a hammock: each of her little children (one twelve months, and the other three years) were carried on the backs of natives, who walked by her side.

When only six miles out from Panama, she breathed her last-drawn sigh. They stopped, dug a grave for the mother by the lonely way-side, and deposited her remains therein. It was a sad spectacle. Well was it for those little orphans that their extreme youth prevented them from realizing the extent of their affliction.

A kind-hearted woman—although the roughest-looking one in the company—volunteered to take charge of the babes until they arrived in New York. Upon arriving at Obispo, a collection of two hundred dollars was taken for the children. Often since, I have thought of that lonely grave by the way-side, with no stone, or even board, to mark the spot, and upon which no tear of affection will ever fall. She buried her husband in San Francisco, three weeks previous to her departure for the Atlantic States. She was getting home by charity; and, being a delicate, feeble woman, could not endure the fatigue of the journey. Deep-seated sorrow had sapped the fountains of life, and she died among strangers, far from friends and home.

Two others of our number died, and were buried on the way. One was a gentleman whose mule had died, and he was footing it along, when he suddenly fell, and expired. Probably his death was caused by disease of the heart. One steerage passenger, who was walking across, died from over-heating himself.

For the distance of six miles, our route lay over a good, paved road, and we galloped along, exceedingly delighted with the scenery, our mules, and the good road. "If this is crossing the Isthmus," said one, "I shall never believe again the horrid accounts I have heard respecting the trip;" but, before the termination of the journey, she thought the one-half had not been told. Soon the road became more rugged, and we began to enter the rocky defiles, ascent the steep mountain passes, and descend into dark, rocky ravines. The sun, which had been shining with tropical fervency, now withdrew his rays, and the rain descended in torrent. The deafening thunder seemed to shake those old mountains to their very base. In an instant we were soaking wet; for, oh, how it did pour! In a short time it was over and the sun shining bright and hot as ever. Two such showers as this we encountered during that mule-back trip.

The scenery through the mountains almost defies description. There are defiles through the solid rock, so narrow as to admit only one mule at a time; while, on each side, the rocks rise to the height of fifteen, twenty, and, in some places, thirty feet. These rocks are surmounted by tall trees, whose dense foliage, blending overhead, completely excludes the sight of the blue sky above.

Sometimes these narrow passes are so descending, as to render it almost impossible to retain your seat upon the mule. In some places there are regular stepping-stones, into each of which little holes have been worn by the mules' feet, that so many times, and oft, have traversed those dangerous passes. I could compare the descent to nought but placing a mule at the top of a flight of stairs, getting upon his back, and riding down.

Those mules are so careful and sure-footed, and so well accustomed to travelling through those frightful places, that there is no necessity whatever of guiding them. You have only to place the bridle over the pommel of the saddle, (those Spanish saddles have a high pommel in front,) and look out for yourself. In descending, we were obliged to lean far back on the animal's back, and grasp the crupper with all our might. It seemed as if our safety depended solely upon the strength of the crupper. How I cried sometimes, with fright! but then I was careful not to let any one see me, and generally took the time for such ebullition of feeling when it was raining hard, and the water would unavoidably be coursing down my face.

How careful those mules were! That day I learned to love them. In going down those rocky flights, they would hold their heads low down, then put one foot over and plant it firmly in one of those little holes, then the other in the same way, then bring their hind feet on to the same shelf. Then go down on to another, and so on to the bottom. Then perhaps commence, and make an ascent equally as toilsome. They have nothing to eat or drink on the way, and never once attempt to nip the herbage that grows in some places, by the way-side.

Once, as there were about fifty mules all in a line, ascending one of those steep mountain passes, the one in advance, which was laden with three large trunks, made a misstep, and fell. These animals are so sure-footed that they never stumble except when giving out, and never fall, unless to die. This one was very weak, and failing fast, but might have succeeded in reaching the top of this dangerous pass, had not the trunks swayed on one side, and hit the rocks, thereby causing him to fall. When passing up those rocky flights, it is utterly impossible for a mule to step backwards, off one of those shelves, without falling, and as utterly impossible to turn the mule about, on account of the extreme narrowness of the way. The fallen mule, in making desperate attempts to rise with those heavy trunks lashed to him, as a natural consequence kept falling back, thereby crowding hard upon those behind him. I was seated on the fifth mule in the rear of the fallen one. Such a shouting and bawling as there was with the natives, who were trying to disencumber the poor beast of the trunks, and, at the same, prevent him from throwing himself any farther back, as, by so doing, he would endanger the lives of those behind him.

How firmly my little mule planted his feet upon the shelf he was on, rounded himself into as small a compass as possible, and awaited his fate. He seemed to comprehend the whole; and, by his looks, I fancied he said, as a token of assurance to me, "I will die here rather than take one step backwards.''" Finally they disengaged the trunks from the animal, and hoisted them up on to the banks above. As the mule was evidently dying, they cut his throat, and lifted him up also. This scene detained us more than an hour; for those natives seemed to make no progress towards extricating the mule from his painful position, but were running to and fro, bawling at the top of their voices, hunting ropes, and ordering one another. The passengers who were far behind were calling loudly to know what was the cause of the detention. Some were cursing the tardy natives; the women were crying with fear; and, if a daguerreotype view could have been taken of the scene, I think it would have had a tendency to deter some from ever crossing the Isthmus of Darien on mule-back.

Upon entering one of those defiles, the natives who are on foot (and there are generally quite a number with each party) go in advance, and keep up a loud shouting, to prevent any party which may be coming in an opposite direction from entering, as it would be death to one or other of the parties' mules, should they meet. We occasionally passed over the carcasses of mules in these places, which had been killed to afford others a passage. We were so fearful that the natives would not make noise enough, that we joined in the shouting, and felt truly grateful when we emerged from the bowels of the earth.

The day previous to our arrival at Panama, the steamer Illinois arrived at Aspinwall, with a load of passengers from New York for California. In crossing, we all met at different points on the way.

Sometimes, upon arriving at a defile, we would hear a loud shouting within; then we would halt, rein our mules out on each side of the way, and wait their egress. Some, upon emerging from the defile, looked very much jaded and fatigued; others were laughing and joking. How earnestly we eyed them, as they appeared one after another, thinking perhaps we might see some friend or acquaintance from home.

Upon thus meeting, each party would accost the other with all the freedom and familiarity of old acquaintances; and some of the remarks which were passed were really laughable. Upon the back of one mule were seated two persons, a young man and an elderly woman. At sight of them, some of the gentlemen of our party hurrahed, which was answered by the woman with a wave of her calash (she wore one of those large old-fashioned green ones,) and a "Hurrah for California!" "That is right," said one, addressing the young man, "take your mother with you; if we had, we might have been spared much suffering." And thus they joked. Some who had been rather unsuccessful advised the emigrants to turn back, even then. "Why?" said they, "is there not plenty of gold in California?" "Yes, there is gold enough; but you may not be lucky enough to get any of it."

They gave us no encouragement as to the route over which they had passed. All said, "Expect to find it as bad and worse than you can possibly conceive of." This was disheartening, I assure you.

Sometimes the trail would be quite passable, and then one could enjoy the scenery. The tropical foliage is beautiful; and among the leaves and branches were hopping birds of beautiful plumage, rendering the woods vocal with their sweetest songs. Monkeys and parrots we saw in abundance.

On the way we passed several hotels,—nothing more than canvas shanties, with large signs attached, bearing the appellations of "Astor House, "St. Charles Hotel," "Revere House," etc. They were kept by Americans, and at them one could procure plenty of fruit and liquors of all kinds; but the wise ones were very abstemious, as a great deal of the sickness on the isthmus is engendered by eating and drinking to excess in a climate so excessively warm.

How tired we grew! And yet, at every hotel, the distance seemed to increase rather than decrease.

Upon first entering the forests on the isthmus, my attention was directed to what looked like ropes hanging from the trees. I soon found them to be vines that had run up on the trees, out on the branches, and were suspended therefrom in every direction. They were leafless, and the color of a rope.

We crossed the Chagres River once only before reaching Obispo. How dark and deep it looked, as we were going down a step declivity directly into it! We were assured it was quite shallow, and not dangerous to fort; and that, if we allowed our mules to take their own course, we should be carried safely across.

Once we came to a little slough, over which was built a narrow bridge of poles. I happened to be ahead at that place, and called to know whether I should cross the bridge, or follow the trail through the slough, which looked very miry. They told me to let the mule act his own pleasure. He first tried the strength of the bridge by placing his foot upon it, and feeling all about, as far as he could reach; then he turned, and went down the trail to the slough, and there reconnoitred in the same way; then he turned to the bridge again. I concluded he thought that the safest way of crossing. Upon reaching it, he stopped, made one leap, and cleared it at a bound, and came very near losing my equilibrium. All the other mules came leaping over except one, which, I expect, was so far gone, he could not jump. He stepped upon the bridge: it broke beneath his weight, and he fell. The lady was thrown from his back; and, altogether, there was quite a scene.

After this, we met two gentlemen on mule-back, and of them we inquired the distance to Obispo. The reply from one was, "I should think it was a dozen miles, and the very worst road you ever travelled."— "Oh, no," said the other, "not so bad as that. This is the gentleman's first trip to California. When he has crossed the Isthmus two or three times, he will not get so quickly discouraged. It is about two miles to Obispo; and rather a rough road, to be sure, but not worse than you have passed, I presume." How those cheering words revived my dropping spirits! I felt (and every lady of the company, I presume, felt the same) as if I could not retain my seat upon my mule but a little longer. Every part of my body ached so hard, I could not tell where the pain was most severe. If I had been placed upon the rack, and every joint drawn asunder, I could not have been much lamer or sorer than I then was.

It was two o'clock in the afternoon, and we had

been riding since five in the morning, without once leaving our mules, over a road which, for its rugged, uneven, and dangerous passes, beggars description.

Suddenly we heard the shrill whistle of a steam engine. Our lagging spirits revived. We toiled on, and reached the top of an eminence which overlooked the beautiful valley of Obispo; and there, far below us, we beheld a scene calculated to inspire the most despondent with renewed hope and courage. There was the terminus of the rail road; and on the track were twelve long cars, headed by an engine, which was puffing and blowing, and sending forth whistle after whistle, long, loud, and clear, its echoes awakening the hitherto unbroken solitude of the primeval forests of New Granada.

Those of the company who had sufficient life and strength remaining to make any demonstration of joy, did so. As we descended the mountain, we were perceived, and welcomed by firing of cannon and loud cheering.

Several hundred United States troops had arrived there, *en route* for California. They were all out on the plaza. Four or five large American flags were floating upon the breeze from the roofs of large temporary hotels which had been erected along the line of the railroad; and, as fast as the road progressed, they were transported along to the terminus. Here I saw a railroad for the first time since leaving Baltimore, a lapse of four years.

When we arrived in the valley, and halted in front of the depot, I suppose our forlorn, jaded appearance excited the sympathy of those there assembled, for many stepped forward to assist us in dismounting. They lifted us from our saddles, and placed us, not upon our feet,—for not one of the ladies in the company could stand,—but flat upon the ground in the mud.

One lady in particular—who rode nearly the whole way, holding her babe on the saddle in front of her—fainted, the moment they lifted her from her mule, and it was a long time before she recovered her consciousness.

Upon leaving Panama, she had consigned it to the care of a gentleman, who was going to take it across the Isthmus on the saddle with himself; but whose mule gave out, and fell with him. In endeavoring to save the infant from injury, he received several severe contusions on his back and head, from the effects of which he did not recover during the journey to New York. This so frightened the mother, that she took the babe herself; and, in consequence of thus exerting her strength to take care of herself and child,—when those who had no child to attend to could scarcely retain their seats,—she came very near dying.

After remaining a few moments in the mud, I made an attempt to walk. I would go a few steps, and then fall; pick myself up again, take a few more steps, and then tumble the other way. I attributed my inability to walk partly to my India-rubber boots slipping on the muddy ground, and partly to the benumbed and stiffened state of my limbs. While I was thus staggering about in the vain endeavor to reach a hotel, a gentleman came along, picked me up, and carried me to the desired haven.

Cars were in readiness to take us immediately to Aspinwall, where the steamer North Star was waiting to convey us to New York. Many of the gentlemen took passage in them; but the ladies were too exhausted to think of proceeding farther that day;

and, as the specie and baggage had not all arrived, there was no danger of the North Star sailing until the next night.

So we all retired, and did not rise again until the next morning. Our accommodations at Obispo were similar to those at Panama, nothing to eat, and not much to lie upon.

In the morning, as we were well-nigh famished, a gentleman of the party invited a friend of mine and myself to breakfast with him, as he had been to the trouble of purchasing something, and hiring it cooked expressly for himself. The breakfast consisted of broiled chicken, fried plantains, and eggs. That meal cost five dollars, and it was the only one I had while at Obispo. That forenoon, our baggage arrived, and, while out on the plaza, it was exposed to one of the hardest showers I ever witnessed. Woe to the contents of those trunks which were not water-proof!

I must not leave the beautiful valley of Obispo without descanting upon its loveliness. It was inclosed by lofty hills, whose sides and summits were clothed with the most beautiful tropical foliage. There grew the tall palm-tree, laden with its milky fruit; the luscious pine-apple; also bananas, and plantains in abundance.

There were, perhaps, twenty native bamboo-huts, thatched with the woven fibre of the palm-leaf, scattered about the valley; around the doors of which, and under the leafy shade of the lime and palmetto, lounged the indolent natives, of both sexes. And why should they exert themselves, when nature has so abundantly supplied their wants?

They appeared perfectly happy and contented in their ignorance. No soaring aspirations for fame caused them to pass sleepless nights and anxious days.

They were slaves to no goddess of fashion; and, if they had any pride, I cannot conceive to what point it tended, unless it was an overweening desire to excel in roasting monkeys. Oh, this was a sunny spot! I can see it, even now, in my mind's eye, as it appeared when viewed from the top of that mountain height, after a day of toilsome travel. That old adage, "It is always the darkest just before day," was never more fully illustrated than when, after such a toilsome, dangerous day's ride as we had accomplished, that lovely, pleasant valley burst upon our view. That last two miles of mule-back travel I shall never forget. Whether it surpassed all other portions of the route in steep and dangerous passes, or whether we were so completely worn out with fatigue, that everything appeared more dark and gloomy than it really was, I cannot say; but that old maxim kept ringing in my ears, and cheering me on—"It is always the darkest just before day." And, certainly, I could not compare that sunshiny valley, at the terminus of our route, to other than the brightest day that ever followed the darkest night.

About four o'clock in the afternoon, we seated ourselves in the cars bound to Aspinwall. Those cars on the Isthmus had cane seats and backs, and were, therefore, not so comfortable for the sick, sore, and lame, as if they had been otherwise.

We were borne over the track quite slowly, as the many short curves which the road made prevented their going with greater speed. The railroad seemed to follow the bed of the Chagres River. We crossed it several times. The scenery was grand and sublime, commingled with the beautiful. On one side of the track, perhaps, a towering mountain raised its rocky sides far above us; while, on the opposite side, the eye might wander far down a steep precipice, causing a shudder to run through the frame at the thought of an accident occurring at such a spot.

How frightened the parrots, paroquets, and monkeys, must have been, when the iron horse first startled those leafy solitudes with his fiery snort! Never again will profound stillness reign triumphant along the course of the Chagres River. Those feathered songsters, of brilliant plumage, lured to its vine-clad banks by the gentle ripple of its tiny waves, will fly, startled from their leafy coverts, at the approach of the iron steed.

By and by, the town of Aspinwall appeared to view. The country all about looked so sunken and marshy, as to impress the beholder at once with an idea of its unhealthy location. It was quite a place, however, and at that time seemed to be all alive with people. We passed from the cars directly on board the steamer, as it was near night, and we wished to get possession of our rooms before sailing. I ascertained the steamer would not get away before midnight, as it was an almost endless task to select the baggage, and get it on board.

Being very weary, I concluded to lie down, and get a nap in the first part of the evening, in order to be awake, and be on deck, when we left Aspinwall.

When next I opened my eyes, it was broad daylight. Aspinwall was far out of sight, and we on the broad Atlantic.

Amid all the bustle and confusion preparatory to sailing, even firing of guns, I had slept soundly. One lady, thinking I would like to see Aspinwall by lamp-light, endeavored to awaken me; said she spoke my name several times, and shook my arm, but still I slept on; and she left me to the enjoyment of my dreams.

Upon going on deck, I met again all the Uncle Sam's passengers, and saw many strangers who had come on board at Aspinwall. On the North Star I had only two room-mates, and was minus baby and parrot.

Now that I was on the Atlantic, I felt that the distance between home and myself would be speedily annihilated. Nothing occurred worthy of note during the passage; and, on the ninth day after leaving Aspinwall, we made Sandy Hook.

J.Bruff July 1851

Some discontented steerage-passengers, got up an indignation-meeting, and paper,—signed by several, in order to publish, at home, they say, because the accommodations and fare, at the two ends of the ship are different. (Cabin passage $350, steerage $125.) The good accommodations at our end, and the accommodating gentlemanly manners of the Officers, elicited from us, a meeting and testimonial of an inverse character to that concocted forward.— Some of the steerage passengers signed with pleasure, our document.

At night, the ship changed her course, to the N.N.E.

July 2d Flying clouds. At 6 ½ A.M. we entered the picturesque anchorage, of Tobago, amongst beautiful verdant islets. Tobago is a small town upon an island of the same name, and largest of the group. Here, bold masses and cliffs, of grey and brown rocks, start up from the midst of feathery palms and dark green foliage—Bright green patches, on the slopes,—of plantains, oranges, bannanas, and spaces, speckled with brown and green, show cultivated patches.

The town, about ¼ mile off, from where we lay, looks exceedingly pretty. Thatched cottages of the natives white-washed adobe structures of gentlemen, with their roofs of red tiles, some modern American-looking residences; the old monkish-looking church, and the graceful cocoa-nut trees, between and waving over them produce a beautiful effect.

There are some fifty-odd vessels laying here; 6 large steamers,—the Constitution, Unicorn, Massachusetts, Carolina, New Orleans, and Fremont; and the rest ships and brigs. The sea around is sprinkled with canoes. In the rear of Tobago arises a range of distant lofty blue, cloud-capped mountains, with many higher peaks. Received Mr. Forbes on board, and after a delay of half an hour, we proceeded, and reached the anchorage off Panama, about one mile from shore, at 7 ½ A.M. Found here, one Propeller, 10 Ships, and 10 Brigs. A sensation of deep regret pervaded the company, on learning that Henry Tracy, Esq. Civil Engineer, and Agent for Law's line of Pacific Steamers, was dead:—a man of noble sentiments and character.

(*Panama.*) The celebrated City of Panama, from the anchorage, looks like most old Spanish towns, dingy and antiquated. The dilapidated walls are crumbling into the sea; sombre-looking rows of houses, with red-tiled roofs, numerous old churches; and in the midst, the tall towers of the Cathedral, whose lofty spires glisten in the sun, with coating of pearl-oyster shells, rise conspicuously. We brought down 205 passengers,—54 of whom were in the Cabins; and 1,200,000 dollars, in gold.

Now is there excitement and confusion, on board:—getting out baggage, and leaving the ship. Swarms of boats and canoes, alongside; and a war of words, in many languages, with the English and Spanish predominating, in the Babal. My old companion,—Mr. Wright, was exceedingly kind to me; he has a Californian wife with him.—waited patiently, till the crowd and confusion abated, and then engaged a snug sail-boat: had our luggage put in, and bade adieu to the good ship California,—which has brought us so briskly and pleasantly down; and to her courteous and worthy Commander and officers, whom I sincerely wish long years of prosperity.

We raised a large sprit sail, and followed by a strong breeze, skimmed rapidly over the green waves. About midway, we were struck by a light squall and shower, which caused our little bark to bound more briskly, over the long swells. We had, however, to steer cautiously, to avoid the numerous sunken rocks in the way. Near the land, a small steamer ran athwart our bow, quite closely.—She plies between Panama and Tobago. We beached our boat, in light surf, in about 20 minutes, after leaving the ship. As soon as she struck bottom, the natives rushed into the water,—some assisting to draw the boat up, but the most of them, grabbing at the baggage, and passengers, to take them ashore. We had to order them peremptorily, to desist, till we were ready for their services. Three darkies now shouldered the passengers,—Mr. and Mrs. Wright, and myself, and bore us up to the dry part of the beach.—Then the luggage was brought ashore, and piled up, and after that, the natives shouldered it, and we closely followed.

In about 100 yards, obliquely across the shingle and pebbles, we reached the entrance to the City, by a dilapidated gateway, through an arched passage, and then a narrow paved street, passing several very narrow transverse streets, till we at length arrived at a large portal, with a sign of "Entrance to the American Hotel". Entering we ascended a flight of broad stone steps, to a large hall,—paved with red tiles, in the back of which was a bar-room. Rooms were promptly assigned us, and our baggage accordingly disposed of. My quarters were a room on the 2nd floor, fronting the street, and opened into a balcony, floored over with red tiles.

Now came the tug of war!—About one dozen natives claimed pay for bringing up our baggage, though we had employed scarcely half that number. They gave us considerable trouble, to ascertain to whom we were actually indebted, and the just amount to pay. I got off by paying, $2.50. When this was settled, I walked down to see the city.

There are many interesting ruins here. A detachment of bare-footed colored soldiers passed us, wearing only shirts and pantaloons, with bright arms, and drum and fife at their head. I visited the Plaza, and examined the front of the great Cathedral; walked over to the guard-house and prison, in the rear of which, stood the stakes where a couple of criminals were shot two days since.—A puddle of bloody sand was at the foot of each: and the wall of the prison,—some 10 paces, behind the place at which they sat was much cut by bullets.

We ascertained, to-day, that there is no steamer yet, on the other side of the Isthmus, and in consequence, we must wait here, a day or so. After supper, Mr. Wright told me, that early to-morrow morning, himself and wife, with a large number of the travellers, intended starting for Cruces; but I had to wait here till the local Agent of Adams & Co.—Mr. Cover, had his packages ready, as he was to furnish me with mules.

The colored population seem to predominate here and a large number are absolute blacks. I noticed a great many very aged females; but saw few handsome ladies. Clothing plentiful, and at reasonable rates. The fare at our hotel, is miserable;—for example,—Dinner,—fried ham, do. beef, boiled beans, molasses, and bread.—Dessert,—sliced pineapple, and a table-spoon-ful, pr man, of bread-pudding.—Supper:—ham, beef, pork & beans, dry toast, bad coffee, and tolerable tea.

The Cathedral has been a magnificent structure, of the kind. There are many other large churches, a monastery, and nunery, and ruins of the old Jesuit College. Most of these are in a ruinous state, covered with vines and moss. The walls and parapets of the City are alike ruinous; and the old stone turrets at the angles, are tottering over their foundations. The method of ornamenting the religious edifices, with pearl-oyster shells, was general, and when perfect, must have had a pretty and brilliant, if not appropriate effect.—Towers, spires, and gables, were thus enriched, the shells bring arranged in regular forms, on stucco grounds, of various colors. I noticed a chain-gang, of criminals, sweeping a street, reminding me of my travels in South America.

There were but 8 deaths known in the City last week-

Here I had the pleasure of meeting Mr. Wallach, formerly of Washington City, who has married a native lady, and is successfully engaged in the carrying business. I walked half a mile out of town, leaving the city by the landgate, which has a bell-fry and bell over it,—to "Cocoa-Nut Grove:" where Capt. Hunter, and some other acquaintances have lodged them selves. Cocoa-nuts and other palm-trees, tropical plants, flowers, and birds, lend their charms, to this pretty spot—The American proprietors have built a neat two-story frame house, in the grove; where board and refreshments can be had; and pleasant repose, in grass-hammocks, under the tall trees, at night.

(*Nunery Gate*) On returning to the City, I resumed my observation of it.—Walked upon the ramparts, which I reached by passing the entrance to the old nunnery, and ascended a small salient angle of the City Wall.—From this point I had an excellent view of the entire range, dedicated St. Francisco—the nunnery, convent, and ruined church. Below this long dingy row, stretched the broken walls of the city, and along its base, a strip of beach, full of canoes.—I sketched the scene, and resumed my travel, along the ramparts. Heat intense.

Reached an Angle of the walls, where lay several long heavy bronze guns, of beautiful proportions: none less than 100 years old. The natives aver that they are exceedingly valuable, on account of containing much silver in the composition; but which I doubt. I judge they are of the calabre of 32 pounders.—In the casemates, below, was a sort of arsenal; containing some mounted brass howitzers, and sundry piles of rusty shot and shell:—around which, lazy non-[com]missioned officers, with soldiers of various hues, were smoking their *papilletoes*. Rambling about all day, in the hot sun, gave me a severe headache; which, with the suffocating heat of the night, almost deprived me of repose.

July 3d At 8 A.M. Mr. Wright bade me good-bye. (*Gate &c.*) In company with Capt. Day, U.S.A. and Mr. Seymour, U.S. Mail Agent,—(who were also passengers in the California, I waked up to the Porto Tierra, or Land Gate, and the Church of La Mercede, just within it:—both of which I sketched. On passing a window, I noticed, upon the iron bars, (no sashes here) a very large and brilliant beetle,—of a golden-bronze hue. On stepping up, to examine it, I saw that it was tied, by a leg, with a cotton-thread, and a handsome Spanish lady within, was watching me.—I saluted the lady, and enquired how I could obtain such a one?—She said that there were plenty in the country, but difficult to catch; and that this one was her pet, and she would not part with it. Small lizzards are quite numerous.

Great prparations are now going on, to celebrate our National Jubalee to-morrow; the civic and military authorities are participating. I noticed that the hairless dog, so common all over S. America and the W. Indies, is also common here.

From 6 to 9 A.M. Travellers, on horses and mules; and on Shank's mare, and long trains of heavily-ladened mules, were wending their way to the Land gate; a short distance beyond which the roads branch,—the left, to Gorgona, and the right, to Cruces.

July 4th 1851 Cloudy, and excessively warm. Native bands of music, have been, since day-light, practicing our national airs of "Hail Columbia," and "Yankee Doodle," which they can perform very well. Children and youths are amusing themselves, and annoying every one else, with fire-crackers, and small rockets.

A great bustle, making reparations for a parade, procession, and oratory. The flags of this, and our own Republic are fraternized. The "Panama Exchange," at the corner of the street leading to the plaza, has a long pole projecting from the arcade, attached to which is a strip of cotton, thus inscribed, with black paint:—

"Let Independence BE OUR BOAST,
Ever mindful What it cost,
Ever greatful for the prize,
Let its Altars reach the skies."

At 10 A.M. the procession was formed, and marshalled, in the Plaza, opposite the Cathedral.— Native officers, with tri-colored ribbons and batons, were galloping about, and I forced my way through the crowd, to see the representation of Americans, in the affair.—Sure enough, there were 6 Yankee Naval uniforms, and friends of mine, and they insisted on my accompanying them; which I did, for a short distance, though I wore a light blouse. If several were surprized to meet here, unexpectedly, that of my friend Rodgers was the greatest, for we had met before, since we parted in the Sierra Nevada, when he was attached to the Relief Party. Occasional showers, and exceedingly warm. A large party left to-day, for Cruces.

I had forgotten to notice, yesterday, the detachment of returned Californians who marched out on foot, early yesterday morning for Cruces. They were from two steamers.—Off they went, in a large body, with blankets and packs; rifles, pistols, and bowie-knives, and long mining boots.—They gave three hearty cheers, as they reached the gate.—This grotesque phalanx, of hardy adventurers, who are well acquainted with the *elephant,* would be tough customers to molest on the route.

At 11 A.M. I accompanied some friends, to the Government Hall, in the Plaza, and listened to an excellent address, by our Consul, which was followed by an explicatione, in Spanish, by a native general officer. The bands in the hall played our National Airs, and the banner of the Two Republics were entwined. Salutes were also fired from the battery, and returned by the shipping.

Our Consul,—Mr. Corwine, gave a general invitation to the Americans, and at 7 P.M. there was a handsome entertainment at his house. From 10 A.M. till 11 P.M. it was very warm, with light showers. Crackers, rockets, Bengal-lights, and other fire-works, with revelry and laughter, continued till late at night.

The people seem to be quite civil, and friendly. I heard a drunken soldier, in the street, sing out "Viva los Americanos!"—American signs are numerous, all over town.

I met a native, dragging a big snake along, tied by a chord around its neck.—The head was gone. It was about 8 feet long, and 18 to 20 inches circumference, at the largest part. It was of a mottled grey color, not unlike some of our rattle-snakes. The native showed me, that about 18 inches, including the head, was gone. I enquired what he intended to do with it? He replied that he would eat it, as it was very good. It came from the interior, where they are not uncommon. As our fare, to-day, has improved, I will notice it:—dinner;—Stewed fresh pork, fried plantains, tough fried beef, fried onions, and raw tomatoes. Dessert, plumb-pudding. The supper of hot cakes, cold meats from dinner, bad coffee, and tolerable fair tea. Some fights, at night, in the streets,—Yankees at the bottom of it.

I am informed that one of the pedestrian-adventurers, who started yesterday morning, for Cruces, a steerage passenger in the Columbus, walked across the Isthmus in long boots, red flannel drawers, loose red flannel shirt, felt hat, and rifle on shoulder—pretty warm work.

July 5th 1851 Awakened at 6 A.M. and started the baggage, for Cruces. At 8 A.M. all the remaining travellers had gone, leaving me alone behind,—awaiting for the agent to close his packages. At 11 ½ A.M., accompanied by Mr. Leavett, (transit agent) we mounted our mules, and started for the gate. I could get neither holsters nor bridle; so tied my pistols together, over the saddle-bow; and hitched a piece of rope around the mules' lower jaw, to guide her.

It is well-known that the road, from Panama, across the Isthmus, was once paved, and some portions of the causeway still remain entire; but most of it, is swept away, or buried in mud. The paving is still good, some distance from the gate. After leaving the gate about 200 yards, we turned to the right. On our left, there was an open space, containing a ruined fountain, and a dilapidated church, of stone, which seems to have been once of considerable importance. A little further on, we rode through a village, of two lines of houses, or rather huts, with mostly colored people. In a couple of miles further the road swept around to the left, being generally of red clay and sand. The sun shone out with great power, and we spurred our mules, in order to compensate for the late starting. Occasionally we passed a native hut, on either side of the road, and mules returning from

Cruces. Hairless dogs and half starved pigs were numerous.

We overtook a Spanish gentleman, on a mule, also travelling over, who spoke some words of English. He is going to New Orleans, to study the English language. Five miles from the City, we passed the train with the U.S. Mail, and I saw our pack-mules with it.—A little further, there was a muleteer reclining beneath a tree, with several packed mules, browsing around him: He hailed us, and on going up, we were informed, that two miles ahead,—at the entrance to a defile, three American brigands were stationed, and armed with revolvers, in wait for stragglers: which was the cause of his stopping,—to wait for more company. As there were three of us, also, we determined that the chances were equal, and proceeded.

The suspicious gorge was soon reached—narrow and deep; and a sort of covered way, of thick foliage. It was muddy, rocky, and sinuous: such a pass as three determined men, with revolvers, might occupy against superior numbers. In some parts, our knees were jostled against one or the other muddy cliff-wall; and I had, occasionally, to raise a foot, in passing a large rock or stump. The mules slipped, staggered, and leaped, through this interesting passage, of several hundred yards. I had sufficient, for hands and head, to preserve my equilibrium and seat; without thinking of banditti, after fairly entering the Pass.

On emerging from the gorge, we rode over small level spaces and undulating surfaces, enclosed by hills, for a short distance; and then entered another defile;—answering as a drain for torrents: it was full of deep pools of mud and water. This passage was, if any thing, more captivating than the first;—being just as crooked as numerous short bends, and right-angled corners, could make it.—Large prostrate trunks of trees lay here and there,—across the top, whose projecting branches and roots kept us constantly ducking our heads, to save our selves, from being unhorsed.—The reeking sides were from 8 to 30 feet high, and in some places, the passage was darkened by the overhanging and woven shrubbery.

Still ascending, About 1 P.M. it commenced raining, and soon after poured down, a perfect deluge, on our devoted heads; accompanied by such thunder and lightning, in blinding flashes and deafening peals, reverberating through the deep gorges and neighboring heights, as are rarely heard even within the tropics. The water ran off my arms and legs, in spouts and frisky fountains; and the old mule laid her ears back, and floundered through it, as if she thought her last hour was now surely come. My chief care, however, was to maintain my seat, and keep my pistols dry, both difficult achievements, under the circumstances of the case. The rain was of short duration.

We passed many return mules, driven by pedestrian natives. The sun occasionally glared upon us as from a reflector; parrots, macaws, and parroquets were constantly flying over, and hopping through the broad foliage, and chattering absurdly; and monkeys and other small animals were heard in the dank forests, alongside, engaged in similar garrulity.

Again we had to thread, narrow and rugged labyrinths—in some places, so contracted, that it was a necessary custom to "halloo" on entering them;—to warn travellers about to enter [the] opposite end of the pass. In several instances, here the walls of the pass were low, I had to throw my body forward, on my mule's neck, to clear a fallen tree, across the top. Fragments of the old Spanish paving, were scattered throughout the gorges; in confused masses; being now stumbling-blocks instead of facilities to the poor mules. Besides which, these narrow passages contained large rocks and huge masses of clay,— fallen from the cliffs; and the intervals were worn in deep round holes by the unceasing travel of mules.

But we shortly entered a gorge—intended to break the monotony of the preceding ones, by its new peculiarities.—The bottom was of that character, called, I believe, in some places,—a *corduroy-road*— loose logs, laid helter-skelter, in mud, for about 50 feet, to the top of a hill. Then a descent, of the same distance, perhaps, but very narrow and crooked.— Steps of stones and earth, deep holes, pools of water, and deep lagoons of red mud; alternating with the loose logs below, and most unship-shape *cross-trees* above. Five resolute men, armed with revolvers and stationed at some angle, in this peculiar passage, could discomfit and capture almost any number attempting to pass.—The foliage above was large and dense, where brigands could secrete themselves, while but one horseman could pass at a time below. In several spots, large masses of earth, rocks, and rush, stood in the centre of the gorge, like islands in the muddy water;—forcing the passage—(for road it could not be called) into branches on either side.

Here and there, where the gorges of the route expanded, I noticed the reed cottages of the natives, with their thatched roofs, peeping from the thick brush and plantain groves, on the eminences; On the top of the *divide*, are three hamlets, some material distances apart, and each has a sign of "The true half-way House." At a native hut, on the left, perched on top of a bank, at the entrance to a defile, a man walked to the edge of the cliff, and asked us in English, Who were coming along? And how many travellers and trains were in the rear? I saw a couple of fellows behind him, and wondered what honest calling these Americans or Englishmen, could find here? What inducement to live in an isolated indian hut, and feed on plantains, in such a climate.

Our Spanish comrade hurried ahead, on hearing interrogatories in English, from cliff, and I told my companion that the case was suspicious, in which he coincided. So I told the fellow, on the bank, that there were many travellers, close in our rear.

Late in the afternoon, at an angle in the road, on the right, I passed a rude wooden cross, decorated with tinsel and ribbons,—opposite to which, on the branch of a tree, hung the sleeve of a white cotton shirt. A bare-footed native coming along, with a budget on his back, and a staff in his hand,—on reaching the cross, doffed his large straw sombrero, made a low bow to it, and proceeded.-

About 5 P.M. my comrade pushed ahead, in a Pass, as evening was closing around us, and he did not like to be caught in these suspicious gorges in the night. My mule was slow, but sure-footed, and I could not urge her to travel faster than she chose to do. At dusk, near the entrance to a deep and dark defile, on my right, about 50 feet high, upon the ban I saw a reed hut, and the dark forms of several men crouching by a fire. I rode near the cliff, and hailed them in Spanish, asking the distance to Cruces? One of them replied, in Spanish, that it was 6 miles, and impossible for me to travel in the night! Another man cried out, "No possible, God d-n, you no can go

Cruces esta night!" I replied, in a determined tone, "Si, possible, Carrahu!" and spurred on to the pass. I thought that those rascals might take a short cut, and head me at some dark turn in the gorge but I was in for it, and there was no use in being skittish.

So I was soon within the walls of the narrow passage, where gloom amounting to darkness obscured every thing.—I had to close my eyes, occasionally, in order to observe the glimmer of the water beneath our feet, when I opened them. I knew not the ramifications of the black pass, but was sure that the mule did; so I dropped the substitute for a bridle upon her shoulders, and secured my seat upon her, by clinging to the saddle, before and behind. The faithful creature, however, went on, plunging, jumping, and stumbling; occasionally rubbing one of my knees against the muddy bank, but bearing me safely through darkness and danger. Had I been unhorsed, in that muddy cold glen, my situation would have been enchanting. I did not now fear robbers, for they could see no better in the dark than myself: and besides, it was not the hour for them to expect travellers on the road. We were rapidly descending; and at about 8 P.M. I was rejoiced to hear American voices, ascending from the town of Cruces.-

The gorge expanded, and I was no longer in total darkness. Soon the hillsides became open space; and while listening to the sounds of laughter, in the town below, a rustle and cracking of sticks, on the cliff near my right, (25 or 30 feet high) caused me to look around, when a panther prowling there uttered so wild a cry, that my frightened mule laid back her ears, and ran down the mountain-slope, like Tam O'Shanter's mare, when closely pressed by the witches,—causing me to hold on the saddle, with might and main, like Johnny Gilpin, expecting momentarily to be projected far over her head, into the middle of next week. On reaching the plain, near the head of the town I managed to catch the rope, and check her speed.

I had now only a short ride, of a few rods, and was about to turn, for a street, which was distinctly marked by a line of light, when a small black animal in the road, which I thought was a young bear, caused the mule to shy, and again start off at full speed, carrying me rapidly into the town; until I brought up at the "American Hotel," and dismounted, leaving half a dozen natives fighting about possession of the mule, though I told them who was the owner.

This so-called Hotel, is an American built frame house, rough and naked in the interior, and kept by a New Yorker. It was crowded, and among the sojourners I had the pleasure of again seeing Major Hobby and Mr. Seymour, besides several other acquaintances.

I was weary and hungry, and obtained something to eat, for 50 cents, and then was shown up into a loft—or entire upper floor of the house, completely covered with cots and sleepers. For another 50 cents I had a cot, and sound repose: The night was drizzly, and cool enough to make a blanket comfortable.

I had put some rolls of bread in my pockets at Panama, but the rain had reduced them to a soft pulp.

July 6th (SUNDAY) Flying clouds and very warm.

A miserable breakfast, and we could not tolerate the stuff they called coffee, so waited till a pot of tea was made. Another half dollar for this meal.

After breakfast I walked up the street,—and on

the same side, a few doors above the hotel, I observed a man dead, with the door of a hut. On approaching the reed-formed tenement, I observed that he was extended on a table, in the centre of the room. He was dark, nearly negro; clad in a full dress-suit of black cloth with black silk stock, white standing collar, and wore black patent leather boots, and his jaws were tied up with a broad black ribbon. On each side of him a candle was burning and several natives—of both sexes, sat around upon the earthy floor. They do not, it appears, use coffins here: but carry the body to the grave in a kind of coffin-bier.—(*Coffin*) One of these stood outside the door;—decently covered with faded purple velvet.

Silently leaving the house of mourning, I proceeded up the street to the church, which stands on an elevated plateau, at the head of the two principal streets, in an open space which I presume is called the 'Plaza." Men, in rows, three deep, were kneeling in the broad doorway, which is the gable-end. These devotees were performing the usual genuflections, and whenever the priest at the altar rang a small bell, they bowed their heads in the dust.

When the services were concluded, a young man of olive complexion, who, as I was informed, was the Acalde, convened all the males in front of the church, and read to them a long list of ordinances of the government, chiefly relating to duties, and transportation, on the routes. About a dozen men listened very attentively to him, and occasionally desired explanations of certain parts. When they dispersed, I walked into the mouldy old church, up to a long bench, which was placed mid-way between the Altar and Portal, and took a seat. Two creole women were at the foot of the altar, apparently doling penance. One knelt upon the lower step, with outstretched arms, audibly muttering her pater nosters. The annoying task imposed upon her, seemed to be to repeat a certain number of Prayers, with extended arms. Her arms became fatigued, and gradually sank, and then she would raise them again, with a deep sigh, and occasionally bow her head, and kiss the dirty edge of the step before her.

It took her about 15 minutes to get through this ordeal, when she arose, made her obesience to a mutilated wooden image, in a cobwebby niche above, drew her serrappa around her head and shoulders, and walked off. Another female then entered, dropped a courtesey to another dilapidated figure full of rags, tinsel, and cobwebs; which appeared to me to have been the representation of some prelate. She then kissed a step of the Altar, blessed herself, and also retired. Being left alone, I walked around this very barn-looking church, to examine it and the mouldy remains of its decorations. The floor, was of earth, and sides and corners full of trash, such as rude frames for transparencies, palanquins, wooden crosses, mutilated wooden crucifixes, broken benches, and coffin-biers, rags, tinsel, and cobwebs. The Altar was chiefly of wood, and very dirty. Ragged common paintings, of Saints and the Virgin, dressed in cheap callicoes, which were dropping from them in moist decay, in unison with the *Irish drapery* [cobwebs?] around.

The plateau in front of the church, was once paved, about 20 paces wide to the front, where it broke off perpendicularly. Between the church and the front of the pavement, on one side, stood a rotten wooden rack or gallows, to which were suspended three very old, warped and split bells, of small size.

One of them, was in fact, half gone, another had lost a large piece, and the third and best, was cracked. To ring them, a boy struck the best one with a pebble. The church is of stone, and stuccoed.—Roof of wood, open in several places, and threatening to fall in. the Buccaneers burnt this town once, when it was a considerable place, hence the unhappy condition of the bells.

The female who had performed the spread-eagle penance within, was now on the platform, outside. She hailed an adjacent house, and the boy whom I had seen ringing the cracked bell with a pebble, came out, bearing in his hand a pair of wooden clogs, which he handed to the penitent—when she knelt, took off her slippers, and strapped on these antique-looking sandals. The fore-part of the soles and the heels were several inches high, like those made for a person with a contracted leg; but taking her slippers in her hand, she walked down the street upon these mud dodgers, with much independence of manner. Another woman passing, looked down at her frail sister's feet.

On the pavement, on the opposite side to the bells, near the church, lay a couple of long and handsomely embellished brass guns, about the calibre of 6 and 9 pounders. One is French, and dated 1737; the other is Spanish, and dated 1809. Near these lay a very ancient looking iron anchor, half-corroded away with rust.—It might have once served a Galleon. About 40 paces in front of the church stands a very neat white structure, with roof of stone, and heavy iron door, resembling a large burial vault: but it is only for the temporary burial of English specie, on its way from Panama to England.

There are 3 long parallel streets, in this place,

being the principal ones, which run down from the church, near the bank of the Chagres river. They are closely built up with reed and thatched houses, and there are a few transverse streets. The town, at a distance, looks like a tolerably symetrical arrangement of hay-cocks.

On my return from a short detour of observation, the defunct darkie was borne in procession, to the burial place,—nearly in the rear of the church.— The padre, with crucifix, led the way, followed by the bearers and crowd, in no particular order. On reaching the grave, they set the bier down, took off the cover, and then canted it so that the dead body rolled into the grave. The bearers then jumped in upon it, and danced about, to straighten it, (perhaps to make sure of his death) and a bottle of wine or aqua-audenta [agua ardiente] was passed around, and the funeral ceremonies concluded with laughter and merriment. There are few white natives here. At night groups gathered around tables in the street, with candles burning, playing Monte, and other games. There is also a negro Billiard Salloon here, which no doubt contributes to the very refined sable sympathies of this miserable place. Heat oppressive, and the town a miserable place.

On awakening, and sitting up in my cot, I was astonished to see a young woman sitting up also in the next cot to me, and fastening the back of her dress; while all around were upwards of a hundred men perhaps, in every stage of rising and dressing. My evident astonishment compelled me to observe to her, that I thought it a very unpleasant predicament for a young lady to be placed in, and she replied that it was; but she had become accustomed to such inconveniences, having crossed the Isthmus several times! I was afterwards informed that she was the wife of the man who recently robbed a jeweller, and a priest, In Panama, and then fled across the Isthmus. She is still in search of him, and says that if she does not meet him in New Orleans, she will proceed from thence to New York. This lady's baggage with some other, has been carried by mistake or villainy, to Gorgona, pulled by four yellow half-naked natives, and owned and commanded by a Long Island negro named Williams, is to take five of us and our luggage down the river to Chagres. Williams is a clever accommodating fellow; has served his three years in the U.S.N. and his boatmen are also very civil. We pay five dollars each-

My companion, of the Express, and two other passengers were acquaintances, and we were prepared to drift down as pleasantly as possible,— having to aid us in this particular, a box of ale, several bottle of claret, and a couple of Brandy, with crackers, cheese, cigars, pipes and tobacco. All hands were cheerful and agreeable, and we drifted down stream right merrily. Captain Williams handled the tiller, and had to steer clear of snags, sawyers, and sand banks, and guide us judiciously down rapids. The rowing was easy, or at least, appeared to be easily performed. We twice grounded, however, on banks, when each time the boatmen leaped into the water and soon shoved off again.

The river is exceedingly crooked, and enclosed between high hills, covered with thick forests and dense shrubberry, down to the water's edge.—Palms, bananas, rich vines, reeds, majestic plants, and beautiful flowers, crowd upon the stream in lavish luxuriance, and the reflection of this mass of verdure, gives the water a rich green and gorgeous aspect.

Florid birds of the parrot kind, and others of brilliant plumage, are constantly flying over, and chattering, in their ridiculous Punch and Judy style of colloquy. I noticed several species of king-fishers,—some very small, and one of a large size. Herons,—blue, and white, and vultures with white shoulders, occasionally added to the diversity of the scene. Monkeys were holding their peculiar confabulations in the woods, at once scream and expectorative. Saw a small alligator, and fired a pistol at him, causing him to grin horribly a ghastly smile, at my folly.

We passed several canoes and barges going up and late in the afternoon we reached Palenkena, where lay a very small steam-boat, just arrived from Chagres, full of California passengers, amongst whom were several wifes, with their little children, going out to seek their husbands. The passengers were taking boats to ascend the river. Soon another small iron Steamer passed, also filed with passengers, endeavoring to get higher up. These little steamers are called the "Milly" and the" Swan".

July 7th About 1 A.M. our gondola ran alongside the bank at Gatoon,—in the midst of a flotilla of barges, launches, & canoes: most of whom were bound up river. We rested here about two hours, and pushed off again. Our passengers, obtained some sleep, in such postures as we could best select for the purpose, where there was a little choice. At about 6 A.M. we reached Chagres, and hauled in to the bank, through legions of boats and canoes, and all sorts of people.

Quickly did we make our way ashore, in search of a breakfast, and was amazed at meeting so many acquaintances and fellow travellers. The principal house of entertainment is called the "Irvine House", and fronts the landing, about 20 paces from it. Breakfast was nearly ready when we reached the house, and a crowd stood around the long table. At the raising of the hand-bell, they rushed into the seats, precluding us most effectually from any chance there, so we walked out and continued around the point to where we were told we could obtain a good breakfast.—We soon found the snug little shanty of old Joe Prince, and in a few minutes were regaled with an excellent and hearty breakfast, for which we paid 75 cents each.

The distances over the Isthmus, are as follows:—
From Panama, to Cruces—25 miles, mule travel.
By water; From Cruces to Palenkina 20 do. , Palenkina to Gatoon 30 do., Gatoon to Chagres *10 do.* Total *85 miles*

After breakfast, I accompanied a few friends across the harbor, to the old town. Passing through the narrow dirty streets, I saw Mr. Wright, who was waiting there, for the arrival of steamer for New Orleans. We were paddled across in a canoe. The main streets have once been well paved. The houses are similar to those of Cruces, except a few dilapidated adobes, and two or three American frames, of two storys. Many American & English signs indicative of eating and drinking establishments, such as "Jack of Clubs," "Davy Crockett,"and Several Billiard houses, with black gamblers around the tables. We followed a street, nearly parallel with the water, to the foot of the tall hill on which stands the moss-grown old castle. Then turned to the right,— in another street, followed it a short distance, and then to the left on a moist and crooked path. The soil here is of the richest black loam. A slight ascent, of about one mile, along the margin of a deep tangled glen, brought us to a beautiful mountain brook. Our guide was my worthy friend Capt Hunter U.S. Revenue Service. He had bathed in this place several years ago. The stream is in some parts 30 to 40 feet wide, but very shallow; and traverses a deep dell, fringed and overshadowed by rank grass and weeds, jungle, and damp forests of large trees, festooned with luxuriant vines, and clothed in mosses. A large number of parasitic plants are here. The bed of the stream is a soft sand stone, worn full of holes, some of considerable depth. The water is clear and cool; a perfect luxury in such a sultry climate. Moisture was weeping upon us from the thick tropical foliage over head; colored women were engaged at every accessable part of the bank, washing clothes; and the slopes were covered with vestments of every kind. On returning, we met several male natives, with machettas, apparently going up in the hills to cut fuel. At the end of the lower street, near the landing, I saw a treasure vault exactly like that at Cruces, and was told that it belonged to the same concern.

Quite a number of small craft are in the harbor and boats and canoes innumerable. There were also several square-rigged craft,—mostly brigs. The Consuls all reside in the old town. The new town is almost entirely American, covering the narrow tongue of land which protects the harbor from the sea. At Meridian I transferred my small amount of luggage to a large row-boat, manned by Englishmen, and full of other returned Californians. We pulled out about 2 miles from land, to the Steamer Brother Jonathan. The swell increased till we reached the ship, where it was considerable, and required some adroit agility to get safely on board, to find my highly esteemed Comrades du voyage, on the other side, who were also to accompany me in this voyage.-

There lay at anchor near us, the British Mail Steamer Trent,—a fine-looking vessel; and Steamer Alabama. On looking down the coast, we saw, standing around a point of land, some 12 ms. off, a small steamer,—towing a brig; perhaps from Porto Bello. A barque is seen on the horizon; and an English cutter sloop lies near us.

The old castle, on the eminence, is a mass of grey stone and dark green moss and shrubbery.—The fortification and the hill on which it stands, are blended in a piece of grey stone and green verdure. Only here and there a short line of coping, an embrasure, or red tiles of a house-top, serve to convince one that there is any of man's work there. I regretted much that I had not visited the old castle. The ruins are exceedingly picturesque, and its history quite interesting. It was once captured by the English Buccaneer, Morgan, who managed to get guns upon the height in the rear, overlooking the castle, and thus reduced. Since then the Spaniards fortified that height also, and the grey and moss-covered lines of that outwork are now all of apiece with the castle and hill. The Buccaneers first captured Panama, then crossed the Isthmus, burning Cruces in the way, and tearing up the paving, to prevent rapid pursuit.

The pedestrian party who left Panama on the 3d joined others already at Chagres, and they took possession of the old castle, to celebrate the 4th— They contrived to clean out several of the heavy old brass canon, fired a salute of 100 guns, and ran up the Stars and Stripes over the ruined walls, where they had never before been displayed. The authorities of the town expressed great indignation at this innovation of the rough Yankees.

When we had descended the Chagres river to where the water was brackish, our boatmen became thirsty, and pulled the boat into a deep glen on the left, where a delightful rill of pure water leaped sparklingly through the foliage, into the river. We entered a little cove, and the men drank from the brook. In the sandy bottom of the cove I saw several large crabs, with one immense claw, like the minute crabs familliarly known as fiddlers. Capt. Williams says that this stream is 3 miles above Chagres.

I am informed that Major Hobby was robbed, at Cruces, of an over coat, and Capt. Moore, of funds, abstracted from his carpet-bag. Capt. Squires, of the Brother Jonathan, informs me that robberies and murders are frequent at Chagres, and the Yankees have established Lynch law in consequence.

The Brother Jonathan is a good sea-boat, with a strong engine, but her accommodations are inconvenient and inappropriate for such service, in such climes: And no regulations usually on board such vessels are enforced. Her burthen is 1400 tons

    Commander Heber Squires,
    Sailing Master, E. McKeige
    H. Dennison—1st Officer
- Miller—2nd Do-
- H. Sandford—Chf: Engineer
- Wm Mills—Purser
- Lemuel Wales—M.D. surgeon

She has on board, 61 first class passengers, 7— second class, 156 steerage and 25 *uncertain* passengers: Total 249 passengers.

The officers of the ship are a very clever set of

men.—Several steerage passengers exchanged their tickets—paying the difference, for places in the cabin.

My kind comrade across the Isthmus—Leavett, left the ship for shore, to return to Panama. About 3 P.M. we dined.

At 4 P.M. the swell increased, and the ship rolled heavily. A sail-boat brought on board our esteemed friend Judge Jones; and Judge Lyons, being in the boat, returned to shore, to await the steamer for New Orleans.

Many years ago, in my rambles over South America and the W. Indies, and Brazil, I had visited Chagres, in a Venezuelan Sloop of War, little dreaming of ever seeing it again.

About 6 P.M. we were heartily glad to find the steamer under way. At 7, the bell summoned us to supper. Hot weather, and a damp and dirty ship. Rain and lightning.

A heavy sea, deep rolling of the ship, and suffocating heat below, entirely precluded all ideas of sleep, in the state-rooms

About 11 P.M. passed a steamer, which from the color of her lights, is supposed to be the 'Crescent City' going into the Chagres.

Heinrich Schlieman—
1851

On the ninth of March at 5 o'clock in the morning we discovered the coast of Central America and at 10 o'clock A.M. we landed 1 mile from Chagres. There came immediately boats alongside, but it took nearly two hours ere I could get away with my baggage, the rush of the passengers being very great. The sea was going very high and not without great danger to lose my luggage or to crush my skull did I get ashore.

    Among all the miserable places I have met with, and it happened to me to see many in different parts of the world, I must give the palm to Chagres. On the left-hand side of the Chagres River live the natives; their houses are mere huts or shelters; four poles are rammed in the ground and entertwined with bamboo-cane, of which equally consists the thatch. One or two hammocks and an iron pot, that is all you see in the interior. On the other side of the river are established a few small wooden houses, occupied by Americans; the whole ground-floors of these houses are filled up with stores of liquors, fruits, clothes, etc. I was immediately busy to engage boats, in which, however, I could not succeed, my fellow-passengers who went before me having taken away all good boats, and therefore thought it best to go by the steamer, its possessors having engaged to dispatch us without the least loss of time in small boats from the place where the steamer would stop. I left Chagres at 1 ½ o'clock; I had about 23 fellow passengers; though we went at the rate of only 2 ½ knots an hour, we soon passed the boats, which had advanced us. The Chagres River is very narrow, and so shallow, that with the greatest difficult only it is possible for small boats to go up, the more so as thousands and thousands of snags (old stems) look up out of the water at every step, and impede the progress.

Nothing more imposing and charming can be imagined than the banks of the Chagres River, covered with incessant and impenetrable forests of Corozo de Lola, orange and limon trees, cocanut palms, palms of corozo de Lola, guayabos, bamboo-cane, leaves of chichica and thousands of others. We stop for some refreshment at Gatun village, consisting of two or three miserable huts of natives. In the evening at 6 ½ o'clock we stop for the night at Vamos Vamos. Eight of my fellow passengers sat gambling the whole night, whilst 12 others went to sleep under a carrozo tree close to a house, and myself with two others, we got hammocks for which we were to pay about 3/6 each. Though the house where we stopped was without any walls and had but a very light cover of dried leaves, yet the heat was insufferable, and I was perspiring the whole night, as if I were lying in a Russian steambath; besides, the noise was immense all the night long, and when at last I fell asleep for one moment, I was immediately again awoken by swine or children who hurt against me. After the heat of the day and the first part of the night, a cold dew rises towards 3 o'clock and from then till sunrise it is quite chilly. In the night I saw many sinister looking natives around me and had consequently continually my revolving pistol in one hand and my dagger-knife in the other. We started in the morning at 5 ½, but scarcely had we proceeded for 1 mile farther, when, owing to a rapid and the shallowness of the water, we were to stop with the steamer altogether and got into the 2 boats, which had been attached to the steamer; it was at that time raining very hard and we got very wet.

The large boat in which I was with about 12 others and the most part of the baggage was rowed by 4 suspicious looking negro-Spaniards, whilst the other boat was managed by 2 negro-Frenchmen, natives of Domingo. At 6 o'clock we met an opposition steamer, 3 times larger than ours and quite differently built, for she had an enormous wheel behind, and had two large decks the one above the other. She had no passengers, for as it takes merely 12 hours to go down from Gorgona to Chagres in open boats, everybody prefers the latter to steamers. Shortly afterwards we came to a point where the railway touches the river, and where a few wooden houses were erected for the accomodation of the railway workmen; about 40 of these came out when we passed; their pale and emaciated faces clearly denoted their sufferings under the horrible effect of this poisonous climate. Under the influence of frequent rain and of a constant heat during the day time of from 100 to 110 degrees (scale of Farenheid) the growth of the vegetation is extremely rapid and causes a strong miasma, which together with the evaporation of the thousand swamps, and ponds with standing water, and the miasma arising from the discomposition of animal and vegetable matter infests the air, and certainly this climate is the most unhealthy on the globe. The constant tremendous thirst, which torments the new arriver, can in no way be quenched, for the water is as warm as the air, and full of insects; to kill these latter and to make the water drinkable, it is always being mixed with brandy, which keeps the nerves in continual excitement and weakens the body. The most beautiful fruit of the tropical clime grows here in wilderness, but it is poison to everyone except to the natives, who are accustomed to it from their earliest youth up.

The natives of this country may be divided in three classes, vis., in Indians of fair brown complexion, usually regular features and long beautiful hair; in negro-Spaniards, who are a mixture of negroes with Spaniards, with curled short black hair, very irregular monkey-like features and thick projecting lips; and finally, in Creoles, or descendents of the Spaniards, who settled here in the beginning of the 16th century. These Creoles have not mixed with any other blood, they are general speaking of fair complexion, but of course sunburnt. The Creoles speak the Spanish language with a beautiful accent, and even in old Spain I never heard this language better spoken than here. The Indians speak also very good and at all events better than the northern provinces of Spain, whilst the negro-Spaniards speak a sort of mixed language.

The railroad (ferro-carril) is being built not from Chagres, but from a bay 3 miles below it, where vessels of every burthen can land. The natives being too lazy for such work, all the laborers are Americans, who come here under an engagement of free passage, housing and victuals and a pay of 35 dollars or 7 pounds sterling per month, and an obligation that after 100 days' work they are to be transported to California or to any other port of the U. S. which they may desire. But with very rare exceptions the Americans cannot stand the climate here for 100 days; for the most part, they catch the fever within the first month after their arrival and die ere they are 6 weeks here. The survivors are of ruined health and disabled for life from enjoying the happiness. We can therefore say that this railway is being built upon the bones of the Americans.

On the 10 March at about 11 o'clock a.m., we landed at some Indian huts to take refreshments; wishing to give to my body a little wholesome exersize, I climbed up a hundred feet high coconut palm tree and threw down some fruit to my thirsty fellow-passengers; afterwards I went up in a orange-tree and shook off hundreds of oranges to my comrades. The Indians charged us a picayune* (1/2 dime) for each cup coffee or milk. The farther we went up the river, the more difficult became the passage, and almost every 5 minutes the negroes were to jump in the water and to drag us over some sandbank. I should certainly not have liked to follow their example, for the river is full of alligators (caymanas) and iguanas (these latter are very like the alligators but have a much longer tail and are of less size). Alligators in the Chagres River are usually from 3 to 10 feet long and seldom more; in a river near Panama they are said to be to 40 feet long by 4 and 5 feet broad. The rays of the burning sun were falling perpendicular upon us, and extenuated by thirst, we landed at 4 o'clock again at some huts for refreshments; all what we could get was some bad black coffee of the worst description. Gorgona was said to be only 4 miles off, and about 9 fellow passengers and I resolved to go afoot. But not being acquainted with the road we soon missed the way and found ourselves in the thicket of the wood without being able to find our way either forward or backward. With immense pain we broke our way through thorny bushes and bahuco and at last we came to some place in the river, whence we saw our boat not far off. I went in it again, whilst my companions went anew for Gorgona conducted by an Indian boy. At last at 10 o'clock in the evening we arrived at Gorgona, a most miserable place consisting of a few wooden houses with gorgeous denominations of "Union Hotel," and "Panama Railroad Hotel." I stopped at the former and received victuals and accomodations of the worst description, though I was to pay very dear; beef is very bad, and I cannot eat it at all; ham is so salted that I were to drink myself to death if I touched it. The only thing I could take was sour stewed apples and weak tea. They located me for the night in a small garret in which besides me slept upwards of 30 persons; the miasma and heat arising from so many people gathered together in a small apartment prevented me from sleeping. In the morning of the 11th March I hired 3 mules, of which one a saddle mule for me and the other two for my baggage; the owner of the mules, Debursio Haramillo went afoot with me. We started at 6 ½ a.m. Although I was to suffer cruelly under the perpendicular rays of the burning sun, yet this journey from Gorgona to Panama is most surely one of the most interesting that I ever made in my life. The way is just broad enough for one mule to pass, but from time to time the traveller encounters little windings and open places, which make it possible for two mules to pass. To prevent embarrassment which would be caused by the encountering of mules going to or coming from Panama, the mule-driver, on entering a narrow pass, always cries at the pitch of the noise in order to give a signal to those who might come in opposite direction. The way leads over the Cordilleras Andes mountains, which are extremely steep and covered with innumerable stones of all possible size, between which it is very difficult indeed to penetrate. They say that Fernando de Cortes has in 1516 established a turnpike road across the mountains, but its traces have almost entirely disappeared. After having with the greatest difficulty reached the top of a steep mountain, the traveller involuntarily shudders when he looks down into the valley which lies 2000 feet down under his feet and into which he is led by a rough path one foot broad and every now and then interrupted by large stones and deep holes. Nothing more beauteous can be imagined, than to behold from the top of one mountain the magnificent production of nature down to the bottom of the deep valley, and abruptly up again 2000 feet high to the top of another mountain. These thousands of feet high and many many miles long amphitheaters made by the hand of nature are filled up with every specimen of southern vegetation. In all their grand majesty the higuerone, the corozo de lola, rice palm, coconut palms, and a thousand others are lifting to the clouds their gorgeous tops, whilst the beautiful orange and limon trees and chichica leaves, as if humbling themselves before their grand neighbors, are offering to the fatigued and exhausted traveller their beautiful fruit. Parrots, cacadous, canaries, paraos, and thousands of other birds of the most beautiful plumage were flying around us. Thousands of monkeys from one foot in size to man's height were playing about and crying in the trees, and the whole nature seemed to sing the praise of the almighty. The Isthmus of Panama is an immense Eden in which the descendants of Adam and Eve seem to have retained the manners and customs of their primitive forefathers; for they go quite naked, and live upon the fruit which the splendid tropical vegetation puts around them in magnificent abundance. Their chief characteristic is a horrible laziness, which does not permit them to occupy themselves with anything; they cannot find themselves happier than lying in their hammocks and eating and drinking. They are very fantastic, but ready to commit any crime which might tend either to enrich their property or to take vengeance for what they think offence. Nobody goes here without being well armed with a 5 or 6 barrelled pistol and a long dagger knife. In coming up the river Chagres, and crossing afterwards the Cordilleras Andes from Gorgona to Panama, the traveller is at every moment disgusted at the horrible smell of animal matter which strikes his organs; this smell arises frequently from the discomposition of mules which fall on the road, or of wild beasts such as iguana, but alas, still much more frequently from dicomposition of travellers murdered on the road by the hand of the natives. When these latter stop for the night with a boat full of passengers, they use to select for their halt a place little above some snag and some rapid; then in the night when all are asleep, the boatmen fling with all their power suddenly the boat down the rapid upon the snag, so that the boat capsizes and all hands perish with the exception of the natives, who are prepared for it and share their spoil. Often, when they are unsuccessful in their attempts to drown their passengers, they stab or shoot them to death and throw them over the banks of the river in the thicket, where the corpses are consumed by insects and by buzzards, which can be seen in myriads on the way from Chagres here.

On the way from Gorgona to Panama they equally shoot or stab them, and throw them down in the abyss, where never a living human being has put his foot. About 16 to 18 individuals of great respectability and very large fortune having a few days ago been killed in the most atrocious manner by the natives on the Chagres River, and their bodies partly thrown in the river and partly burried on the bank of the river, so that the arms and legs looked wide out of the water, and were horribly mutilated by the buzzards, the scorn of the Americans residing in this place was roused to the highest degree; a petition was made to the governor, and a party of Americans accompanied by some soldiers went immediately down to Chagres in pursuit of the murderers. They got hold of the latter, who were brought in here on the day of my arrival (11 March), and will be shot in a few days. Had it not been for the stringent exertion of the Americans, nobody here would have taken the slightest notice of the murder.

The Tropics seem to be the fatherland of the vegetable world; every plant, every tree of Europe I find here, a thousand times more grand, more beautiful. The butterflies have here almost the size of a pigeon, and are of the most beautiful colors in blue and yellow.

I arrived here at Panama on the 11 March at 3 in the afternoon and stopped at the Louisiana Hotel, which (except in Chagres and Gorgona) is the dearest and worst I ever met with in my travels, but the best in this city. Panama is a most miserable dirty place, with about 2000 inhabitants, of whom certainly ¼ are Americans, 1/2 negro-and Indian-Spaniards, and ¼ Spanish Creoles. The streets are narrow, and have the common sewer in the midst, which is very convenient in the rainy season. The houses are all built so as to hang some six to eight feet over in the streets in order to protect against rain and against the burning sun. It is indescribably hot here, and all day long I perspire as if I were sitting in a Russian steam bath. The perspiration excites the thirst, and I know no means to quench it; for the only thing I can drink here without fear to poison myself is brandy and water.

Panama was built about 8 miles from here in 1516 by Fernando de Cortes, and about 250 years ago it had a flourishing commerce and about 100,000 inhabitants. About 200 years ago it was overtaken and devasted by pirates, and the whole population was murdered; only a few fled and rebuilt afterwards the present miserable town. The soldiers here are all colored people and are said to be the greatest rascals: as their employ is to contribute to public safety, so their crimes pass under the mantle. They go barefeeted and look like rovers with their old roasted [rusted] guns. The government seat is in Bogota, about 1000 miles from here. Here are printed twice a week two English papers (called the Panama Star and the Panama Echo) and one Spanish (called el Panameño). In my hotel I have to sleep together with 6 other persons, and the heat of the apartment is certainly 110 degrees, though we keep all doors all the night wide open. Windows and window-glass are things quite unknown here in Panama. Every room of the houses opens by large doors upon galleries. Good Panama straw-hats cannot be bought here.

On the 13th at 7 ½ p.m. I went to the theater, a small roughly made building, which resembles more a barn than a theater. As usual in Spanish theaters I was to pay first for admission and then for my seat (6 reals for the former and 2 reals for the latter). I got a place in the pit, which instead of chairs was filled up with bad banks [benches]. They represented "El Alcalde de Salamanca" and "La familia improvisada," and the play being to the benefit of the poor, the house was crowded to excess. There were many Spanish "belles" in the theater; they have black hair, black eyes, yellow pale complexion, but generally very interesting features. There were equally a large number of stout colored ladies in the house, who, with their blunt strong features presented a great contrast against the fine and thin Spanish ladies. Under the influence of this burning climate the Spanish beauties fade still far quicker than the Americans. On my left were sitting two young Spaniards, and I employed all my power of conversation to gather from them as much as possible useful information about this country and the mode of its government. But I found their education on a very low degree, and all I could learn from them was, that a president stands at the head of the government; that the country is divided into about 30 provinces, and that each province sends 2 representatives and 1 senator to Congress, which takes place once a year at Bogotà, and lasts 3 months. This latter place, though only about 1000 miles from here, takes about 20 days to the traveller, for the way leads continually through the Cordilleras Andes, and is connected with immense danger and hardships, as it goes sometime over 12,000 feet high mountains through eternal snow, and then again through desserts under the burning sun of the tropics. The characteristic of the Spaniard in this country is a great inclination to the frivolous and amusing, a great laziness, and a great lightness of character. Everybody wears night and day a dagger-knife with him, and besides a pistol, when going out of town. As could be foreseen, the actors and actresses plaid very bad, knew very badly their parts, and the prompter's voice could always distinctly be heard. In the coffe-house opposite the theater I got the best coffee that I ever tasted since I left Liverpool; in the coffee-room is written "Aqui non se fia."

On the 14th March early in the morning, I hired together with a fellow passenger two mules for $3 a peace, and set off to the place where the city of Panama had formerly been. With the utmost difficulty and cruel sufferings under the burning sun we traced the mules' tracks through forests, underwood and thickets and arrived after 1 ½ hours ride to the sea-shore in sight of and not far from the ruins of old Panama. On the sea coast we had again to battle and struggle with thousands of difficulties and hardships; the heat of the sun was so great, that we could scarcely breathe; our mules were always sinking deep in the loose sand; sometimes we came to places where our beasts fell to the belly in the mud, then again had we to find our way through large and pointed pieces of rocks, where a single false step of the mule would have brought instantaneous death to his rider. Then again had we to descend and to drive our mules over high and steep rocks. At last we arrived and were very disappointed to find but very little to satisfy our curiosity. The old city has about 200 years ago entirely been devastated and destroyed by the Buccaneers. In this burning heat, the dicomposition is as it were keeping pace with the vegetation, and thus little or nothing can be seen of the old city. Here and there was visible something of an old wall or the ruins of some houses; then a stone bridge over a small canal and at last a steeple; the walls, though composed of granite stones and cement, were covered with thousands of trees of all dimensions and I saw them to 100 feet high.; I don't know how trees can grow from out a stone wall, and I cannot cease to wonder at the splendid vegetation of the Tropics. The walls of the steeple were equally all over covered with underwood. Judging by the ruins, the old town must have had from 80 to 100,000 inhabitants. Fatigued and exhausted by hardship and thirst, we found with the utmost difficulty our way to the end of the ruins, where we rested a ½ hour in a forest of orange-trees, which had certainly formerly been a park, and had served as place for refreshment and recreation to the inhabitants of old Panama. In a moat near the wall I saw an alligator of more than 7 feet length. Myriads of musquitos trouble here both men and beasts, and thousands of iguanas which come forth at every pace disgust the view of the visitor to this country.

On the way home we met still much more difficulty than on going out, for the tide was fast running up, and sometimes it rushed upon us with great fury. At last, we reached an Indian house, where we put up for some refreshment; but there was no fruit to be got, and all we could obtain was a little bad water which we swallowed away to satisfy our burning thirst. At 2 o'clock we came home; our beasts were quite exhausted with fatigue, and no spurring with the heels or beating with the whip could prevail upon them to go anything faster than at a slow pace.

On the 15th March, [1851], at 10 o'clock in the morning I got my luggage carried down on negroes' back to the sea-coast; another negro brought it in the boat, and as the latter could not quite come up to the shore, I got myself also carried on negroes' shoulders in it. We had to wait about 1 hour in the boat, and only came on board the steamer "Oregon" at 11 ¾. This steamer has very good accomodations, and pleases me a good deal better than the Crescent City. There is only one deck, covered with canvass, and no supper deck; the saloon serves all at once as assembly-room and dining hall. The staterooms and berths are very nice and clean.

16 March. We started yesterday by 5 ½, for it took a long time to take all the passengers and luggage on board. We steered S. W. Taboga island in sight. It was a delightful evening. A fresh sea breeze had cooled the air. Full moon was shining perpendicular upon us, and such is her brightness here in the Tropics that hardly a single star was perceptible on the cloudless sky.

Nothing excells the beauty of Taboga island with its thousands of feet high mountains covered with forests of palm trees, orange trees, when seen from on board a steamer in a moonlight night; nothing more majestic than the aspect of the calm ocean when reflecting the full moon in the Tropics. Till a late hour all passengers were on deck and enjoyed the fresh evening air together with the splendid spectacle of nature. I asked for a bath, but had no little difficulty to get it, the colored man, who takes care of it, being just as indolent as he is lazy and arrogant. The table on board the Oregon is far from what it was on board the Crescent City, for there being no ice on board, we have no means to preserve fresh meat; all dishes of meat which are brought on the table consist therefore of salt proc and corned beef. But I see we have got 3 living oxen on board, which most likely will be slaughtered to supply us when we run shorter of meat. We have about 100 passengers in the first and about 40 in the second cabin; we have all to take the meals at the same table, and the latter being but very short, ½ of the passengers sat first and the rest afterwards. The tea and coffee is most excellent on board this steamer. The staterooms are very small; I have F where I am together with two others.

In the night the heat was intolerable, and neither of us could sleep, though we all lay naked. Unfortunately, we could not open the window, owing to the spray of the sea, our stateroom being close to the wheel. Though ventilators have been put to operate all through and over the ship, yet the heat is awful. We all go in the thinnest possible clothes and with large straw-hats. Our Captain Pearson and a lady-passenger are caught by and suffering from Panama-fever. This morning I experienced again much difficulty to get a few buckets of seawater for my bath, for which I have now agreed with the negro to pay always 50 cts. All the morning we have been in sight of the mountainous coast of the American continent, and I think by 12 o'clock we shall come out of the Bay of Panama and come in the open ocean. It is a hot and calm day. Off Panama we met yesterday the English ship "Antelope," formerly a steamer, now converted into a sailing-vessel, which arrived in 70 days from San Francisco with passengers.

During my stay at Panama I visited the Mass in the Catholic church, and was a little disgusted at the blind fanaticism of these ignorant people. The Catholic priests of this country are said to be all greatly subjected to despondencies and dissipation; nothing more shocking than the stupid features of a Catholic priest, worn out and emaciated by prostitution. One of the ecclesiastics who officiated had about 4 months ago made an attack upon the pudor of a girl less than 9 months old and effected to rape her. For this outrage he was merely condemned to 3 months' emprisonment, and had only last week left prison to continue his profligate life. In the foregoing pages I forgot to insert that on the 13th inst. I visited the Governor of Panama, who received me with great politeness, and with whom I had a long conversation. To-day (Sunday 16 March) we were according to the bulletin stuck up on deck latitude 7° 16' No, long. 81° 03' W. and the distance run from Panama was 170 miles.

Personal Memories of Capt. U.S. Grant: 1852

In the spring of 1851 the garrison at Detroit was transferred to Sackett's Harbor, and in the following spring the entire 4th infantry was ordered to the Pacific Coast. It was decided that Mrs. Grant should visit my parents at first for a few months, and then remain with her own family at their St. Louis home until an opportunity offered of sending for her. In the month of April the regiment was assembled at Governor's Island, New York Harbor, and on the 5th of July eight companies sailed for Aspinwall.

We numbered a little over seven hundred persons, including the families of officers and soldiers. Passage was secured for us on the old steamer Ohio, commanded at the time by Captain Schenck, of the navy. It had not been determined, until a day or two before starting, that the 4th infantry should go by the Ohio; consequently, a complement of passengers had already been secured. The addition of over seven hundred to this list crowded the steamer most uncomfortably, especially for the tropics in July.

In eight days Aspinwall was reached. At that time the streets of the town were eight or ten inches under water, and foot passengers passed from place to place on raised foot-walks. July is at the height of the wet season, on the Isthmus. At intervals the rain would pour down in streams, followed in not many minutes by a blazing, tropical summer's sun. These alternate changes, from rain to sunshine, were continuous in the afternoons. I wondered how any person could live many months in Aspinwall, and wondered still more why any one tried.

In the summer of 1852 the Panama railroad was completed only to the point where it now crosses the Chagres River. From there passengers were carried by boats to Gorgona, at which place they took mules for Panama, some twenty-five miles further. Those who travelled over the Isthmus in those days will remember that boats on the Chagres River were propelled by natives not inconveniently burdened with clothing. These boats carried thirty to forty passengers each. The crews consisted of six men to a boat, armed with long poles. There were planks wide enough for a man to walk on conveniently, running along the sides of each boat from end to end. The men would start from the bow, place one end of their poles against the river bottom, brace their shoulders against the other end, and then walk to the stern as rapidly as they could. In this way from a mile to a mile and a half an hour could be made, against the current of the river.

I, as regimental quartermaster, had charge of the

public property and had also to look after the transportation. A contract had been entered into with the steamship company in New York for the transportation of the regiment to California, including the Isthmus transit. A certain amount of baggage was allowed per man, and saddle animals were to be furnished to commissioned officers and to all disabled persons. The regiment, with the exception of one company left as guards to the public property—camp and garrison equipage principally—and the soldiers with families, took boats, propelled as above described, for Gorgona. From this place they marched to Panama, and were soon comfortably on the steamer anchored in the bay, some three or four miles from the town. I, with one company of troops and all the soldiers with families, all the tents, mess chests and camp kettles, was sent to Cruces, a town a few miles higher up the Chagres River than Gorgona. There I found an impecunious American who had taken the contract to furnish transportation for the regiment at a stipulated price per hundred pounds for the freight and so much for each saddle animal.

But when we reached Cruces there was not a mule, either for pack or saddle, in the place. The contractor promised that the animals should be on hand in the morning. In the morning he said that they were on the way from some imaginary place, and would arrive in the course of the day. This went on until I saw that he could not procure the animals at all at the price he had promised to furnish them for. The unusual number of passengers that had come over on the steamer, and the large amount of freight to pack, had created an unprecedented demand for mules. Some of the passengers paid as high as forty dollars for the use of a mule to ride twenty-five miles, when the mule would not have sold for ten dollars in that market at other times.

Meanwhile the cholera had broken out, and men were dying every hour. To diminish the food for the disease, I permitted the company detailed with me to proceed to Panama. The captain and the doctors accompanied the men, and I was left alone with the sick and the soldiers who had families. The regiment at Panama was also affected with the disease; but there were better accommodations for the well on the steamer, and a hospital, for those taken with the disease, on an old hulk anchored a mile off. There were also hospital tents on shore on the island of Flamingo, which stands in the bay. I was about a week at Cruces before transportation began to come in.

About one-third of the people with me died, either at Cruces or on the way to Panama. There was no agent of the transportation company at Cruces to consult, or to take the responsibility of procuring transportation at a price which would secure it. I therefore myself dismissed the contractor and made a new contract with a native, at more than double the original price. Thus we finally reached Panama. The steamer, however, could not proceed until the cholera abated, and the regiment was detained still longer. Altogether, on the Isthmus and on the Pacific side, we were delayed six weeks. About one-seventh of those who left New York harbor with the 4th infantry on the 5th of July, now lie buried on the Isthmus of Panama or on Flamingo island in Panama Bay.

One amusing circumstance occurred while we were lying at anchor in Panama Bay.

In the regiment there was a Lieutenant Slaughter who was very liable to sea-sickness. It almost made him sick to see the wave of a table-cloth when the servants were spreading it. Soon after his graduation, Slaughter was ordered to California and took passage by a sailing vessel going around Cape Horn. The vessel was seven months making the voyage, and Slaughter was sick every moment of the time, never more so than while lying at anchor after reaching his place of destination. On landing in California he found orders which had come by the Isthmus, notifying him of a mistake in his assignment; he should have been ordered to the northern lakes. He started back by the Isthmus route and was sick all the way.

But when he arrived at the East he was again ordered to California, this time definitely, and at this date was making his third trip. He was as sick as ever, and had been so for more than a month while lying at anchor in the bay. I remember him well, seated with his elbows on the table in front of him, his chin between his hands, and looking the picture of despair. At last he broke out, "I wish I had taken my father's advice; he wanted me to go into the navy; if I had done so, I should not have had to go to sea so much." Poor Slaughter! it was his last sea voyage. He was killed by Indians in Oregon.

By the last of August the cholera had so abated that it was deemed safe to start. The disease did not break out again on the way to California, and we reached San Francisco early in September.

Crossing The Isthmus In 1852

REPORT OF THE REGIMENTAL

SURGEON, FOURTH INFANTRY, U. S. A.

General George H. Davis, first Governor of the Canal Zone, recently chanced upon a report of a transit of the Isthmus of Panama made by the fourth regiment of infantry, U. S. A., in 1852, during which there was a severe outbreak of cholera. In his letter transmitting the report, General Davis says: "The regiment in question, the Fourth Infantry, was one that has had a very distinguished personnel in its history, and one of the officers of that regiment in 1852, referred to in this report by name, was Captain, afterwards General and Commander-in-chief, Ulysses S. Grant."

The report follows:

SAN FRANCISCO, CALIF.,
September 14, 1852
SIR: The occurrence of malignant cholera in the Fourth regiment of infantry, which I accompanied from New York to California, seemed to me to require that I should make a special report to you upon the subject. I have, therefore, made a report of the sick of that regiment up to the 31st of August, and beg leave to accompany it with the following remarks:

The regiment was concentrated at Fort Columbus, New York, in obedience to orders from the War Department, the last company having arrived on the 23d June. On that day 243 recruits were received and examined. On the evening of the 2d July, about 150 more recruits were received and examined. On the 5th July eight companies of the regiment, with the band and headquarters, were embarked on the United States mail steamer *Ohio,* bound for Aspinwall, New Granada. We had a good deal of diarrhoea among our men during their stay upon Governor's Island, but it was quite manageable, and when we embarked I did not consider it necessary to leave but one man in the hospital; he was recovering from a broken leg, and would not have been able to march across the Isthmus. The *Ohio* was a large ship, as to tonnage, and in that respect, capable of carrying our whole command; but her room is so badly distributed that we should have been crowded had there been no other passengers. Our command, including women and children, was about 800. We had, however, all told, passengers, crew, etc., 1,100 on board. This was altogether too many people for her accommodations of that season of the year, and in a voyage to the tropics. We, however, reached Aspinwall on the 16th July, without losing a man. We had a number of cases of both diarrhoea and constipation, and a few cases of fever on the voyage. Our sick report, nevertheless, was very small upon landing. One man (the bandmaster), sick with chronic diarrhoea, had sunk so much on the voyage I was obliged to leave him on the ship, where he died two days afterward.

On the voyage I had endeavored to impress upon the commanding officer the necessity of preventing the men from eating the fruits of the country, and from indulging in any of the liquors they would meet with on the march. A very judicious order, embracing these views, was issued previous to our debarkation. I am sorry to say, however, it was not observed on the march. Had it been strictly obeyed, I think we should have been spared much suffering. It being the height of the rainy season when we reached the Isthmus we were much embarrassed by the state of the roads; by rains every day; by the extreme heat, and by the epidemic in influences prevailing.

Cholera existed at Aspinwall when we

landed. It had been very fatal a short time previously among the laborers on the railroad, in consequence of which they had very generally abandoned the work. Forty laborers out of one hundred, I was told, had died at one station. It was existing of both Cruces and Gorgona on the route—points we were obliged to pass and at both of which we were unfortunately detained. We found it also at Panama upon our arrival there.

Notwithstanding all this, and the cautions in the order of march, the men had no sooner been permitted to land to procure water, than numbers of them sought the first tavern they could find, to indulge their fatal craving for liquor. Many were brought back on board that night intoxicated and drenched with rain. Fruits were also eaten with avidity whenever they could be procured.

As we did not reach Aspinwall until after the departure of the daily train of cars we were obliged to remain there until next morning. Our baggage, however, was principally landed, and stowed in the cars that afternoon, and this operation was completed early the next morning. When the hour arrived for starting, it was found that the locomotives were too light to carry more than half our men in one train. They were accordingly dispatched in two trains at intervals of an hour, and then the baggage had to be left to be brought up by a return engine. Arrived at Barbacoas, the present terminus of the railway, Colonel Bonneville informed me that it was determined to march the main body of the men from Gorgona to Panama; that the sick, the women, the baggage, and one company would proceed to Cruces, where the mule transportation would be provided, and whence they would also proceed to Panama. I was ordered to accompany this last detachment. Colonel Bonneville then proceeded at once in boats to Gorgona. Colonel Wright was to follow when the baggage came up. The baggage did not arrive till after dark; too late to transfer it to the boats.

In the morning it was discovered that the hospital stores were not contained in those cars. I had a special messenger sent back to bring them up immediately. Colonel Wright went on with his battalion, leaving me, a subaltern, and a small guard, with the sick. My messenger did not return till late in the afternoon, and then brought up but four packages out of thirty, declaring there were no more to be found. This made it necessary for me to return to Aspinwall, which I did that night upon a hand car. I found my stores in the first baggage car I met with in the depot, and the next morning carried them to Barbacoas in a special train furnished me by Colonel Totten, the engineer of the road. I proceeded at once up the river to Cruces, a distance of twelve miles, against a rapid and dangerous current, in a small boat, propelled by setting poles only; and by dint of great exertion and determination succeeded in reaching that point at about 9½ at night. My hospital boat did not get up until next morning. At Cruces, very much to my surprise, I found the regimental quartermaster, about seventy men, and all the women and children. This was Monday night. He had been there since Sunday morning, and no transportation for the baggage had yet been furnished by the contractors. The detachment was encamped on the river, at the landing place and all the baggage piled up in the vicinity. At this time all were well, and my sick had entirely recovered. Transportation was promised in the morning, and I determined to push on as rapidly as possible, to overtake the main body, at that time probably at Panama.

In the morning we were again disappointed in transportation. This was Tuesday, 20th July. While endeavoring to get from the contractor mules for myself and necessary stores, I was called to see a soldier said to be ill of cramps. I found a case of malignant cholera, of the most aggravated character. The man died in six hours. Upon instituting a rigid inquiry I found that the disease was, and had been, for some time prevailing in the town; that numbers had died, and were still dying there; and that a physician had been sent there from Panama for the special purpose of treating such cases. It was of course impossible for me to leave the detachment under such circumstances. I, therefore, decided to remain until the men were all started, and this more especially, as I was informed from day to day by passengers from Panama that the main body had gone on board the transport in Panama bay, and that there was no disease among them. I thought it but prudent, however, to urge the quartermaster to as speedy a movement from the place as possible; and by my advice he determined if the requisite transportation was not furnished by the next morning, to procure it himself of anybody, at any price, and require the contracting parties to pay for it. It must be observed that a subcontractor had agreed to furnish mules for 11 cents a pound, and all this time they were in demand for private transportation at 16 to 20 cents. We had the vexation of seeing hundreds of citizens forwarded, with scarcely an hour's detention, while our men were kept at the most unhealthy point of the Isthmus for five days, with no adequate effort on the part of the contractors to forward us to Panama. The next morning we were no better off. Captain Grant then went into the market, and succeeded in completing a contract before night with a responsible person, for the requisite number of mules, to be ready early the next day. In the meanwhile several cases of cholera occurred, and we had four more deaths. One man convalesced from the disease, but too ill to move, I was obliged to leave in charge of the alcalde and the town physician. I recommended, under the circumstances, that the whole detachment should be furnished with mules, lest the fatigue of marching over so desperate a road should excite the disease in men predisposed to it, and they should perish, without the possibility of my aiding them, on the way. That was done, but notwithstanding every precaution on our part, three fatal cases did occur on the road.

In compliance with Captain Grant's contract, a large number of mules, both saddle and cargo, were brought up in the morning, and despatched as fast as possible with riders and burdens, respectively; by 1 p.m. about one-half our men and nearly one-half our baggage were on the road. The usual rain then coming on operations were necessarily suspended for the day. I must here remark that the preservation of anything like order or organization in the forwarding of troops or baggage on mules across the Isthmus is altogether out of the question. The moment a rider or a cargo is placed upon a mule's back that moment he must set out, or the muleteer strips his mule and carries him off. Our movement was, therefore, of necessity, a straggling one, each man making his way to Panama as he best could, when once mounted. The next morning, before 10 o'clock, the last of our men was on the way, and most of the remaining baggage and I then set out myself. I reached Panama before dark, but too late to go the ship that night. I learned that she was lying off Taboga, 12 miles down the bay; that cholera had broken out on board and carried off a number of men. A small steamer communicated with her once a day only, leaving Panama at 5 p.m. I was therefore, detained at Panama until that hour the following day. Here I learned that six of the cabin passengers by the *Ohio* (our ship) had died in Panama of cholera contracted on the Isthmus.

I proceeded to the ship on the first opportunity, and there was informed that the main body had passed three nights on the road between Gorgona and Panama without shelter; that they were drenched by the rains every day; that the order relative to fruits and drink had been entirely disregarded, and in consequence several men had been attacked by cholera, and died on the way. After their arrival upon the ship, the surgeon of that and of two other ships of the same line had been constant in their attendance upon the sick, and abundance of hospital stores and medicines had been furnished by the company. That day (Saturday) the sick had been removed to a hulk anchored near, and a detail of men to nurse them, under the charge of an officer, had been sent on board by the commanding officer. I went on board the hulk and passed the night there. Several new cases were sent on board from the ship during the night. The next day, Dr. Martin, of the *Columbia*, kindly volunteered to take my place, and I got some sleep. I passed the next night again on board the hulk, besides frequent visits during the day. The next day I was obliged to apply to the commanding officer for assistance. It was impossible for anyone to endure such an amount of physical and mental exertion any longer. We had, fortunately, among our passengers, Dr. Deal, of California, a physician of experience and intelligence, with whom a contract was made to perform the duties of an assistant surgeon on board the *Golden Gate*, from that time until she reached San Francisco, for the moderate sum of $250. Had we known what was before us we could not have secured his services for ten times the amount.

Tuesday, 27th July, the disease was evidently subsiding. No new cases had occurred during the night, and the sick were, for the most part, improving. I entertained strong hopes that as soon as our baggage was all received we should be in condition to prosecute our voyage. In this hope, however, we were doomed to be disappointed. In the afternoon of that day we had a heavy rain, against which many of our men were but ill protected. Upon the arrival of the small steamer in the evening about a dozen knapsacks were received, that had been lying and moulding somewhere on the Isthmus for a long time. The men to whom they belonged seized upon them immediately with great eagerness, and opened them to get a change of clothing. I was afterwards informed that some of these men fell sick while in the act. Be this as it may, in about 20 hours afterwards they were all taken ill of cholera in its worst form and within an hour of each other, and most of them died. The disease having thus reappeared, it was determined to land the troops. There being shelter for the sick upon the island of Flaminco, about six miles from Panama, the debarkation was effected upon the 20th; the sick were placed in huts, and the well in a few tents and under sails stretched over poles. On the 1st August, Brevet Major Gore was attacked, and died on board the *Golden Gate*. His was the last case of cholera that occurred, and he the only officer we lost. I recommended to Colonel Bonneville to destroy any other knapsacks that might be received from the Isthmus, and to have the ship fumigated with chlorine, which was done. Several other officers were threatened, but, by timely means, escaped a decided attack. Upon the island a number of those previously ill died, but no new cases appeared to show itself, which made all anxious to leave Panama as soon as possible.

On the 3d August, the *Golden Gate* determined to go sea the next day, but refused to take on board more than 450 of our people, and expressly declared that she would not receive a single sick man. To this extraordinary demand we were forced to submit, and I was accordingly ordered to remain on the island with the sick, most of the women and children, and one company of troops to act as nurses, etc., until the next steamer should sail. I approved of the proposal to divide the command between two ships, but could not agree as to the propriety of leaving all the sick for another steamer, as a similar objection would probably be made to their reception on board of her. I was, however, overruled, and on the 4th August, the *Golden Gate* sailed with 450 well men, Dr. Deal acting assistant surgeon. The three months' supply for the regiment being stowed away in the hold of the ship, I placed it in charge of Dr. Deal, with the packer's list, that he might use such of the medicines and store that he should need on the voyage; the remainder to be left with the medical purveyor at Benicia. Dr. Deal was discharged at the termination of the voyage, and I have not seen him since, nor have I had any report from him. I have ascertained, however, that he had ninety cases of fever and diarrhoea on the voyage, and three deaths. These are embodied in my report. I have also learned that, not being able to find the box containing the sulphate of quinine, he had purchased two ounces at Acapulco and borrowed more of the ship, which has since been returned.

Upon the 7th of August it was announced that the steamer *Northerner* would take us on board and sail the next day. The surgeon of that ship was sent on shore to inspect our men; and although he thought there were several cases of fever that would die, still, as not infectious disease was prevailing, he made no objection to receiving them on board. Arrangements were accordingly made for embarking. The sick were to be first sent on board and accommodated before the ship should be crowded with the well. By a mistake of the agent a scow was sent to the island this evening to take us on board. In this scow our luggage was first stowed, and the sick placed upon it. In a few minutes the whole was flooded away, owing to the leaky condition of the scow. Our sick and baggage were hastily transferred to boats alongside, and thus sent to the steamer. It was this accident that caused the damage to the instruments that were afterwards condemned by a board of survey.

It appeared afterwards that it was not intended we should be embarked that evening, and the consequence of the blunder was a remonstrance on the part of the other passengers against our sick being permitted to remain on board. After a great deal of negotiation it was finally agreed that a few of the worst cases might be left in hospital at Taboga, under the special charge of the agent of the company, he guaranteeing that every comfort and suitable medical attendance should be provided for them, and they forwarded as soon as possible. I considered it of the greatest importance that we should leave that climate, as our well men were daily sickening with the fever. Accordingly four men were selected to be left, by the ship's surgeon, which satisfied the passengers, and on the 8th of August, we embarked the remainder and put to sea.

We arrived at Benicia on the 26th of August, having lost but one man on the voyage. He died on the secondary fever of cholera. Upon my arrival at Benicia I found a large sick report from among the men shipped on the *Golden Gate*. They were ill of diarrhoea, dysentery, and typhoid fever. The men were destitute of clothing, and were in tents, exposed to intense heat by day and to very cold nights. By the advice of Assistant Surgeon Griffin they were ordered from the tents into some new cavalry stables just finished, and with marked good effect. The character of the fever was decidedly typhoid, and the dysenteries generally assumed the same type.

With regard to the treatment of the cholera as it prevailed among us, I have only to say that all the usual means were tried, and with the usual want of success. The first cases were nearly all fatal. I think the free exhibition of brandy with capsicum and chloride sodium was about as successful as anything. We found the acetas plumbi, in doses of five to ten grains, a valuable means of restraining the diarrhoea. I feel sure many cases were relieved by it that would have terminated in malignant cholera without speedy relief. Mustard and bottles of hot water with frictions of the surface externally, camphor, calomel, and quinine internally, were freely used. But, as I have already remarked, and as usually happens in severe epidemics, the chances are that the cases first attacked will die, and that the ratio of the mortality will diminish with the duration of the epidemic. In this epidemic we lost about eighty men.

Very respectfully, your obd't serv't,
CHAS. S. TRIPLER,
Surgeon, U.S. Army

BRIGADIER-GENERAL LAWSON,
Surgeon-General, Washington, D.C.

L.M. Schaeffer—1852

On Saturday, May 22d [1852], we reached the anchorage about ten miles, *more or less*, from Panama. Now all was excitement and confusion; the passengers forgot all concern about cabin or steerage accommodations. The question was how to reach Panama, and when?—The day was fast declining; a thick mist was lowering upon us, but we could perceive small boats making for the ship. At length the boats of various size and design reached us, and the natives cried out—"go ashore;" "me take you 'shore for two dollars"—"hah! Signor, take my boat, me go quick!["]—but Uncle Samuel's mails had first right, then the lady passengers came next, and finally the privilege was extended to all the passengers to "vamose in double quick time." . . . I climbed down the side of the vessel and alighted in an old mud scow, just in time to secure a delightful sail to the ancient city of Panama. There were about a dozen of us on board, all strangers to each other; but we soon formed a community of social and friendly travelers; our old scow seemed to have been distanced by the other boats; our boatmen looked as though they could murder and pitch us overboard as easily as they poured forth their horrid oaths; and it was not until dark night overshadowed us, that we reached the outside of the remains of a dilapidated wall, which I believe once encompassed the city; but our troubles were not yet ended; the boatmen demanded extra compensation to carry us through the mud, at the same time ordering us out of the boat in true Spanish fashion, to the infinite amusement of the hang-dog looking crowd of natives who were standing around watching a chance to pilfer; the mud was at least two feet deep to the landing, a distance of about two yards, and things looked equally; but seeing a big fellow about to wade through for the purpose of fastening the boat rope to a post, I leaped upon his back and compelled him to carry me ashore "*nolens volens.*" . . . at last we reached the centre of the city, where we found a "numerous delegation" of "Los Yankee;" and when I heard my name called, I turned, and was agreeably surprised to find some of my acquaintances from California, who at once introduced me to the landlord of the "American House," who accommodated me with a room in which only fifty men were to sleep! After partaking of a supper fit only for an aboriginal to enjoy, I ventured forth to "see the sights," but as the night was dark, and the authorities not approving of lighting the streets, I retraced my steps, and feeling jaded and wearied, I sought rest on my cot.

 Saturday, May 22, 1852— . . . There were about fifty men lodged in one room. We slept on cots, or rather reclined on cots, hardly two of which were alike.

"Slap, flap, bang"—"confound these musquitoes;" "slap, slap, bang," "what's that?" . . . "Who can sleep in such an insect-infested hole as this?" And in truth, forbearance ceased to be a virtue. I tried the expedient of covering myself with bed clothes; that wouldn't answer, for I came near being melted. I threw off the sheets; an army of insects attacked me "fore and aft." However, daylight at length condescended to peer through the dirty, prison-looking windows, and such a tumbling down stairs was only familiar to the quercitron-dyed landlord, who flourished at the American.

It was the rainy season on the isthmus, and were I not homeward-bound, I might have felt most uncomfortable. My bill for supper, lodging and breakfast was only one dollar and fifty cents. I strolled around the city, and noticed that in the business portion of the town the houses were three-storied, "*originally*" white-washed, balconies running along the second story which had been painted red about ninety years ago—more or less, the streets were very narrow, filth abundant, and the markets remarkable only, for a want of order and cleanliness . . . .

. . . I was so favorably impressed with the attractions of the ancient city of Panama, that I determined to leave for Gorgona on foot and alone, despite the heavy shower that was beating down.

I had not proceeded far out of the city ere I began to wish that the others would follow. I stopped at a mud hut, drank coffee, and by the time I was ready to depart, there came along a crowd of Americans, each one, like myself, traveling on "shanks' mare," and a merry party we were; away went, now tumbling into mud deeper than we desired, and again picking our way over solid rock by a rugged path wide enough for a mule to pass . . . .

The rain poured down furiously, but on we traveled; and anon the clouds would break away and the glorious sun shine forth, even here. About every five miles we came across thatched huts, in which brandy and coffee was dispensed at ten cents a swallow, and the natives seemed to be well encouraged, for the wayward travelers needed refreshments. We continued our slow and wearisome march up hill and down hill, through mud and over rough stones, until we reached the ""Half-way Settlement," where we concluded to hold up until the following morning.

The house, or rather the tent, at which we stopped was conducted by an American woman, who was as gentle and kind-hearted as an enraged tigress. Her face must have contained 90 per cent of brass, and her heart have been composed of stone. Here we were privileged to "pile ourselves" on top of a load of wood, and if any of the party were comfortable that night, I never heard of it.

Sunday, May 23.—I should not have known it was the Sabbath day only for the regular posting in my journal. We ate breakfast—and such a breakfast!— settled bills, and left the inhospitable "Half-way House" with no friendly feelings to our hostess or her miserable shanty.

Away we trudged for Gorgona . . . .

Towards the close of the day we espied Gorgona, and the first hut we reached I entered, ordered supper, and sat down to rest myself with all the importance of a steamboat captain. My hotel had no floor, no beds, not a table, and I was curious to know how my host would arrange matters. After considerable delay, he brought in an old box, covered it with *unbleached* muslin, and then placed my meal on it, which consisted of fried bananas, eggs, and a bottle of claret wine. I enjoyed the repast, (charge, sixty cents,) and soon after sallied forth in quest of novelty, and was surprised to find "further down the road" quite a settlement, several hotels conducted by enterprising Americans, the principal houses being the Union and the St. Louis, and at the end of the lane I discovered the Chagres River, not near so formidable a stream as I had been led to expect. Finding most of the Americans quartered at the Union and St. Louis hotels, I concluded to retrace my steps, procure my bundle, and board at the Union.

. . . I was in a short time standing on the balcony of the Union hotel watching the vast crowd of homeward-bound travelers gathered around, not two of whom were dressed alike, and each sadly needing the barber.

Understanding that the cots were nearly all taken, I made application to the landlord, who secured me one just in time, or I should have been compelled to sleep on the damp floor, as a goodly number did.

The sky was overcast, and the temperature moist and chilly. I would have preferred a seat in the kitchen to dry my clothing, but there was no alternative. I had to lounge about the only spare place, the bar-room, which was damp, overcrowded, and *not* perfumed with either the rose or jessamine.

Monday, May 24, 1852.—Overcome by fatigue, I slept well last night; arose early this morning, partook of a tolerable breakfast, and then paid $2.80 for supper, lodging and breakfast to the landlord of "Union hotel," Gorgona.

Now commenced another unpleasant task, to select out of the many "dug-outs," one to convey my honorable body down the river to a place called Tivoli. After bargaining some time with the half-clad natives, I at length selected one in which I found several Americans . . . Our fare was four dollars each; distance not over twenty miles . . . .

Taking a last, and I hope eternal farewell of Gorgona, our boatmen sang out, "all ready," and off we sailed about as fast as the current was pleased to take us, no thanks to the copper-colored boatmen. We had not proceeded very far, and had hardly become familiar with our unsymmetrical "dug-out," when the "gentleman from Ohio" fell forward in my lap, very nearly upsetting our rickety old craft. The frequent indulgence in "Darien fruits" put him "*hors du combat*," to the serious annoyance of our native boatmen, who cared as much for the sick man as they did for a log of wood . . .

About noon we reached the *great city* of Tivoli, and had the sick man placed in "Old Joe's" hotel, where he was as comfortably provided for as circumstances would permit. I found Tivoli the dirtiest, meanest, most contemptible fever and ague breeding hole it ever fell to my lot to visit. There were about a dozen thatched huts, with accommodations a shade better than a decent pigpen.

As soon as possible I purchased a ticket for Aspinwall, distant eighteen miles, fare, five dollars; but unfortunately we received intelligence that some accident had happened, and we should be compelled to wait here until the succeeding day.

Hundreds of homeward-bound Americans were quartered here awaiting the arrival of the cars, consequently they "ate and drank" everything the shiftless natives could muster. This place was the first way station and terminus, at that time, of the Panama railroad. Many of the natives were unfriendly to the road, because it deprived them of a fine revenue from boating, etc., . . .

In my walks around, I chanced to enter a dirty-looking shanty, and make the acquaintance of the proprietor. He was a young man from "down east," who had ventured out here for the purpose of "bettering his finances." The unhealthy climate, the miasmatic effluvia arising from the damp and filthy village and its surroundings, had seriously impaired his health; he looked to be more dead than alive. I suggested the propriety of leaving this death-inviting place; but he replied, "I have a fine chance to accumulate money here, and if I go away, what can I do? I came here to make money, and I am bound to see it through." . . .

The Ohio traveler soon recovered his usual health, and agreed with me, that his illness was occasioned by indulging too freely in tropical fruits.

While I discountenanced the habitual use of brandy, still, in journeying through such places as Panama, Gorgona, and Tivoli, it were better to use brandy moderately than to indulge in the tempting tropical fruits.

Tuesday, May 25.—There were no sleeping accommodations for the passengers; some slept on the railroad track, because it was cleaner than the village; others secured seats in the cars, and I walked, talked, and occasionally nodded during the night, which seemed almost interminable . . . .

"Hark! what's that?" "Three cheers, men, the cars are coming!" and true, here comes dashing along the train—the cars crowded with men, women and children, bound for California . . .

As soon as the California gold-seekers were out of the cars, we homeward-bound travelers rushed to the seats, and it is unnecessary to say, anxiously waited for the train to move off. The cars were built in the United States expressly for the climate of Darien, were cheerful in appearance and very comfortable. Soon the conductor sang out, "all aboard," and away we went in gallant style for Aspinwall. The road was in excellent condition, so far as I was able to judge. The thick, luxuriant shrubbery which lined the road on either side precluded an opportunity of "seeing the country."

About mid-day we arrived at Aspinwall, being the only place this side of California which bore any resemblance to the "land of the free and the home of the brave." The railroad company had erected a long, well-covered shed, extending a considerable distance out into the bay, which allowed steamers to anchor alongside, to the great convenience and gratification of travelers.

Upon our arrival at Aspinwall, we found several steamers "up for the States," . . . As I had no baggage to trouble me, I hastened at once to the first steamer lying most conveniently to the railroad wharf—sought out the purser's office, and purchased a cabin ticket for New York for twenty-five dollars. I was most agreeably disappointed in finding the fare so much reduced; the usual rate had been from eighty to one hundred dollars for cabin fare; but the unusual number of opposition steamers meeting there at the same time caused the reduction . . .

On the wharf, the first sight that reminded me of my return to civilized communities, was that of observing Irishmen selling apples and cakes! . . .

Louis M. Gottschalk
April 12, 1865

In sight of Aspinwall.

During our dinner a second-class passenger has written for amusement a bill of fare... which he has nailed to the quarter-deck.

The heading is a tortoise, very well drawn, with chimney on his back and a wheel on each side, representing the steamer *Ariel*, on which we are, and which is known as the slowest steamer on the line.

This proves little in favor of the table. From the first cabin I can judge of the second, and the satire is just and true.

SECOND CLASS—THREE HUNDRED DOLLARS (Nothing extra for meals) BILL OF FARE D i n n e r *S o u p s* T u r t l e , (s c r a t c h e d o u t) Vanderbistallen, Oyster. (scratched out) *Roast* Turkey (scratched out) Lamb, (scratched out) Gutta Percha, Goose, (scratched out) Beef.

(scratched out) *Boiled*Chicken (scratched out) Owl, Ham. (scratched out) *Fried*Oysters, (scratched out) Boot Heels, Ham and Eggs, (scratched out) *Vegetables*Green Peas, (scratched out) Jerusalem Artichokes, Beets (diseased), Cauliflower. (Scratched out) *Side Dishes*Baked Beans, (scratched out) Hardtack (a la Monitor), Pilot Bread (a la Ironsides), Lobster Salad. (scratched out)*Dessert*Minced Pie, (scratched out) Antediluvian Pie, C.S. Army Pie, Custard Pie, (scratched out) Dried Cucumber Pie.*Extras*Tomato Ketchup, Ice Water. Please report any civilities on the part of waiters

APRIL 12

Eleven o'clock in the morning. Land in sight. We see the mountains of New Granada rising up on the horizon. At two o'clock we can see Aspinwall; some white houses, in the midst of which the American flag floats in the breeze; a little farther on a Protestant church of cut stone and Gothic architecture presents a singular effect in the midst of the palm trees and bamboos that surround it. Aspinwall is still only a village; its population does not exceed one thousand souls, two-thirds of which is composed of Negroes; but, thanks to the flux and reflux of travelers, who every five or six days cross the isthmus from one ocean to the other, it has a certain commercial importance and extraordinary animation. It wakes up immediately on the arrival of a steamer. Hardly at the wharf, the steamer is invaded by Negro porters with large pointed bonnets on their heads which recall those of the astrologers, made from the stringy bark of a tree, and are of the color of tow. We have great trouble to keep off this turbulent, officious swarm, who seize by force every package that is in sight, and without disquieting themselves about the proprietor, and, whether you are willing or unwilling, carry it on land. At a hundred yards from the wharf we find ourselves in a street, about five hundred yards long, in which every house is a hotel. There are twelve or fifteen, one after another, all American. Each is a two-story frame house with a porch. The roof extends above the porch, which is sustained by beams, and forms a veranda on the ground floor.

The Negress fruit sellers abound. They are clad in white muslin gowns, low in the neck, with short sleeves. The color of the dress is sullied by the dust, scorched by the sun, and rumpled by the rain. Eight or ten rows of flounces are ranged one above the other as high as the waist. Bare feet. They follow us, offering us, in poor English, bananas, coconuts, oranges, and some cigars, for which they make us pay ten times their value. I buy some bananas. "How much?" I say to her. "Fifty cents," she answers me. I give her a dollar note, which she returns to me, preferring not to sell to taking paper money.

The sun is burning hot. While awaiting the departure of the train we enter the Howard Hotel, kept by Mrs. Smith, an American. Unfortunately for me, there is a piano in the large hall. The passengers assemble and force me to play. The instrument is from the factory of Raven & Bacon, of New York. One lives fast under the tropics; the strings have not resisted the climate. Some low notes remain. I utilize them by playing a semblance of my *Banjo* and clear out.

The train leaves. It is full. The road is lined with thick jungles of mangroves, bindweed, bamboos, and palms. Sometimes the road widens; then we see one or two farmers' huts. Their architecture is primitive: there are four beams on which is placed, four or five feet from the earth, a roofing of palm leaves. The soil around the cabin is still black from the fire that, by burning the forest, has opened a clearing in the midst of this chaos of vegetation, which grows so rapidly in this warm and humid soil.

The crossing is made from ocean to ocean in two hours and a half. We are running alongside a pretty little river. Six o'clock in the afternoon. Arrived at Panama.

Salvo Atlantic! Garrison in full dress; six Negroes and one mulatto under arms form in line near the wharf. We embark in great confusion on a boat that transports us to the steamer, which is two or three miles out at sea. The city of Panama, proper, extends for some distance. The houses are of Spanish architecture, heavy, massive, and square, which the laziness of the inhabitants leaves to fall in ruins. An American resident assures me that ten houses have not been built since the departure of the Spaniards. Two clock towers overlook the city; it is the cathedral. It is as dilapidated as the rest. The roof lets the rain pass through. The statues of the saints in the interior, of painted wood, are rotten and worm-eaten. The doors are off their hinges and hang on one side at the entrance of the church.

A clever prestidigitator, I was told, found the means of drawing four or five hundred dollars last week from this miserable borough. He announced two performances in the following style:

"Homage of the all-Powerful Devil. Mr.—
will give two performances of *magic*, the

> product of which, after deducting all expenses, will be consecrated to repairing the cathedral roof and making new doors."
> The hall was filled. The receipts were eight hundred dollars, of which the devil (or his disciple) took one-half under pretext of expenses. Someone assured me that wax lights are wanting for the service of religion, and that there is no money to buy them. Apathy, laziness, and filth everywhere; nobody is willing to work. When their houses (built by the Spaniards, whom they execrate, and to whom nevertheless they owe the little civilization that remains to them) fall into ruins, they prop them up with planks or build them up again as well as they can; they stop up the gaps with stones, which they take from the wall that encircles the town, and which today is everywhere tumbling down under the double attack of time and of the wretched builders who have made a quarry of it.

On board the steamer *Constitution*. A splendid steamer, which makes a still grater contrast with that nutshell—the *Ariel*—which we have just left. The heat is excessive, and produces a malaise that we feel doubly from the absence of ice. Here, as on the Ariel, the water is lukewarm. We have to pay twenty-five cents extra for a few small pieces of ice, and again the bar has to be closed, like last night, at ten o'clock.

A pearl fishery exists on a small island (Isle of Pearls) one mile from the coast; few are now found, nevertheless lately a pearl was fished up that was sold for eight thousand dollars to the Prince of Wales.

The fishery has become dangerous on account of the number of daring sharks that are found swimming close in to shore.

I have said that the *Constitution* is the finest, steamer that I have yet seen, but I am not on that account willing to say that there might not be many improvements in various things that concern the interior.

THE RETURN—OCTOBER 1

Landed at Panama. The steamer cast anchor before the island of Tobago, two miles distant from the town. The site is ravishing; the island is a broken coast whose steep and precipitous declivities plunge perpendicularly into the blue sea. A boat comes for us, it will have to make three trips, for it cannot carry at once four hundred passengers, and we are at least four hundred. The wharf is crowded. The Negro porters, sellers of fruit and cigars, quarrel among themselves, as usual, for their prey. Each of us is assailed by six or eight of these ragged monkeys, who offer us their services in English, French, and Spanish, and often impose themselves imperiously upon us by seizing, whether we are willing or not, our trunks. The women sell lemonade, rum, and parrots. It is enough to drive one wild; we are jostled, squeezed, tossed about from one end of the wharf to the other. The first train is just starting for Aspinwall; it is for the steerage passengers.

I succeed in collecting three of my trunks, which are running at random on the shoulders of three busybodies who were in quest of a job and who consent, by means of a forced contribution, to permit me to take possession of my property. A hatbox and small trunk are still missing, but after the departure I shall probably find them, because I took the precaution of writing on them "Panama," which signifies that I stop there and takes from the porters the hope of keeping them with impunity. There remains to them the consolation in perspective of skinning me under the pretext of having had to watch my baggage for two hours.

An omnibus, drawn by two sorry-looking horses sagging in the back, driven by a Negro, takes me to the town properly so-called, which is a mile off. On our road we pass wretched cabins, Negroes in tatters, ruins of stone houses, some tottering walls, the stones of which served for building the few new tottering hovels built in his decrepit town. On a hut a sign in French: "French gentlemen travelers are informed that Jean Francois, from Paris, washes and does everything pertaining to his trade."

A large square building of cut stone, the whole of which is broken down, and the interior of which has become a medley of climbing plants and trees, is the old Jesuit college. This is the old town, the title might lead one to suppose that the remainder is less in ruins. Vain illusion. Ruins! Ruins! Ruins! The cathedral is falling down. The wooden balconies of the houses lean toward the street with an evident tendency of throwing into it those who might be so imprudent as to venture into them. The dismantled roofs are covered with vegetation. The clock tower of the cathedral is covered instead of slate with pearl-oyster shells incrusted in the masonry, which sparkle in the burning rays of the sun. The streets are narrow and crooked, and the pavements resemble the brim of a well. The porches serving for entrances to the shops are dark: they sell in them a lot of rags and other mean dirty things.

The Aspinwall Hotel is kept by a Frenchman. The hotel is dirty and dilapidated; the dinner is passable, although I found many flies in my soup and omelet.

Opposite the hotel a Frenchwoman keeps a shop of super-annuated dresses.

I have been walking on the promenade of the ramparts on the edge of the sea. An old cannon, which keeps itself in equilibrium on half of a gun carriage, is what remains of an immense barrack of cut stone. The walls have crumbled and the roof is falling in. the ground floor still remains. The windows are grated, serving for a prison. A crowd of unfortunates stretch out their hands to me through the bars. "*Un medio, señor.*" I throw some small pieces of money to them. "*Dios lo bendiga,*" covered with benedictions, I was about to leave, but the soldiers, allured by my generosity, are at my heels, and I am soon surrounded by a score of black and yellow ringtail monkeys in red caps, who have come out of the guard house. By their caps I guess that I have business with the invincibles of the army of occupation. The uniform consists of a scarlet cap, cotton drawers, no shirt. Some have bayonets at their sides, others a cartouche box hung by a shoulder strap, and no shoes. They were fighting three weeks ago.

PANAMA, OCTOBER 7

A concert, organized by subscription, given in the hall of the *hotel de ville*. The tickets are a dollar. Receipts one hundred forty dollars. The audience appears to be charmed, while I am playing on a cottage piano that I suspect was the product of an illicit union between a jew's-harp and a large kettle. The climate is so hot and damp that the best piano is not playable at the end of three weeks. Besides they have no tuner. The only person who meddles with them is an unfortunate French secretary at the consulate who has one-half of his face and nose eaten off by a frightful cancer.

Today I have seen the president of the state, Sobrerano, of Panama. He is a dark mulatto, who received me in his shirt sleeves and slippers, in a nasty, miserable, and unclean little house. His mother is an old Negress who sells preserved guava, which she makes herself, and who goes every morning to market, barefooted, in her chemise. The president is the son of the old Bishop of Panama.

Yesterday I was admiring a pretty girl, eleven or twelve years old, who was making some purchases in the French Bazaar opposite the hotel. She is, I am told, the daughter of the priest—this was said artlessly, as if we had been only speaking of the mayor. Besides her, the priest has also six others—all pretty. She did not hesitate in saying when she made her purchase: "Place that on the account of Papa, el Señor Cura."

The French consul, having heard of very rich discoveries, wrote lately to his agent at Chiriqui, ordering him to buy all the ornaments found in the recent excavations. The latter complied, and the consul received at the end of a few days a very heavy box full of shapeless golden ingots—the agent having had the happy idea, he said, of flattening all the objects with a hammer so that they might take up less room!

The church is dilapidated . . . There are some

farmers who pay the priest for permission to sweep the church out after High Mass on Sunday. They carefully gather up the dust and spread it over their fields, persuaded that it is an excellent fertilizer and that it blesses their crops.

Nothing could give you an idea of the ignorance and apathy of these people, who constantly see the progress of the civilization of the Americans, and who nevertheless continue to isolate themselves better than the Chinese do behind their Great Wall. They have a horror of innovations. The foreigner is repugnant to them because he represents a summary of ideas and customs different from those which have been transmitted to them by their ancestors. They take great care not to expand their views beyond their small sphere of action, in which they are so circumscribed that they have finally lost all idea of social proportion or historical perspective. They depreciate all foreign events that take place, and exaggerate all those which pertain to themselves.

Their views never extend beyond the circle of little intrigues and petty passions in which they take part. Through constantly occupying themselves only with themselves, they finally lose every idea of proportion; the imperceptible sphere in which they move becomes the center of the world; the universe looks at them—they think themselves great.

SS Ancon Transit— 1939, 25th Anniversary

More than 800 residents of the Isthmus and retired employees and their families who had returned to the Canal Zone for the occasion helped to make history Tuesday when the old Panama Railroad steamer *Ancon* reenacted its memorable Canal transit of 25 years ago, in connection with the 25th anniversary of the opening of the Canal to the commerce of the world.

Bedecked in all its flags and following the anniversary ceremonies on Pier 6, Cristobal, the *Ancon*, piloted by Captain K. M. Wikingstad, veteran Canal pilot, backed out into Cristobal Harbor and started its commemorative voyage at approximately 9:30 o'clock in the morning.

As the vessel started into the Canal Channel, to repeat its historic voyage of August 15, 1914, when it led the parade of craft through the Canal to open the waterway to the commerce of the world, the Standard Fruit and Steamship Company's S. S. *Cefalu,* which had arrived in the breakwater just as the *Ancon* started from the pier, saluted the vessel with three whistle blasts, and was answered in the like manner by the *Ancon.* The *Cefalu*'s salute was the first of about a dozen salutes the vessel was to receive before it docked at Balboa in the afternoon.

As the *Ancon* started its commemorative transit, 35 patrol bombers from Patrol Wing 3, Fleet Air Base, appeared in the sky, in an aerial demonstration as a tribute to the historical occasion. The demonstration continued until the vessel had entered the lower east chamber of Gatun Locks, where the tribute was taken over by the Atlantic side silver employees and their families.

As the *Ancon* approached the Gatun Locks, passengers aboard the vessel could see the residents of both silver and gold communities pouring through the fields in the direction of the lock enclosures. With the closing of the lower lock gates and as the vessel was being raised to the level of the middle chamber, passengers on the vessel received their first idea of what was to come during each lockage during the transit and as the vessel passed along the banks of the Canal.

With tears in their eyes and waving United States flags, practically the entire population of the nearby silver communities sang and cheered, while a band, composed of colored boy scouts, played appropriate military and sentimental songs.

As the vessel reached the middle chamber of the locks several red, white and blue streamers were tossed aboard the vessel and tied to the rails, while a small girl and boy carried the other end along the wall of the lock chamber, preceding the center towing locomotives.

Arriving in the upper chamber of the locks. It appeared that every resident of the Atlantic side of the Isthmus, not aboard the vessel, was within the lock enclosure to greet her. With the assistance of the 14th Infantry Band, from Fort Davis, which had boarded the vessel after participating in the initial anniversary ceremonies on pier 6, everyone on shore and aboard the *Ancon* joined in singing a song to the *Good and Faithful Old Ancon*, to the tune *of Darling Nellie Gray*, and, as the vessel entered Gatun Lake, the refrain of *Auld Lang Syne* resounded from the ship and shore.

The Gatun celebration for the vessel was slightly dimmed by a light rain and just as the voyage across Gatun Lake was started by the *Ancon*, with the U. S. Navy destroyer J. Fred Talbot leading the way, and The Panama Canal Lighthouse Subdivision tug S. S. *Favorite* bringing up the rear, the rain became heavier and continued until the vessel had passed Barro Colorado Island and had entered Gamboa Reach.

As the *Ancon* approached Gamboa, the banks of the Canal were lined with people from the nearby silver and gold communities wishing to pay tribute to the old vessel on its commemorative voyage.

Passing Gamboa at about 12:30 o'clock in the afternoon the vessel received salutes of three whistle blasts from the various floating equipment of the Dredging Division, which it answered in turn, the last answering blast coming just as the *Ancon* turned into Gaillard Cut from Gatun Lake.

It was within the walls of the Cut that most interest was displayed by the passengers aboard the vessel, many of whom began pointing out to their children and grandchildren various points of interest and places in which during the construction days, they sweated and labored that the engineering miracle of the age might be accomplished.

Pedro Miguel Locks were reached shortly before 2 o'clock in the afternoon, and hundreds of persons were lined along the banks from Paraiso to the lower end of the locks on the outside of the locks enclosure.

Clearing the Pedro Miguel Locks and entering Miraflores Lake, the *Ancon* and its passengers were greeted with numerous small motorboats, which continued to buzz around the vessel like little flies until the approach to the Miraflores Locks had been made.

The vessel entered the upper east chamber of Miraflores Locks at approximately 2:30 o'clock in the afternoon to be greeted by what appeared to be the entire population of the Pacific side of the Isthmus.

With the arrival of the vessel, the 11th Engineers Band, from Corozal, played the national anthem of the United States, with the entire gathering, led by Rev. H. Christy Scheveland, singing. The band followed with several military selections while the vessel was being lowered to the level of the lower chamber, after which a group of small children carried a chain of flowers to the side of the locks and the flowers were pulled aboard the vessel.

As the *Ancon* left the upper chamber of the locks, the assembled populace sang *Farewell to Thee, Ancon*, to the tune of *Aloha Oe*, closing the Pacific side ceremonies.

The *Ancon* left the Miraflores Locks at approximately 3:30 o'clock in the afternoon after a slight delay due to a fouled towing locomotive cable, which had caught on an eyebolt on the side of the vessel, and which had to be cut in order to be released. The vessel proceeded to Balboa, where it tied up at about 4 o'clock.

Several hundred persons awaited the arrival of the steamer at the Balboa pier, and, as it approached, a U. S. Navy band and the band aboard the ship played the national anthem of the United States, followed by several other military numbers while the gangplank was being placed in position.

One of the many interesting items concerning the commemorative transit of the *Ancon* was the last-minute passage granted Mrs. Joseph Fink, widow of a construction days worker.

According to Mrs. Fink's own story, she was unaware that the *Ancon* would be open to the public for the commemorative voyage until late Monday night when friends informed her of that fact. Having made the return voyage from Balboa to Cristobal aboard the *Ancon* on August 23, 1914, she was particularly anxious to transit the Canal on the commemorative voyage. However, all reservations had been accepted many days before and, for a time, it looked hopeless that she would get to board the vessel for Tuesday's trip. With the cooperation of some of her friends she went through a trunk containing souvenirs of the early days of the Canal and unearthed the original pass which she and her husband had been granted for the 1914 voyage.

Shortly before time for the train to leave for Cristobal, Mrs. Fink called at the residence of C. A. McIlvaine, Executive Secretary of The Panama Canal, and explained the situation to him, whereupon a notation was made upon her original pass, permitting her to board the *Ancon* for Tuesday's commemorative voyage.

The oldest Isthmian resident, from the standpoint of initial residence, aboard the *Ancon* Tuesday was J. D. Maxwell, resident of Panama City, who first arrived on the Isthmus in 1899. The founder of what is now the Kelso-Jordan Company. Mr. Maxwell represented the Bureau of Clubs and Playgounds aboard the vessel in the sale of a native souvenir ivory nut.